Review and Evaluation of the Substance Abuse and Mental Health Services Block Grant Allotment Formula

M. Audrey Burnam, Peter Reuter,
John L. Adams, Adele R. Palmer,
Karyn E. Model, John E. Rolph,
Joanna Z. Heilbrunn, Grant N. Marshall,
Daniel F. McCaffrey, Suzanne L. Wenzel,
Ronald C. Kessler

Prepared for the Center for Substance Abuse Treatment,
Substance Abuse and Mental Health Services Administration

Health Program • Drug Policy Research Center

RAND

RA
790.6
.R48
1997

PREFACE

This report represents the results of a study designed to evaluate the equity of the formula used to allocate federal Block Grant funds to the states for the provision of substance abuse and mental health services. This study was mandated by Congress under the Alcohol, Drug Abuse and Mental Health Administration Reorganization Act of 1992, and was conducted in 1994 under a contract from the Center for Substance Abuse Treatment.

The study examined the concept of equity represented in the current formula, reviewed empirical literature that could inform an evaluation of the state-level measures used in the formula, conducted analyses of existing data to develop improved state-level measures of formula components, and compared the distribution of Block Grant funds under the current formula to the distribution that would result from using alternative empirically based measures.

This report presents a full description of the study, including a series of appendixes providing supplementary methodologic details and analytic results. It provides information relevant to the question of whether and how the formula for distributing substance abuse and mental health Block Grant funds should be modified. In addition, the study represents an approach to developing a Block Grant allocation formula that is relevant to other federal Block Grant programs.

CONTENTS

Preface	iii
Figures	ix
Tables	xi
Summary	xv
Acknowledgments	xxi

Chapter One
INTRODUCTION: BACKGROUND AND PURPOSES OF STUDY	1
The History of the Block Grant Formula	2
The Current Formula	4
Mental Health	6
Substance Abuse	7
Analytic Strategy	7
Caveats to This Study	9
Time	10
Missing Data	10
Incentives	10
Hold-Harmless Provisions and Other Constraints	10
Outline of the Report	11

Chapter Two
PRINCIPLES FOR ANALYSIS OF ALLOCATION FORMULA	13
Concepts of Equity	13
What Funds	15
Treatment and Prevention	16

Chapter Three
POPULATION IN NEED OF TREATMENT FOR MENTAL ILLNESS	19
Overview	19
Mental Illness Literature Review	20
Definition of Mental Disorder	20
Correlates of Mental Disorder in Adults	22
Correlates of Mental Disorder in Children and Adolescents	24
Analyses of Factors Predicting Need for Community Mental Health Services	26

Definition of Population in Need of Community Mental Health
Services 26
Operational Definitions of Population in Need of Community
Mental Health Services Based on Survey Measures 28
Analysis Methods.. 30
Results 33
State-Level Estimates of Needs for Community Mental Health
Services 35

Chapter Four
POPULATION IN NEED OF SUBSTANCE ABUSE PREVENTION AND
TREATMENT 39
Overview.. 39
Substance Abuse Literature Review 40
Predictors of Alcohol Abuse 41
Predictors of Drug Abuse 43
Analyses of Factors Predicting Need for Substance Abuse Prevention
and Treatment Services 45
Definitions of Population in Need of Substance Abuse Treatment
and Prevention Services 46
Operational Definitions of Populations in Need of Substance
Abuse Treatment and Prevention Services Based on Survey
Measures 47
Analysis Methods... 49
Results 51
State-Level Estimates of Need for Substance Abuse Prevention and
Treatment Services 55

Chapter Five
COST OF SERVICE INDICATORS 59
Overview.. 59
Evaluation Criteria 62
The Current COS Measure 63
Issues in Measuring Resource Prices 64
Wages 64
Rents 71
Prices of Miscellaneous Resources 72
Implications of Revising the Price Measures 73
Weights for Combining Resource Prices 74
Resourcing Patterns Observed in SA and MH Services Survey
Data 75
Using SA and MH Services-Based Experience to Develop
Standardized COSIs 78
Conclusions Regarding the Current Weights 79
Overall Implications of Improving the COSI Methodology 81

Chapter Six
MEASURING STATES' FINANCING CAPACITY 85

Overview	85
Why Not Use Actual Funds Allocation?	86
A Standardized Measure	87
Evaluation Criteria	87
Volatility	87
Availability	88
Reliability	88
Alternative Measures of Fiscal Capacity	88
Personal Income	88
Total Taxable Resources	89
The Representative Tax System (RTS)	92
Comparing Indicators—Does It Matter?	94

Chapter Seven

EVALUATION OF THE EFFECTS OF ALTERNATIVE COMPONENT DEFINITIONS IN ALLOTMENT FORMULAS	97
Overview	98
Evaluation Methodology	99
Effects of Revising the Population Needs Component	101
Population Needs for Mental Health Services	101
Population Needs for Substance Abuse Services	103
Cost Component	106
Fiscal Capacity Component	108
Interaction of Population in Need and Cost of Services Components: Expenditure Need	108
Poverty and Population Need for Services	112
Summary	116

Chapter Eight

CONCLUSIONS	117

Appendix

A. CONCEPTUAL ANALYSIS OF THE BLOCK GRANT FORMULA	123
B. ALTERNATIVE MEASURES, STATISTICAL ISSUES	131
C. COST OF SERVICE REGRESSION ANALYSIS	165

Bibliography	177

FIGURES

3.1.	One-Year Rates of Severe Mental Illness, by State, ECA Data	38
3.2.	30-Day Rates of Less Severe Mental Illness, by State, NCS Data	38
4.1.	Percentage of Population Meeting RAND Criteria for Drug or Alcohol Dependence, by State, NHSDA Data	57
4.2.	Percentage of Population Meeting RAND Criteria for Drug Dependence Only, by State, NHSDA Data	58
5.1.	Percentage Differences Between (Rescaled) Mean and Median Nonmanufacturing Wage Indexes for 1990	66
5.2.	Percentage Differences Between (Rescaled) Indexes of Manufacturing and Nonmanufacturing Wages	67
5.3.	1990 (Rescaled) Indexes of All Nonmanufacturing Wages Versus Wages in SA and MH Services-Related Industries and Occupations	68
5.4.	Numbers of States with Alternative Index Values	69
5.5.	State Wage Index Rankings, 1990 Versus 1980 Median Nonmanufacturing Wages	70
5.6.	Percentage Effects of Using Revised Wage and Rent Measures in the Current Formula	74
5.7.	Index Comparison of Reported Funding per Client, Substance Abuse Versus Mental Health Services	76
5.8.	Comparison Between the Standardized Substance Abuse Cost Index and an Index Constructed from Actual Funding Data	79
5.9.	Percentage Differences Between the Experience-Based Indexes for Mental Health and Substance Abuse Services	80
5.10.	Current and Alternative Cost of Services Indexes	82
6.1.	Percentage Change in States' Total Taxable Resources (TTR), 1986–1988	90
6.2.	State TTR Rankings, 1988	91
6.3.	TTR 1991 Versus Three-Year Average TTR, 1989–1991	91
6.4.	Percentage Change in States' RTS, 1986–1988	93
6.5.	State RTS Rankings, 1988	93
6.6.	Fiscal Capacity, 1991, TTR and RTS	94
7.1.	Percentage Change in the Mental Health Allocation Under the Preferred Alternative Measure of Population Need, by State	103
7.2.	Percentage Change in the Substance Abuse Allocation Under the Preferred Alternative Measure of Population Need, by State	105

7.3. Percentage Change in the Mental Health Allocation Under the Preferred Alternative Measure of Expenditure Need, by State 110
7.4. Percentage Change in the Substance Abuse Allocation Under the Preferred Alternative Measure of Expenditure Need, by State 112
7.5. Percentage Change in the Substance Abuse Allocation from an Allocation Based Only on Population Size Under the Current Formula and the Preferred Alternative Measure, by State 113
B.1. Percentage of Population Meeting RAND Criteria for Drug or Alcohol Dependence, by State, NHSDA Data 134
B.2. Percentage of Population Meeting OAS Criteria for Drug or Alcohol Dependence, by State, NHSDA Data 135
B.3. Percentage of Population Meeting RAND Criteria for Substance Dependence, or Making Heavy Use of a Substance, by State, NHSDA Data 136
B.4. Percentage of Population Meeting RAND Criteria for Drug or Alcohol Dependence, by State, NHSDA Data 137
B.5. Percentage of Population Meeting OAS Criteria for Drug or Alcohol Dependence, by State, NHSDA Data 138
B.6. Percentage of Population Meeting RAND Criteria for Substance Dependence, or Making Heavy Use of a Substance, by State, NHSDA Data 139
B.7. Alternative Model of the Percentage of Population Meeting RAND Criteria for Dependence 158
B.8. Alternative Model of the Percentage of Population Meeting RAND Criteria for Dependence, by State 159

TABLES

3.1.	Operational Definitions of Adults with Serious Mental Illness	29
3.2.	Percentage of Persons with Serious Mental Illness in Adult Household Population	30
3.3.	Variables Examined as Predictors of Serious Mental Illness	31
3.4.	Final Models: Factors Predicting Serious Mental Illness in ECA Study	33
3.5.	Final Models: Factors Predicting Serious Mental Illness in NCS Study	34
3.6.	Predicted Prevalence of Serious Mental Illness for States: Summary Statistics and Correlation Coefficients for Eight Alternative Definitions of Need for Treatment	37
4.1.	Operational Definitions of Persons Needing Substance Abuse Treatment Services	48
4.2.	Percentage of Persons with Substance Dependence in Household Population	48
4.3.	Operational Definitions of Risks to Youth for Developing Substance Use Problems	49
4.4.	Variables Examined as Predictors of Need for Substance Abuse Treatment and Prevention Services, National Household Survey of Drug Abuse	50
4.5.	Final Models: Factors Predicting Drug or Alcohol Dependence or Drug Dependence Alone	52
4.6.	Final Models: Factors Predicting Risks for Developing Substance Use Problems	53
4.7.	Prevalence of Substance Dependence for States: Summary Statistics and Correlation Coefficients	56
5.1.	Simple Correlation Between Population Urbanicity and Percentage Differences Between Current and Alternative COSI Values	84
7.1.	Effect on Mental Health Allocations of Changing Population Needs Index Only	102
7.2.	Correlation of State Characteristics with Mental Health Allocations, Changing Population Needs Index Only	102
7.3.	Effect on Substance Abuse Allocations of Changing Population Needs Index Only	104

7.4.	Correlation of State Characteristics with Substance Abuse Allocations, Changing Population Needs Index Only	105
7.5.	Effect on Mental Health Allocations of Changing Cost of Service Index Only	106
7.6.	Correlation of State Characteristics with Mental Health Allocations, Changing Cost of Service Index Only	107
7.7.	Effect on Substance Abuse Allocations of Changing Cost of Service Index Only	107
7.8.	Correlation of State Characteristics with Substance Abuse Allocations, Changing Cost of Service Index Only	108
7.9.	Total Effect on Mental Health Allocations of Changing Population Needs and Cost of Service Indexes	109
7.10.	Correlation of State Characteristics with Mental Health Allocations, Changing Population Needs and Cost of Service Indexes	109
7.11.	Total Effect on Substance Abuse Allocations of Changing Population Needs and Cost of Service Indexes	111
7.12.	Correlation of State Characteristics with Substance Abuse Allocations, Changing Population Needs and Cost of Service Indexes	111
7.13.	Total Effect on Mental Health Allocations of Changing Population Needs and Cost of Service Indexes and Restricting Population Need to Poverty Population	114
7.14.	Correlation of State Characteristics with Mental Health Allocations, Changing Population Needs and Cost of Service Indexes and Restricting Population Need to Poverty Population	114
7.15.	Total Effect on Substance Abuse Allocations of Changing Population Needs and Cost of Service Indexes, and Restricting Population Need to Poverty Population	115
7.16.	Correlation of State Characteristics with Substance Abuse Allocations, Changing Population Needs and Cost of Service Indexes, and Restricting Population Need to Poverty Population	115
7.17.	Percentage Shift in Grant Allocations Due to Need and Cost Components	116
B.1.	Operational Definitions of Persons Needing Substance Abuse Treatment Services	132
B.2.	Prevalence of Substance Dependence in Household Population	132
B.3.	Final Models: Factors Predicting Substance Dependence/Substance Abuse	133
B.4.	Predicted Prevalence of Substance Dependence/Problems for States: Summary Statistics and Correlation Coefficients	134
B.5.	Effect on Mental Health Allocations of Changing Population Needs Index Only	140
B.6.	Correlation of State Characteristics with Mental Health Allocations, Changing Population Needs Index Only	140
B.7.	Total Effect on Mental Health Allocations of Changing Population Needs and Cost of Service Indexes	141

B.8.	Correlation of State Characteristics with Shifts in Mental Health Allocations, Changing Population Needs and Cost of Service Indexes	143
B.9.	Effect on Substance Abuse Allocations of Changing Population Needs Index Only (20 Percent Prevention)	145
B.10.	Effect on Substance Abuse Allocations of Changing Population Needs Index Only (50 Percent Prevention)	146
B.11.	Correlation of State Characteristics with Shifts in Substance Abuse Allocations, Changing Population Needs Index Only (20 Percent Prevention)	147
B.12.	Correlation of State Characteristics with Shifts in Substance Abuse Allocations, Changing Population Needs Index Only (50 Percent Prevention)	147
B.13.	Total Effect on Substance Abuse Allocations of Changing Population Needs and Cost of Service Indexes (20 Percent Prevention)	148
B.14.	Total Effect on Substance Abuse Allocations of Changing Population Needs and Cost of Service Indexes (50 Percent Prevention)	150
B.15.	Correlation of State Characteristics with Shifts in Substance Abuse Allocations, Changing Population Needs and Cost of Service Indexes (20 Percent Prevention)	152
B.16.	Correlation of State Characteristics with Shifts in Substance Abuse Allocations, Changing Population Needs and Cost of Service Indexes (50 Percent Prevention)	153
B.17.	Final Model: Factors Predicting Drug or Alcohol Dependence (RAND)	156
B.18.	Predicted Prevalence of Substance Dependence for States: Summary Statistics and Correlation Coefficient Between Alternative Models of Need for Treatment Defined as Drug or Alcohol Dependence	157
B.19.	Predicted Prevalence of Mental Illness and Substance Dependence for States: Summary Statistics and Correlation Coefficients Between Weighted and Unweighted Models of Preferred Definitions of Need for Treatment	160
B.20.	Predicted Prevalence of Mental Illness and Substance Dependence for States: Summary Statistics and Correlation Coefficients Between Individual and Aggregate-Level Estimates	161
B.21.	Census-Tract Variables Examined as Predictors of Need for Drug or Alcohol Abuse Treatment	162
B.22.	Final Model: Factors Predicting Drug or Alcohol Dependence Using Census-Tract Variables	163
C.1.	1990 Wage and Rent Indexes	169
C.2.	Descriptive Statistics for Substance Abuse Analysis Variables	170
C.3.	Descriptive Statistics for Mental Health Services Analysis Variables	172
C.4.	Substance Abuse Regression Statistics	172

C.5.	Substance Abuse Regression: Analysis of Variance	172
C.6.	Substance Abuse Regression: Coefficient Estimates	172
C.7.	Mental Health Regression Statistics	173
C.8.	Mental Health Regression: Analysis of Variance	173
C.9.	Mental Health Regression: Coefficient Estimates	173
C.10.	Substance Abuse Urbanicity Regression Statistics	174
C.11.	Substance Abuse Urbanicity Regression: Analysis of Variance	174
C.12.	Substance Abuse Regression: Coefficient Estimates	175
C.13.	Normalized Cost of Service Indexes	176

SUMMARY

INTRODUCTION

In 1992, Congress passed the Alcohol, Drug Abuse and Mental Health Administration Reorganization Act, which, among other things, revised the formula that the federal government uses for distributing Block Grants to the states to provide substance abuse (SA) and mental health (MH) services. To distribute the Block Grant funds equitably across the states, the current SA and MH formulas calculate shares based on three formula components that are measured for each state: the size of population in need, the costs of providing services, and the state's fiscal capacity. Congressional debate has continued, however, about whether the specific measures used to represent these components are appropriate. In particular, the measure of population need for substance abuse services, which heavily weights youth living in urbanized areas, has been the subject of debate in the Senate.

The purpose of this study, mandated by the 1992 authorizing legislation, was to inform Congress about the appropriateness of measures used in the current allocation formula and to identify factors that Congress might wish to take into account in the formula to attain greater equity. The study was not intended, however, to recommend or generate specific alternative formulas.

To this end, we first examined the concept of equity represented in the structure of the current formula to understand the intent of Congress in choosing this formula to distribute funds among the states. Second, we reviewed the epidemiological literature to determine what factors might be predictors of populations in need of SA and MH services. But because of limitations in drawing conclusions from the available literature, we analyzed major national datasets to identify factors predicting population need for services and developed our alternative measures based on these. Third, we examined the data sources and methodology used to measure interstate variations in cost of services for the current formula. Again, observing limitations in the information used to develop these measures, we turned to additional data sources to develop alternative cost measures. We also reviewed the literature on fiscal capacity measurement, and evaluated the existing measures of that component. Finally, we compared these alternative measures of the three formula components with the measures specified in the currently legislated formula by analyzing how the 1993

Block Grant allocations would be redistributed to the states under the improved, alternative measures.

CONCEPT OF EQUITY

The current formula structure implicitly embodies the concept of taxpayer equity. That is, it aims to equalize the rates that taxpayers would have to pay to support a standard level of service. This study does not question the taxpayer equity approach. However, the current formula fails to consider non-Block Grant federal funding of SA and MH programs (e.g., Medicaid and Medicare). Nor does it take into account differential population needs due to availability of private insurance coverage that may vary across states. Thus, it may not equalize, or address variations in, total public and private funding for SA and MH services across states. Because Block Grant funds are largely used to provide treatment to uninsured and poor persons, states with similar total population needs for SA and MH services may nonetheless have different needs for Block Grant services because of differences in the extent to which their populations are uninsured. Given the focus of the formula on the equitable allocation of only Block Grant funds, rather than on equalizing total federal and private funds for SA and MH services, the structure of the current formula is appropriate for equalizing taxpayer burden across states. What is at question is whether measures for the three components in the formula can be improved; this question was the major focus of our analysis.

POPULATION IN NEED OF MENTAL HEALTH SERVICES

To identify factors predicting need for MH services, we conducted analyses of two major psychiatric epidemiologic datasets (the Epidemiologic Catchment Area Study and the National Comorbidity Study). From this analysis, we developed multivariate models of social demographic and community-level factors associated with serious mental illness. Data regarding predictors of need among children were unavailable. For adults, results indicate that need for MH services is higher among women, the unmarried or separated, those who are disabled or receiving welfare, and those without a high school diploma. However, the current formula uses only age as an indicator of differential need for MH services.

After an analysis of need predictors, we used indirect estimation techniques to project needs for all states based on their population characteristics reported in the 1990 Census. We assumed a constant rate of need among children across states. Then we examined how the projected needs varied among the states. We found that the proportion of the population needing MH services tended to be higher in southeastern states and lower in northwestern states but was not strongly related to state population size, urbanicity, or poverty population.

Our preferred alternative indicator of MH needs was based on predictors of recent serious mental illness among adults from the National Comorbidity Survey and on a crude estimate of youth needs based on 3.2 percent of a state's population under age 16. Holding other elements in the grant formula constant, using this preferred alternative measure of population needs, rather than the current one, would shift only 5 percent of the federal funds across states; the shares of about 20 percent of the states (containing 12 percent of the U.S. population) would change by more than 10 percent. Overall, shares would shift toward states with a higher percentage of their populations in poverty if improved measures of needs for MH services were included in the formula.

POPULATION IN NEED OF SUBSTANCE ABUSE SERVICES

To identify factors predicting need for SA prevention and treatment services, we analyzed data from the 1991 National Household Survey of Drug Abuse. Again we developed multivariate models of social demographic and community-level factors associated with population need for services. Persons in need of prevention services were defined as youth (aged 12–20) weighted by their risk of using substances (alcohol, drugs, or tobacco). Persons in need of treatment services were defined as those with recent alcohol or drug dependence. SA prevention needs among youth were associated with increasing age, having lower family income, not attending school full-time, living alone, and working. SA treatment needs were found to be higher for males, white non-Hispanics, persons separated or unmarried, those aged 18–44, high school and college drop-outs, and residents of the Western United States. Additionally, living in a nonmetropolitan area was associated with *higher* needs for SA treatment; this was due largely to the higher needs for alcohol treatment found in nonmetropolitan areas. In fact, urbanicity was unrelated to need even when we considered drug dependence treatment need separately from alcohol dependence treatment need.

We developed alternative measures of SA prevention and treatment needs by indirectly estimating rates of need for the states using 1990 Census data. With these alternative measures, state-level rates of need for treatment services (per 100 population) tended to be higher in less urbanized states but were not related to state population size or poverty population. Findings on state-level rates of need for prevention services showed no strong relationships to states' population size, urbanicity, or poverty population.

Our preferred alternative SA needs measure was based on a definition of treatment need that targeted any drug or alcohol dependence among adults and a definition of prevention need that weighted the number of youth in each state by the probability of any substance use among those youth. Compared to the population needs measure used in the current formula, our preferred alternative measure would shift about 18 percent of the total Block Grant funds for SA services across states. This calculation assumes that prevention need constitutes a 20 percent share and treatment need an 80 percent share of total population need and that the other components of the formula are equal. Furthermore, the shares of nearly three-quarters of the states (containing 65 percent of the U.S. population) would change by more than 10 percent. If the current formula were to be improved by incorporating SA service need measures similar to those we developed, allocation shares would tend to shift away from larger and more urban toward smaller and more rural states. This reflects in part the dominance of alcohol dependence in the population needing SA treatment and the higher rate of alcohol dependence in nonmetropolitan areas.

COST OF SERVICES COMPONENT

Even if all the states had the same populations in need of both SA and MH services, their *expenditure* needs could differ sharply due to cost differences. To account for this, Congress introduced a cost of service (COS) index as a component of the formula in the Block Grant legislation of 1992. The current COS index, which applies to both MH and SA services, is a weighted sum of indexes of interstate wage and rent variations. We examined each COS element (weights as well as wages and rents) in terms of timeliness (i.e., applicability to current costs), relevance to measuring SA- and MH-specific services, and sensitivity to interstate differences in delivery settings.

The COS methodology in the current formula uses a wage index based on median nonmanufacturing wages in each state. Using 1990 Census data, we found that this measure does not adequately represent interstate wage variations in occupations and industries related to SA and MH services. By using a more relevant wage indicator (one that represents interstate wage variations in occupations and industries related to SA and MH services), we found that the COS index would rise in most lower-wage states while noticeably declining in a few states that have high nonmanufacturing wage indexes. We also updated the rent index, which is currently based on 1980 Census and market rent data, by using 1990 data. Though using timelier estimates appears warranted, we found that the rent index rose or fell more than 10 percent in only a very few states. Even in those states, the overall effect on the COS index was not large because rents contribute only modestly to the overall cost of providing SA and MH services.

The COS methodology in the current formula also combines the wage and rent measures using weights derived from a general survey of physician practice costs. However, these weights are not specific to SA or MH services and do not recognize potential differences in the cost of providing care in urban versus rural settings. To judge whether those weights fairly represent SA and MH service costs, we examined data on the actual provision of SA and MH services from the 1991 National Drug and Alcoholism Treatment Unit Survey (NDATUS) and the 1992 National Reporting Program for Mental Health Services (NRPMHS). Recognizing criticism that the NDATUS does not fully capture funding and other data, we selected a sample of NDATUS reporting units that provide complete information, tested those records for consistency, and found the selected data suitable for the analyses we performed.

Regressions relating funding per client to labor and facilities costs proved to be very good predictors of both SA and MH service interstate cost differences. These also showed that states systematically spend more to provide both SA and MH services in rural areas. We used this evidence to predict what SA and MH service costs would be if all states used a standardized combination of labor and facilities and translated that into a standardized cost index. Compared to the current COS index, these new COS indexes give higher standardized cost values to states that are more rural relative to those with highly urban populations. When we compared states' allocation shares under the current Block Grant formulas with shares using these alternative COS indexes (other components of the formula being equal and not applying any restriction on the range of the COS index), 7 percent of the MH and 8 percent of the SA allocation shares were shifted across states.

FISCAL CAPACITY COMPONENT

The fiscal capacity component included in the current formula reflects the notion that, all other things being equal, a state with a greater ability to raise revenues ought to require fewer federal funds to provide a standard level of services. Since the Block Grants supplement states' internal allocations for public SA and MH services, it is desirable for equity-based formulas to account for a state's revenue-raising abilities. After examining several alternative measures of fiscal capacity, we concluded that the measure currently used in the formula, total taxable resources, is the least volatile and most reliable indicator of fiscal capacity currently available. It accurately captures a state's ability to raise revenues; its relative stability suggests that it is not contaminated by large measurement errors.

COMBINED POPULATION NEED AND COST OF SERVICES COMPONENTS

Because the population need and cost of service components in the current Block Grant formulas are related multiplicatively, we examined the effect of using improved measures for both components on allocation shares. If both the population needs and cost of service measures were changed to our preferred alternative measures, 22 percent of the allocation for substance abuse services would shift across states, generally moving shares from larger urban states toward smaller rural states, and 7 percent of allocations for mental health services would shift, generally going toward states with larger poverty populations. The relatively large shift from urban to rural is a combination of undoing the current urban overweighting and our higher estimates of rural needs. Because of the multiplicative effects of the population needs and costs of service components, improvements in measuring both will have a much greater effect on the SA than the MH Block Grant formulas.

CONCLUSIONS

To evaluate the appropriateness of the current MH and SA Block Grant formulas, this study analyzed recent national data to develop improved alternative measures for the population needs, cost of services, and fiscal capacity components composing these formulas. Taking these alternative measures as the best available standards for an equitable distribution of funds across states, it becomes apparent that the current formula would be more equitable if improvements were made in two component measures: population needs and costs of services. Improvements would have a large effect on the distribution of SA Block Grant funds across states, with shares tending to shift from larger urban to smaller rural states. Improvements would affect the distribution of MH Block Grant funds modestly, with shares tending to shift toward poorer states.

In interpreting the results of this study, certain data limitations should be kept in mind. First, use of probability samples of the national population to identify factors predicting population need for services cannot be expected to estimate needs accurately for states where local conditions are unusual or unique. Second, household population surveys miss institutionalized and homeless persons, many of whom have substance abuse or mental health treatment needs; in excluding these populations, the national population data likely underestimate population need for services in urban areas, where homeless and criminal populations are more concentrated. Third, the complete absence of national epidemiologic data on prevalence of serious emotional disturbances among children is another limitation to developing a MH Block Grant formula that considers state variations in needs of children. Finally, the study does not explicitly address the question of what alternative indicators are available on an annual basis to implement improved formula measures—accessibility and timeliness of data would need to be considered in improving existing formula measures.

While the scope of existing data is an inherent limitation in any effort to improve block grant allotment formulas, this study represents an approach that should be of interest not only to those who are concerned about the equitable distribution of funds for the SA and MH Block Grant program but to those who would like to improve distributional equity of other existing or newly legislated federal Block Grant programs. The current SA and MH Block Grant formula has evolved into a conceptually sophisticated formula; its structure is appropriate to consider in other health, human service, and welfare contexts. This study represents an empirical approach to the development of measures of components that could be used in efforts to develop formulas for other Block Grant programs.

ACKNOWLEDGMENTS

We gratefully acknowledge the extensive statistical programming carried out by Bernadette Benjamin, Karen Spritzer, Cindy Foster, Jinyun Liu, Katherine McGonagle, Christopher Nelson, and Shanyang Zhao; the editorial assistance provided by Anita Spiess and Ruth Goldhor; and the secretarial support and production assistance provided by Patti Sue Thompson and Nelie Gill. We also appreciate reviews and helpful suggestions from Daniel Relles and G. Richard Smith.

Chapter One

INTRODUCTION: BACKGROUND AND PURPOSES OF STUDY

In 1992, Congress passed the Alcohol, Drug Abuse and Mental Health Administration Reorganization Act. This act, among other things, revised the formula by which the federal government disbursed funds as Block Grants to the states for the provision of services dealing with substance abuse and mental illness. Alcohol and drug abuse were lumped together as substance abuse for the first time but then were separated from mental illness. In addition, important technical changes were made in the formula used to distribute moneys.

These changes were the subject of debate in the Senate; some Senators argued that the new formula unfairly penalized their states. Though the conference committee's formula was adopted without change, it was agreed that the Secretary of Health and Human Services should contract for a study to review and evaluate the new formula. To put an evaluation of this Block Grant formula in a larger context, consider what is at stake with the formula. The federal government distributed $1.1 billion dollars to states for substance abuse prevention and treatment in 1993, and $280 million dollars for mental health treatment. This represented a significant contribution to states' expenditures on substance abuse prevention and treatment (25 percent on average across states) and a much smaller but notable share of states' expenditures on mental health services (4 percent on average). Not surprisingly, then, the debate surrounding the formula has been most intense regarding specification of that portion of the formula governing the distribution of funds for substance abuse prevention and treatment.

In August 1993, the Center for Substance Abuse Treatment, identified in the legislation as the responsible agency within the Department of Health and Human Services, contracted with RAND's Drug Policy Research Center to conduct the congressionally mandated study over a period of six months.

This is the final report of the study called for by the legislation. The study team of psychologists, economists, and statisticians (1) examined a variety of new databases to estimate the population need for treatment and prevention services; (2) reviewed the literature on the epidemiology of mental illness and substance abuse; (3) used new data to estimate the variation in costs of providing services among states; (4) interviewed Congressional staff, GAO and Substance Abuse and Mental Health Services Administration (SAMHSA) officials to learn more about the goals and implementation of the formula; (5) developed a more explicit analysis of the equity and policy issues involved in the formula; and (6) built simulation models to examine the consequences of incorporating relevant epidemiological and fiscal factors in estimating state-level need for services.

This chapter covers a number of background matters before the substantive analysis: It describes the evolution of the formula, including a detailed description of the current formula, the analytic strategy pursued, and the constraints of this study, and outlines the remainder of the report.

THE HISTORY OF THE BLOCK GRANT FORMULA

The Alcohol, Drug, and Mental Health Services (ADMS) Block Grant was one of seven Block Grants established by Public Law 97-35, the Omnibus Budget Reconciliation Act (OBRA) of 1981, to be administered by the Department of Health and Human Services (57 FR 31682). The ADMS Block Grant consolidated categorical grants for substance abuse and community mental health services that had been sanctioned under four prior authorizations: the Community Mental Health Centers Act of 1963; the Mental Health Systems Act of 1980; the Comprehensive Alcohol Abuse and Alcoholism Prevention, Treatment, and Rehabilitation Act of 1970; and the Drug Abuse Prevention, Treatment, and Rehabilitation Act of 1970 (Carnevale and Fastrup, 1991; Institute for Health and Aging, 1986; Pope, 1990). Consolidation of categorical grants into Block Grants was intended to provide state and local governments with more flexibility and control over funding to enhance their ability to meet localized needs, to end duplication of effort in delivering services, and to enable better coordination of services (Carnevale and Fastrup, 1991; U.S. Senate, 1981, 1984).

The OBRA legislation authorized ADMS Block Grant funds for fiscal years 1982 through 1984 in proportion to the historical funding patterns of the original categorical programs. States' allocations were based on alcohol and drug funding that each had received in 1980 and on mental health funding that each had received in 1981 (Carnevale and Fastrup, 1991; Pope, 1990; U.S. GAO, 1990).

The 1981 legislation resulted in wide variation in per capita funding among states (Pope, 1990). Legislators recognized historical inequities in the allocation of substance abuse and mental health funds and hoped for the development of a more equitable formula (U.S. House of Representatives, 1981). The 1981 legislation directed the Secretary of Health and Human Services to conduct a study that would produce a formula to more equitably distribute funds among states. The study was to consider "(1) the financial resources of the various States, (2) the populations of the States, and (3) any other factor which the Secretary may consider appropriate" (P.L. 97-35).

The secretary's report recommended population and fiscal capacity measured in terms of per capita personal income (PCPI) as appropriate indicators of need (U.S. DHHS, 1982). In a later study, the GAO concurred that population and per capita income were better indicators of need than the 1981 allocation level (U.S. GAO, 1984, as cited in Institute for Health and Aging, 1986).

The Alcohol Abuse, Drug Abuse, and Mental Health Amendments of 1984 (P.L. 98-509) renewed the ADMS Block Grants for three fiscal years. The amendments also mandated a "minor equity adjustment" (U.S. Senate, 1984) on allocations in excess of 1984 appropriations. The Committee on Labor and Human Resources (U.S. Senate, 1984) had reported concern over the equity of the distribution of ADMS Block Grant funds to the states. Although a complete formula revision was considered unacceptable (U.S. Senate, 1984), funds above the 1984 hold-harmless level[1] were to be allocated using a formula based equally "(i) on the population of each State, and (ii) the population of each State weighted by its relative per capita income" (P.L. 98-509). To further address the concerns about equitable distribution of ADMS Block Grant funds among states, the amendments required that a nongovernmental entity review the formula to determine "whether a more equitable formula [could] be designed" (P.L. 98-509).

The Alcohol, Drug Abuse, and Mental Health Administration contracted with the Institute for Health and Aging at the University of California, San Francisco, and the Institute for the Study of Family, Work and Community in Berkeley to examine the allocation formula. The institutes reported that the method of allocating funds used in the Alcohol Abuse, Drug Abuse, and Mental Health Amendments of 1984 (P.L. 98-509) led to inequities resulting mainly from the hold-harmless benchmark of the 1984 amendments (Institute for Health and Aging, 1986). Phasing out the hold-harmless provision was therefore recommended. The institutes also concluded that an allocation of funds based on populations at risk of substance abuse and mental illness would produce a more equitable distribution of funds. Since the ADMS legislation intended equalization of Block Grant resources, the institutes also recommended inclusion of a fiscal capacity measure (Institute for Health and Aging, 1986).

Funding for the ADMS Block Grant was reauthorized and changes in the allocation formula were specified in the Comprehensive Alcohol Abuse, Drug Abuse, and Mental Health Amendments Act of 1988, a subtitle under the Anti-Drug Abuse Act of 1988 (P.L. 100-690). Congress made two formula revisions based in part on the 1986 report by the Institute for Health and Aging (Pope, 1990). First, total taxable resources (TTR) replaced PCPI as the measure of fiscal capacity. TTR (the average of PCPI and gross state income) is considered a more comprehensive measure than PCPI (Carnevale and Fastrup, 1991; U.S. Department of the Treasury, 1985, as cited in U.S. GAO, 1990) because it takes account of the fact that some income received by a state's residents is generated elsewhere.

Second, Congress incorporated a population measure consisting of a weighted sum of a state's high-risk population age cohorts and its urbanized area population (Carnevale and Fastrup, 1991). Age cohorts used in the formula are identical to the age cohorts determined in the 1986 Institute for Health and Aging study to be at high risk of alcohol abuse and dependence (25–64), drug abuse and dependence (18–24), and selected mental disorders (25–44). Prevalence rates for disorders were reported

---

[1]This hold-harmless provision prevented redistribution of allocations across states if these would reduce any state's allocation below its 1984 level.

by age cohorts in the Institute for Health and Aging Study, but these rates were not used in the legislation.[2] The weights the legislation assigned to each of these age cohorts (.20) and to the urbanized area population (.40) were arbitrary (Fastrup, 1991). The higher weight for the urbanized population reflected the belief that the prevalence of drug abuse was higher in urban areas.

The 1988 legislation also provided for a phase-out of the hold-harmless provision from 1989 through 1992, so that an increasing proportion of each fiscal year's Block Grant funds would be allocated using the formula (Carnevale and Fastrup, 1991). The hold-harmless provision was to be eliminated in fiscal year 1993 (U.S. GAO, 1990). Although a reduction in the hold-harmless provision was enacted, another formula constraint was introduced in the 1988 legislation guaranteeing that small states would share in the ADMS Block Grant funding increase between 1988 and 1989 (Carnevale and Fastrup, 1991; U.S. GAO, 1990).

The formula enacted in the 1988 Anti-Drug Abuse Act improved the targeting of Block Grant funds, but later studies indicated that inequities would remain even after phase-out of the hold-harmless provision (Fastrup, 1991; Pope, 1990; U.S. GAO, 1990, 1991). First, arbitrary weighting of high-risk and urban population groups in the formula reduces the influence of populations at risk of mental health and alcohol disorders and produces a bias against rural states (Fastrup, 1991; U.S. GAO, 1990, 1991). Second, percentages specific to each state were used to allocate funds between mental health and substance abuse services. Because these within-state percentages varied across states, there may have been an inequitable distribution of mental health and substance abuse Block Grant funds even if overall ADMS funds were allocated fairly (Pope, 1990; U.S. GAO, 1991). Third, although states' public treatment systems primarily serve the poor, states' allocations were based on their total populations rather than their poverty populations (Pope, 1990). Fourth, there was no adjustment in the formula for variation among states in the cost of providing services (Pope, 1990; U.S. GAO, 1991).

THE CURRENT FORMULA

The 1992 Alcohol, Drug Abuse and Mental Health Administration (ADAMHA) Reorganization Act (P.L. 102-321) changed the ADMS Block Grant formula in several significant respects. Earlier reports had proposed separate Block Grants for mental health and substance abuse as a potential improvement to allocation of funds (Pope, 1990; U.S. GAO, 1991). The ADAMHA Reorganization Act instituted separate Block Grants to be allocated to states using separate formulas: Subpart I—Block Grants for Community Mental Health Services; Subpart II—Block Grants for Prevention and Treatment of Substance Abuse. The use of separate allocation formulas was in-

---

[2]The 1986 Institute for Health and Aging study included (1) a detailed table giving specific prevalence rates for alcohol abuse and dependence, drug abuse and dependence, and selected mental disorders for ages 18–24, 25–44, 45–65, and 65+, and (2) a table derived from the first, listing high-risk age groups and genders for each disorder. The derived table indicated that people aged 18 to 24 are most at risk for drug abuse and dependence, men 25 to 64 are at most risk for alcohol abuse and dependence, and people aged 25 to 44 are most at risk for selected mental disorders.

tended to better reflect the population in need of mental health services (U.S. GAO, 1991) and provide for more uniform within-state allocations between mental health and substance abuse (Pope, 1990).[3]

To remove what was now viewed as the overstatement of urban drug abuse while recognizing some urban-rural differences in drug use among 18- to 24-year-olds in the substance abuse formula, the 40 percent weight on states' urbanized area population was eliminated and their urbanized area population of 18- to 24-year-olds was double-weighted (Carnevale and Fastrup, 1991; U.S. GAO, 1990, 1991). The current mental health formula uses the following age cohorts: 18–24, 25–44, 45–64, and 65 or older.[4] The age cohorts were weighted by the prevalence rates for total selected mental disorders reported in the 1986 Institute for Health and Aging study. A "cost-of-services" index, bounded to within 10 percent of the national average, was included in both formulas to reflect the assumed higher cost-of-service provision in urban areas (U.S. Senate, 1992). The 1992 legislation did not maintain a small-state minimum, although it did preserve a hold-harmless provision. Under the hold-harmless provision within the mental health Block Grant, each state must be allotted at least 20.6 percent of its 1992 allocation for mental health for fiscal years 1993 and 1994. Within the substance abuse (SA) Block Grant, each state must be allotted at least 79.4 percent of its 1992 allocation for substance abuse for fiscal years 1993 and 1994. The 1992 legislation did not act on the recommendation to consider states' poverty populations in allocating funds (Pope, 1990).[5]

The current formula has a similar structure for the SA and MH grants to the state. In each case, there are three elements to be estimated: population in need (P), cost of service (C), and fiscal capacity (N). The formulas differ primarily in the equations for estimating the size of the population in need.

In each case, the allotment formula can be written as

$$G_i = A(X_i / \sum X_i), \tag{1.1}$$

where

G_i = grant amount for the ith state
A = total funds appropriated for distribution among the states
X_i = score for ith state

---

[3]In interviews with RAND staff, two Substance Abuse and Mental Health Services Administration (SAMHSA) representatives noted that the mental health constituency viewed separating the mental health and substance abuse Block Grants as a way to preserve mental health services funding.

[4]Due to a typographical error, the age cohort 45–64 originally appeared as 25–64 in the mental health formula of the ADAMHA Reorganization Act. The Public Health Service Act Technical Amendments Act of August 26, 1992 (P.L. 102-352) corrected "25–64" to read "45–64."

[5]A legislative staff member interviewed by RAND stated that inclusion of the poverty population in the formula was attempted; however, the shift in the balance of Block Grant allocations among states was too large to be acceptable to some states.

and the summation is over the 50 states plus the District of Columbia. The numerator, referred to here as the state score, is the product of P, C, and N.

Mental Health

The state population at risk (P_i) is the weighted product of various age categories:

$$P_i = \sum W_j A_{ij}. \tag{1.2}$$

The weights W_j are derived from the 1986 Institute for Health and Aging study and are intended to represent the relative risk for each age group. They are specified in the legislation as

$$W_1 = .107 \qquad W_2 = .166 \qquad W_3 = .099 \qquad W_4 = .082.$$

The A_{ij} are the numbers of persons in state i in age group j; i.e.,

A_{i1} = number of persons in state i, aged 18 to 24
A_{i2} = number of persons in state i, aged 25 to 44
A_{i3} = number of persons in state i, aged 45 to 64
A_{i4} = number of persons in state i, aged 65 or older.

The cost factor, intended to adjust for differences among the states in the cost of providing mental health and substance abuse services, is derived from the 1990 report of Health Economics Research Inc. (HER). Costs are decomposed into labor (L), rental (R), and "other supply" costs.

$$C_i = .10 + .75 L_i + .25 R_i. \tag{1.3}$$

In the HER report, the labor index was based on median hourly nonmanufacturing wages obtained from the 1980 Census, and the rental housing index was based on the Department of Housing and Urban Development measure of "fair market" apartment rents. The cost of other services (drugs, office equipment, etc.) was assumed to be uniform across the nation and adds the constant .10 to the index value. The legislation specifies that the range of variation for C is limited: No state can have a C of less than 0.9 or higher than 1.1.

The third element of the formula (N) is intended to adjust for differences in state capacity to pay for mental health or substance abuse services.

$$N_i = 1 - .35 \, (R_i\% / P_i\%), \tag{1.4}$$

where $R_i\%$ represents the state's share of national total taxable resources, adjusted by the cost index, i.e.,

$$R_i\% = [TTR_i / C_i] / [\sum TTR_i / C_i], \tag{1.5}$$

where TTR_i is the total taxable resources of state i, to be calculated from the latest three-year average of arithmetic means.[6] In the equation for N_i, the denominator $P_i\%$ is the state's share of the population at risk:

$$P_i\% = P_i / \sum P_i \qquad (1.6)$$

(i.e., it takes account of the weighting of different age groups in the population). If a state's share of the at-risk population equals its share of total taxable resources, then N_i will equal 0.65. The higher N_i, the higher the state's share of the Block Grant. The statute puts a lower limit on N_i of 0.4.

N_i can be thought of as the share of a standard benefit per person at risk that the federal government will pay. For a state that has the mean total taxable resources, the federal government will pay 65 percent, with the state paying the other 35 percent.

Substance Abuse

The substance abuse formula differs from that for mental illness only in its definition of the state population at risk, which gives additional weight to the percentage of young adults living in urbanized areas:

$$P_i = 0.5 \, [(A_i / \sum A_i) + (B_i / \sum B_i)], \qquad (1.7)$$

where

$$\begin{aligned} A_i &= T_i + U_i \\ T_i &= \text{number of persons in the ith state, aged 18 to 24} \\ U_i &= \text{number of persons in ith state, aged 18 to 24 and living in urbanized areas} \\ B_i &= \text{number of persons in ith state, aged 25 to 64.} \end{aligned}$$

The double weighting of 18- to 24-year-olds living in urbanized areas was a compromise, giving less weight to urbanicity than did the prior formula but still giving some additional weight. It appears that this may have been driven by beliefs that treatment service costs were higher in urban areas (U.S. GAO, 1990).

ANALYTIC STRATEGY

The authorizing legislation specified five tasks for this study. The first of the five ("an assessment of the degree to which the formula allocates funds according to the respective needs of the States and territories") raised the question of what constituted a state's "needs." As interpreted to date, this term has been synonymous with the estimates of the number of persons suffering from substance abuse or mental disor-

---

[6]For the District of Columbia, total personal income is substituted for total taxable resources.

ders, adjusted by costs of provision of service. In fact, there are reasons for looking much more closely at the concept of need. For example, should the formula take account of the cross-state distribution of other federal or private programs that provide funds for the same kinds of services? After all, the Block Grant accounts for a modest share of federal, let alone total government, funding of SA and MH services; should these funds not be taken into account, so that the Block Grant is distributed on the basis of remaining need? Most of the Block Grant money goes to programs that serve only the poor who are not covered by other sources; should the formula take account of the cross-state distribution of the poverty population? We considered the advantages and disadvantages of including these factors in the formula.

Need also imbeds a concept of equity that merits examination. Thus, we considered what concept of equity was implicitly being used in the current formula and how it related to possible alternatives.

The next two clauses of the statute both require a review of the epidemiological literature. Clause 2 ("a review of relevant epidemiological research regarding the incidence of substance abuse and mental illness among various age groups and geographic regions of the country") asks for such a review, focused on two specific sets of correlates (age and geographic region). Clause 3 ("the identification of factors not included in the formula that are reliable predictors of the incidence of substance abuse and mental illness") also requires such a review before any data analysis is undertaken. We conducted a comprehensive review of the relevant epidemiological literatures, giving primary emphasis to those related to the major national datasets.

The new analyses of this study are primarily generated in response to Clauses 4 ("an assessment of the validity and relevance of factors currently included in the formula, such as age, urban population and cost") and 5 ("any other information that would contribute to a thorough assessment of the appropriateness of the current formula"). An assessment of validity and relevance of the currently included factors cannot be conducted simply through a literature review. No doubt other variables will be found that have, in some studies, improved the prediction of the prevalence of substance abuse and mental disorder in some population. The question is whether these would make a substantial difference to the distribution of funds among the states, if they were to be included, either in place of or as additions to the current variables. For example, there may be substantial differences between males and females in the prevalence of these problems; however, the gender distribution of the states is so similar that this need not be included in the formula. To identify relevant correlates, we use the most appropriate existing data to compare the outcome of including other variables on estimates of the distribution of the population in need among the states, using the approach known as "synthetic estimation."

For cost and fiscal capacity we faced no similarly complex conceptual issues and had access to more refined datasets (cost-of-service provision) or the opportunity to conduct more refined analyses (fiscal capacity). We developed new cost-of-service indexes and compared the current fiscal capacity measure (three-year average of TTR) with a variety of other measures.

After estimating models to predict variation in the prevalence of substance abuse and mental illness among populations, these models were then incorporated into simulation models to examine the effect of these indicators, compared with the current formula, in distributing the population in need among the states. Similarly, alternative cost of service indicators were compared with the current one in terms of the distribution across states, taking account of the legislatively imposed constraint on the variation; the same was done for fiscal capacity measures. The result was a set of alternative measures for each formula component that is intended to provide Congress with guidance about the consequences of making different choices of equity and targeting.

In conducting these analyses, we have made use of several new databases. The current mental health formula depends heavily on research conducted in 1986, using some early results regarding lifetime prevalence of psychiatric disorders from the Epidemiological Catchment Area (ECA) study, all that were available at that time. The ECA provided the first data on the prevalence of mental disorders for the general population of adults, collected from samples in five sites; it also included data on the prevalence of alcohol and drug abuse. When the pivotal 1986 Block Grant analysis was done by the Institute for Health and Aging, the complete ECA database was not available. Since then, not only have more ECA data become available but an additional national sample survey of mental disorders has been completed. The National Comorbidity Study (NCS) is a national sample of 8,098 persons, who were interviewed by the University of Michigan between September 1990 and February 1992. Our report makes extensive use of both the full ECA and the NCS to estimate the correlates of need for mental health services, operationally defined as the presence of recent serious mental illness.

The 1986 study also relied on the ECA for estimation of substance abuse problems. Since 1986, the National Household Survey on Drug Abuse (NHSDA) has been modified in ways that make it more useful for analysis of state variation in SA. First, its sample size has almost quadrupled, from 8,000 in 1985 to over 32,000 in 1992. Second, it now includes more questions about problems related to use of alcohol and illicit drugs that are reasonable indicators of substance dependence as defined by current diagnostic criteria of the American Psychiatric Association (DSM-III-R). Hence we have relied on the 1991 NHSDA in developing models of the correlates of need for substance abuse treatment and prevention services.

CAVEATS TO THIS STUDY

A study of the MH and SA Block Grant formulas could have been conducted in a number of ways. Certain choices we made were dictated by available time and resources; others were necessitated by gaps in the available data; still others were a consequence of the specifications of the legislation. Below we set out a number of caveats.

Time

The short time (five months to draft report) provided by the contract for this study limited the analyses that were possible. Certain datasets could not be obtained in time. For example, the Bureau of the Census maintains a 20 percent sample dataset, but that agency could not conduct special runs for our use in the time available. Thus, our analysis of cost-of-service indexes, which is reported in Chapter Five, had to be performed using the 5 percent sample that is available as a public use tape. This limited the refinement of the models that could be developed. Similarly, certain models of the prevalence of substance dependence in Chapter Four would have been better estimated by combining the 1991 and 1992 data from the National Household Survey on Drug Abuse. Instead, time limitations and late access to the 1992 data required that we restrict our analyses to the 1991 data.

Missing Data

The act specifically identifies serious emotional disturbances among children as one of the Block Grant targets, the first time this has been introduced into the Block Grant. Thus, it would be desirable to estimate the variation among states in the prevalence of serious emotional disturbances in childhood. Unfortunately, there are no national data on this problem and few small area studies that would provide any guidance. Consequently, the distribution of severe mental illness among adults was supplemented by an estimate of the rate of serious emotional disturbance among children that was assumed to be constant across states.

Incentives

The current Block Grant formula does not attempt to provide incentives for states to increase or decrease their own funding of SA and MH programs. For example, actual expenditures by the states do not enter into the formula directly, though the act, like its predecessors, does impose maintenance of effort requirements to ensure that states do not substitute federal funds for state funds. In considering alternative specifications of each element (population in need, cost of services, and fiscal capacity), we accepted that the formula had to be neutral with respect to incentives.

Hold-Harmless Provisions and Other Constraints

The ADAMHA Reorganization Act included strong hold-harmless clauses for the first two years (FY 1993 and FY 1994), earmarks for various program types, as well as two other constraints (in the extent of variation allowed for costs and fiscal capacity in the formula) on the implementation of the Block Grant formula. The hold-harmless clauses essentially limit the formula from changing a state's 1992-level allocation except through a budget increase. The hold-harmless clauses were intended to minimize the dislocation to the states arising from the implementation of a new allocation formula, while the other constraints were intended to limit the extent of variation in state allocations even after implementation.

Introduction: Background and Purposes of Study   11

All these constraints are political decisions. We interpreted the statutory language calling for this study as not inviting inquiry into the desirability of these decisions. This is particularly significant for the hold-harmless clauses, which, in a time of minimal growth in federal discretionary social spending, have the effect of minimizing the allocative influence of the new formulas; indeed, the 1993 Mental Health Block Grants were essentially frozen at 99 percent of 20.6 percent (the share going to mental health) of the 1992 ADMS Block Grant levels. Presumably, Congress saw the formulas becoming effective in outyears and sought an evaluation for a period in which the hold-harmless clauses would not be the principal determinant of allocations. Thus, our analysis evaluates the current formula as it would operate without the hold-harmless clauses.

The act also included a series of earmarks. For example, states are required to spend at least 35 percent of the SA Block Grant on drug abuse services. These earmarks are not characteristics of the formula as a redistributive device; they only influence the manner in which funds are spent within a state rather than their allocation across states. Consequently, we did not take these into account in our analyses.

The two other constraints (on variation in cost and fiscal capacity measures) present a different issue. These appear to be intended as permanent components of the formula; consequently, we took them into account when we considered alternative specifications of components of the formula.

OUTLINE OF THE REPORT

Chapter Two deals with a variety of conceptual issues: What is the appropriate concept of equity to apply to the formula, what sources of funding should be considered in developing measures of the population in need, and how should diverse interests, such as the balance of need for SA treatment versus prevention, be weighted in considering differences in population need among the states?

Chapters Three (Mental Illness) and Four (Substance Abuse) have identical structures. The first section of each chapter is a review of the literature, identifying the correlates of mental disorder and substance abuse that might be relevant to the Block Grant formula. The second section then describes how we defined variables and developed empirical models to estimate the importance of these correlates. The third section presents the results of our analyses of epidemiologic databases to identify factors associated with population need for services, and to estimate rates of need (per 100 persons) for each of the states.

Chapter Five uses more current and refined data to measure the variation in cost of providing services across states. Particular emphasis is given to finer 1990 Census data on earnings in occupations known to be of importance for treatment of substance abuse and mental disorders. The final section of Chapter Five shows how this more refined assessment of costs of services varies among the states and how it compares to the current formula's specification of the cost-of-service index.

Chapter Six deals with fiscal capacity issues. The current formula uses a three-year moving average of total taxable revenue to compare states' capacities to pay for services themselves. In this chapter, that formula is compared with three other alternative measures of states' fiscal capacity.

Chapter Seven presents the results of analyses that compare shares of the Block Grant allocations received by states under the current formulas with shares based on the preferred alternative measures of population in need and cost of services developed by this study. Alternative fiscal capacity measures were not indicated from analyses presented in Chapter Six, and are therefore not considered in this set of comparisons. Chapter Seven concludes by summarizing the implications of these analyses for refinements to the formula.

A series of technical appendixes present more detail about data sources and methods.

Chapter Two
PRINCIPLES FOR ANALYSIS OF ALLOCATION FORMULA

This chapter deals with some major conceptual issues that affect our analysis. First, what is the underlying standard of equity of the formula and should other standards be considered? As it turns out, the current formula can be viewed as embodying an acceptable standard of equity. Second, what, if any, funds other than the Block Grant funds should be considered in developing the Block Grant formula? We suggest that other funds should indeed be considered but that Congress has clearly chosen not to do so, and this makes it difficult to ascertain how successful the formula is in accomplishing its goals. Finally, how can a single formula take account of the fact that the SA Block Grant funds are intended for both prevention and treatment, given that the notion of "population in need" is very different for the two program types? We suggest that the extent to which prevention versus treatment needs are emphasized is a policy decision, not subject to empirical analysis, and consider two alternative decisions regarding that emphasis for further analyses.

CONCEPTS OF EQUITY

Assessing how well an allocation formula functions requires specification of a notion of equity. Congress has not addressed this question directly but its choice of formula has implicitly embraced the concept of taxpayer equity, i.e., that the federal government should pay a fixed share of an estimated cost of providing a standard package of services.

Putting aside for the moment issues of measurement, what constitutes an equitable distribution of the Block Grant money? One possibility is that each person should receive the same amount, regardless of which state that person resides in or whether or not treatment is needed: Per capita allocations would be constant across states. That is not an appealing allocation because the federal government then is playing a purely pass-through role, unrelated to the goals of these grants; it could accomplish the same goal by reducing federal tax rates correspondingly. Moreover, that criterion ignores at least three obviously relevant factors, namely variation among the states in:

1. the needs of the population for SA and MH services. More funds should go to those states that have greater problems;

2. the capacity of the citizens of the states to pay for the services themselves. For redistributive reasons, the federal government should award more funds to states that are less able to finance services themselves; and

3. the cost of providing services. States in which less money is needed to provide a given level of services should receive fewer funds.

The current Block Grant takes these three factors into account and does so in a more sophisticated fashion than is the case for other Block Grant formulas, such as those used to distribute funds under the federal Maternal and Child Health program or Older Americans Act. It implicitly embodies one of two plausible concepts of equity for transfer programs, i.e., taxpayer equity. A detailed conceptual analysis of the Block Grant formula demonstrating its basis as a taxpayer equity approach is provided in Appendix A. While this study does not challenge the taxpayer equity approach, it does raise questions about whether Congress might consider a more refined implementation of this concept of equity.

An insightful GAO analysis of equity (U.S. GAO, 1992) in another context (maternal and child health) has suggested two alternative standards of equity on which grant allocations may reasonably be based. One, described as "beneficiary equity," would equalize the federally funded share of the cost of providing a standard level of service to all persons in need of those services. The alternative, "taxpayer equity," equalizes the potential tax rates taxpayers would have to pay to support that standard level of service.

Both standards have their weaknesses. Beneficiary equity takes no account of differences in state capacity to pay. On the other hand, taxpayer equity may result in an extremely uneven distribution of payments, with wealthier states receiving negligible funds, a politically unattractive consequence. Fortunately, it is also possible to combine the two standards into a single formula that gives a specific weight to each consideration.

It turns out that a well-defined generic specification allows the formula to represent the contending concepts of equity through the choice of three parameters: overall federal funding, the federal share of expenditure need, and the state and local tax burden. Those choices are policy decisions, and while there may be debate about their social and political implications, they do not raise questions of fact that need to be resolved empirically.

The central concept of both standards is "expenditure need" (hereafter E), representing the aggregate expenditure within a state necessary to provide the standard level of service to all persons in need; this expenditure might be financed by any combination of federal, state, and local funds. The beneficiary equity criterion is that federal funds should be allocated to support a constant share of E in each state. The taxpayer equity standard is that federal funding should make up the difference between E and the portion of E that could be funded by state and local governments, assuming that they taxed their fiscal capacities at a common rate.

Expenditure need is a concept that includes two of the three elements of the Block Grant formula, namely, population in need and cost of service. Though we develop estimates of the two separately at some stages of the analysis (i.e., Chapters Three, Four, and Five), for purposes of formula evaluation it is essential that they be combined in the single E measure (as they are in Chapter Seven). That leaves the fiscal capacity measure for separate consideration (in Chapter Six).

The bulk of our empirical analysis is concerned with the effects of using alternative measures of the three components of the formula—population in need, cost of services, and fiscal capacity. The basic questions we address are: (a) Do conceptual or empirical arguments favor one measure over another? (b) Is it feasible to use the superior measure? (c) If there are practical limitations, is a compromise possible? (d) Are the differences in the measures large enough to affect the components of grant awards substantially?

WHAT FUNDS

The discussion here has so far not addressed which federal funds should be included in allocation decisions. The Block Grant program represents only one of multiple federal sources of funding for public mental health and substance abuse programs. In particular, federal Medicaid and Medicare programs finance substantial mental health treatment services and some substance abuse treatment. In 1988, for example, approximately $1.9 billion was spent on mental health treatment as part of the Medicaid program (including federal, state, and local shares), and another $700 million was spent by Medicare on mental health treatment (U.S. DHHS, 1992). There is reason to believe that such federal funding from non-Block Grant sources could vary substantially across states, whether measured per capita or per person in need. To equalize federal funding contribution under either standard, the federal government might look at total federal funds allocated in this programmatic area and allocate the Block Grant to equalize either the total federal contribution to E or the total taxpayer contribution.

Interviews with Congressional staff, as well as the silence of the Congressional debate on this issue, indicate that Congress has not considered this possibility. The Block Grant funds are treated in isolation from other federal funding. One justification for ignoring other federal expenditures is that the data to measure the distribution of non-Block Grant federal funds across states are difficult to obtain. Whatever the justification, however, the consequence is that it is not possible to determine whether the Block Grant funds in fact equalize, by any criterion, total federal funding for SA and MH services.

Not surprisingly, then, it also appears that Congress has not considered private coverage for SA and MH treatment, though in fact significant funds are expended for these and such coverage may vary greatly among the states. This may cause problems of equity if in some states the share of the population in need receiving treatment under private coverage is higher than that in other states. Again, we note the lack of good data to measure variation among the states in the extent (and depth) of private insurance coverage, but a more appropriate measure of population in need would subtract out the privately covered population.

Most of those served by Block Grant funds are at or near poverty. Thus, one heuristic that could be used to obtain a more meaningful measure of the population in need is to relate it to the distribution of the poverty population among the states. Again, interviews with Congressional and SAMHSA staff suggested that this was not considered a politically acceptable approach, though it would help cut through the issue of what sources of funding to include.

In summary, the existing population-in-need measures, by ignoring the availability of funding from other federal and nongovernmental sources, adopt a highly stylized version of whom the funds serve. We have not challenged that stylization but believe that it is worth Congress's consideration.

TREATMENT AND PREVENTION

SA and MH Block Grants help fund different types of services for different subpopulations: persons with different types or degrees of mental illness and persons who are dependent on alcohol or drugs. Furthermore, the SA grant supports substance abuse prevention (including tobacco prevention) as well as treatment.

Both the technical debate (e.g., as reflected in U.S. GAO, 1984, 1991, and numerous other U.S. GAO studies), and the political debate have focused exclusively on differences in treatment needs among the states. Yet the demand for SA prevention services is almost certainly differently distributed by age, if not by other characteristics, than is the demand for SA treatment services. Some users may be in need of treatment at age 14 and others may not start use until age 25, but both of these are quite rare; initiation usually occurs during adolescence and the need for treatment generally manifests itself in adult life. Thus, one challenge of the analysis is to determine how to merge consideration of both treatment and prevention needs into one formula for allocation among the states. The detailed analyses are presented in Chapters Four and Seven. Here we deal only with the conceptual issues.

Despite the differences in the subpopulations to be served, both the mental health and substance abuse grant formulas use a single overall measure of each state's population in need. The formulas count people in various subgroups that might differ in service needs and then combine those counts in a single weighted sum for each state. Specifying the formulas in that manner makes it appear that the weighting of various population subgroups is essentially a measurement issue, implying that it can be resolved in the context of estimating overall population in need.

However, if the objective in specifying a Block Grant formula is to distribute federal funds under the taxpayer equity concept, then

- The choice of weights is fundamentally a policy issue: It might be influenced by information about benefits and costs of treatment versus prevention but cannot be made solely on empirical grounds;

- Implementing weights by embedding them in the calculation of overall population in need requires a specific assumption about the costs of different types of services—and that assumption may not be valid; and

- The general effects of alternative weights can be evaluated analytically—without embedding them in a measure of population in need and without quantifying a range of alternatives.

We do not consider differences in mental disorders within the domain of serious mental illness as presenting separate funding needs. Community Mental Health Centers provide the bulk of community mental health services funded under the Block Grant. Furthermore, providers of community mental health services do not generally restrict themselves to serving persons with specific types of disorders within the domain of serious mental illness. We do separate needs for treatment and prevention services for substance abuse. These involve different populations, providers, and technologies. After estimating the variation among states in the expenditure need for SA treatment and prevention, we combine them into a single measure using two alternative weights for each one, based on the set-asides specified in the formula for prevention and our judgment about the maximum share that might reasonably be assigned to prevention.

The prevention programs funded under the SA Block Grant explicitly target tobacco as well as alcohol and other drugs. This is not only explicit in the statute but reflects the reality of most prevention programs; we employ measures of tobacco use (as well as alcohol and drug use) to estimate variations in need for prevention services across states.

Chapter Three

POPULATION IN NEED OF TREATMENT FOR MENTAL ILLNESS

The size of the population in need of community mental health services differs from state to state. The current practice of weighting various age groups by the lifetime prevalence rates for total selected mental disorders reported in the 1986 Institute for Health and Aging study may not provide the best estimate of those populations. Federal funds for mental health services are targeted at persons with serious mental illness. In this chapter, we develop state-level measures of need for these services. First, we examine the literature and analyze recent databases to determine what demographic and community-level factors can be used as predictors of serious mental illness. Because data are not available to directly estimate state-level rates of serious mental illness, we then use indirect simulation methods to estimate these rates, based on the best predictors of serious mental illness in existing national surveys.

In the first section of this chapter, we describe the correlates of serious mental disorder found in previous studies. Next, we report the results of the analyses of the ECA and the NCS that we conducted to estimate the importance of these correlates. The third section presents the results of simulations to estimate state rates of serious mental illness. These are then used to derive alternative measures of need for mental health services. In Chapter Seven, preferred measures will be compared with those generated by the current Community Mental Health Block Grant formula.

OVERVIEW

In our analysis of the ECA and the NCS, we used four definitions of serious mental illness: All included DSM-III-R criteria for schizophrenia and schizophreniform disorder, bipolar illness, major depressive disorder, panic disorder, and dementia of the Alzheimer's type; two included additional severity criteria for depression and panic disorder; and the definitions varied in the reference time period—two referred to the past year and two to the past month. The additional severity criteria and a briefer time period of one month allowed us to focus on the most severe and persistent problems.

Results from the literature review and our logistic regression analysis generally agreed: Serious mental illness is higher among women, the unmarried or separated, those who are disabled or receiving welfare, and those without a high school diploma. Predictors in only one study or for only some of the definitions included age (25–44), living alone, and the interaction of gender with marital status (suggesting that among women, marriage is *not* associated with lower rates of serious mental illness). The effect of race was inconsistent across the two studies and not robust enough to be identified as a predictor across all definitions. Community-level variables, including urbanicity and region of the country, were not predictive.

State-level rates of serious mental illness, which we determined using the method of indirect estimation, showed no systematic relationship to the size or urbanicity of a state's population. There is, however, a strong relationship between rates of mental illness and poverty.

MENTAL ILLNESS LITERATURE REVIEW

This section examines existing epidemiologic studies concerning the prevalence and correlates of mental illness. The aim of this review was to identify factors associated with state-level variation in need for mental illness treatment services. Therefore, we focused on sociodemographic variables that would be readily available to states. These variables include both individual-level data such as age, sex, and marital status and aggregate data reflecting regional variation in factors such as population density. In examining available studies, we considered the correlates of mental disorder in children as well as adults. Although children are not currently counted in the population need index of the current Block Grant formula, the act does mandate their inclusion in program coverage.

For several reasons, the literature reviewed below provides suggestive evidence—rather than definitive guidance—regarding factors to include in the Block Grant formula's population needs component. First, the literature typically examines the correlates of specific categories of mental illness and does not yield information that can be directly extrapolated to severe mental illness in the aggregate. Second, most studies tend to examine small subsets of potential predictors of need, or even individual factors, in isolation from one another. More definitive conclusions regarding predictors of need require simultaneous examination of multiple factors. As yet, few studies of this sort have been conducted. Thus, our review of the literature might best be viewed as serving to identify factors for inclusion in our own empirical analyses of the correlates of need for services. Before reviewing the existing empirical literature, we provide an overview of the definition of the general term "mental illness" and then review specific diagnostic criteria associated with key mental illnesses.

Definition of Mental Disorder

Within the DSM-III-R (American Psychiatric Association, 1987), a mental disorder is defined as "a clinically significant behavioral or psychological syndrome or pattern that occurs in a person and that is associated with present distress (a painful symptom) or disability (impairment in one or more areas of functioning) or with a significantly increased risk of suffering death, pain, disability, or an important loss of freedom. In addition, this syndrome or pattern must not be merely an expectable response to a particular event, e.g., the death of a loved one" (p. xxii).

As suggested by the foregoing definition, mental disorder is a generic term subsuming numerous discrete diagnostic syndromes. Each specific disorder is characterized by a unique set of defining clinical symptoms or symptom clusters. Disorders also vary with respect to numerous other factors including their course, associated level of functional impairment, and treatment.

For two reasons, our efforts focus on identifying correlates of specific disorders rather than on the correlates of mental disorder in general. First, the heterogeneous nature of mental illness has prompted researchers and clinicians to distinguish among types of mental illness. Thus, most available data are not aggregated to the level of mental illness but instead focus on discrete disorders. Second, given that Block Grant funds are intended to serve persons who have severe mental disorders, the most useful estimates of state-level variation in need for treatment focus on persons with more serious disorders rather than persons with milder disorders.

The Center for Mental Health Services (CMHS) definitions of severe mental illness in adults and severe emotional distress in children seek to identify persons with the most serious forms of mental illness. Two of the most serious forms of mental illness are schizophrenia and the major mood disorders. Certain forms of anxiety disorder, particularly panic disorder, can be also associated with significant functional impairment. Finally, dementia of the Alzheimer's type is, by definition, associated with marked impairment. In recognition of this impairment, dementia of the Alzheimer's type was expressly included in the CMHS definition as meeting conditions for severe mental illness.

In examining the correlates of mental illness, we focus on the five previously mentioned disorders: schizophrenia and schizophreniform disorder, two of the major affective disorders, i.e., bipolar illness and major depressive disorder, panic disorder, and dementia of the Alzheimer's type.[1]

---

[1]*Schizophrenia* is a disorder characterized by psychotic symptoms including delusions and/or hallucinations, deterioration from a previous level of functioning, and continuous signs of the disturbance for at least six months. The diagnosis of schizophreniform disorder is reserved for persons meeting all criteria except for duration. The best available evidence suggests that 1.5 percent of persons have met criteria for either schizophrenia or schizophreniform disorder at some point in their lifetimes, and 1.2 percent of persons have met criteria within the past year. *Panic disorder* is characterized by recurrent panic attacks that are not triggered by social situations and are not associated with exposure to a situation that would normally cause anxiety. Attacks generally last a few minutes and are experienced as a sudden onset of intense fear and related anxiety symptoms. The lifetime prevalence of panic disorder is estimated at 1.6 percent, and the one-year prevalence rate is 1.3 percent. *Major depressive disorder* is characterized by either depressed mood or loss of interest or pleasure in all, or almost all, activities, and associated symptoms, for a period of at least two weeks. Associated symptoms include appetite disturbance, change in weight, sleep disturbance, psychomotor agitation or retardation, decreased energy, feelings of worthlessness or excessive or inappropriate guilt, difficulty thinking or concentrating, recurrent thoughts of death, or suicidal ideation or attempts. The one-year and lifetime prevalence rates for major depression have been estimated at approximately 2.7 percent and 4.9 percent. *Bipolar disorder* is characterized by manic episodes, usually accompanied by one or more episodes of major depression. The most salient feature of a manic episode is a distinct period during which the predominant mood is either elevated, expansive, or irritable with associated symptoms such as inflated self esteem or grandiosity, decreased need for sleep, being more talkative than usual, distractibility, and excessive involvement in pleasurable activities that have a high potential for painful consequences. The lifetime prevalence of bipolar disorder is estimated at 1.3 percent and one-year prevalence rate at 1.2 percent. *Dementia of the Alzheimer's type* is characterized by progressive and gradual deterioration of intellectual abilities including memory, judgment, abstract thought, and other cortical functions, as well as changes in personality and behavior. Onset typically occurs after 65 years of age. Relative to other disorders, dementias are difficult to diagnose because there

Correlates of Mental Disorder in Adults

For adult disorders, the review relies heavily on data from the ECA study. The ECA study, sponsored by the National Institute of Mental Health, is the largest and most comprehensive study of the prevalence and correlates of mental disorder in the United States. During the early 1980s, a stratified random sample of approximately 20,000 adults aged 18 or over, drawn from five metropolitan areas, was interviewed using the Diagnostic Interview Schedule (Robins, Helzer, Croughan, and Ratcliff, 1981). The DIS is a fully structured psychiatric interview, designed for use by trained lay persons. The DIS yields specific psychiatric diagnoses using algorithms derived from DSM-III criteria (American Psychiatric Association, 1980). We also review initial findings from the NCS study (Kessler et al., 1994), the first survey to administer a structured psychiatric interview to a national probability sample in the United States. The NCS is based on a stratified, multistage area probability sample of over 8,000 respondents drawn from noninstitutionalized persons aged 15 to 54 years in the 48 contiguous states. For the NCS, psychiatric diagnoses were established using a modified version of the Composite International Diagnostic Interview (CIDI) (World Health Organization, 1990). Derived from the DIS, the CIDI is a fully structured instrument designed for administration by trained lay persons and yielding DSM-III-R psychiatric diagnoses (Robins, Wing, Wittchen, and Helzer, 1988). The NCS was fielded between September 1990 and February 1992.

The ECA and NCS studies have a few notable limitations. First, both studies focused on the prevalence of adult disorders. Thus, no information concerning rates of childhood disorders is provided. Second, neither study provide good data on the prevalence of Alzheimer's dementia. The ECA provides information on the prevalence of serious cognitive impairment; we used these data as a proxy for Alzheimer's dementia. The NCS did not attempt to diagnose either Alzheimer's dementia or cognitive impairment. For reasons noted previously, ECA data are likely to overestimate the prevalence of Alzheimer's dementia. Third, ECA respondents were sampled from five metropolitan areas and thus are not a nationally representative sample. This shortcoming makes examination of several key issues problematic. For example, the small number of sites with rural populations makes examination of possible rural-urban correlates of mental illness difficult. However, inasmuch as the NCS focuses on a nationally representative sample, the NCS offsets this limitation of the ECA study. Third, minority representation in the sample is somewhat limited. For example, the Hispanic sample was drawn primarily from Los Angeles residents of Mexican heritage and is therefore not representative of the national Hispanic population.

The ECA and NCS studies provide data regarding the sociodemographic correlates of mental disorder. We will review data concerning the relationship between one-year prevalence estimates for key mental illnesses and five demographic characteristics.

---

must be corroborative history, physical exam, or laboratory findings. These diagnostic complexities render prevalence estimation using conventional epidemiologic methods exceedingly difficult. Severe cognitive impairment, a reasonable proxy for dementia, has a prevalence rate of 2.3 percent among persons 55 years of age or older.

These characteristics are age, gender, race or ethnicity, marital status, and socioeconomic status.

Age. ECA data reveal that schizophrenia, panic disorder, major depressive disorder, and bipolar disorder occur most commonly among young persons (Keith et al., 1991; Weissman et al., 1991; Eaton et al., 1991). NCS data show a similar pattern of findings with respect to affective and anxiety disorders (Kessler et al., 1994). By contrast, severe cognitive impairment is much more common among older persons (George et al., 1991).

Gender. ECA data reveal a mixed relationship between gender and the prevalence of serious mental disorder. Panic disorder and major depression were more common among women (Eaton et al., 1991; Weissman et al., 1991), a pattern also reported by the findings of Kessler et al. (1994) from the NCS data. By contrast, rates of bipolar illness (Weissman et al. 1991; Kessler et al., 1994), schizophrenia (Keith et al., 1991), and severe cognitive impairment (George et al., 1991) are comparable in males and females.

Racial/Ethnic Status. Available evidence from the ECA study suggests that rates of certain severe mental illness may vary as a function of racial or ethnic status. Schizophrenia appears to occur somewhat more commonly among African-Americans than among either non-Hispanic Caucasians or Hispanics (Keith et al., 1991). Panic disorder is less prevalent among Hispanics than among non-Hispanic Caucasians or African-Americans (Eaton et al., 1991). Data from both the ECA and NCS studies indicate that African-Americans and non-Hispanic Caucasians experienced panic disorder with equal frequency (Eaton et al., 1991; Kessler et al., 1994). A recent analysis of lifetime prevalence using ECA data (Horwath, Johnson, and Hornig, 1993) also reported comparable rates for African-Americans and Caucasians. Although Kessler found higher rates of affective disorder among Hispanic respondents in the NCS (Kessler et al., 1994), no significant racial or ethnic differences were found in the ECA with respect to one-year prevalence rates for major depressive disorder (Weissman et al., 1991). Similarly, no significant racial or ethnic differences emerged with respect to the rate of bipolar disorder (Weissman et al., 1991), a finding consistent with the NCS study (Kessler et al., 1994). Race is related to prevalence of severe cognitive impairment (George et al., 1991). African-Americans are much more likely to suffer from severe cognitive impairment than are either Hispanics or Caucasians.

Marital Status. In general, being married is associated with lower prevalence of mental illness. Schizophrenia (Keith et al., 1991), major depression (Weissman et al., 1991), bipolar illness (Weissman et al., 1991), panic disorder (Eaton et al., 1991), and severe cognitive impairment (George et al., 1991) occur more frequently among never-married persons, divorced persons, or separated persons relative to married or widowed persons.

Socioeconomic Status. In general, severe mental illness appears more common among persons of low socioeconomic status. Although findings vary somewhat as a function of the manner in which socioeconomic status is measured, rates of schizophrenia (Keith et al., 1991), severe cognitive impairment (George et al., 1991), and panic disorder (Eaton et al., 1991; Regier, Narrow, and Rae, 1990) appear higher among persons with lower status. ECA evidence with respect to bipolar disorder and major depression was equivocal, with higher prevalence associated with some indexes of socioeconomic status but not with others (Weissman et al., 1991). Results from the NCS study (Kessler et al., 1994) reveal that socioeconomic status is linked to higher prevalence rates of both affective anxiety disorders, although data were not presented with respect to specific disorders.

Urban-Rural. ECA results concerning the association between place of residence and the prevalence of mental disorder are equivocal. Evidence with respect to major affective disorder is mixed, with some evidence suggesting that rural rates may be higher and other evidence suggesting that rates in urban area may be higher (Weissman et al. 1991). ECA data also suggest that persons in rural areas may have higher rates of severe cognitive impairment (George et al., 1991). As judged by one-year prevalence rates, severe cognitive impairment does not appear to vary as a function of place of residence (George et al., 1991). Nevertheless, a slightly different analysis of ECA data, which focused on six-month prevalence estimates, suggests that severe impairment may be more common among rural residents (George et al., 1991). We were not able to identify published ECA prevalence estimates for panic disorder or schizophrenia. Results from the NCS provide little evidence of a link between degree of urbanicity and prevalence of mental disorders.

Summary: Correlates of Mental Disorder in the ECA and NCS Studies. Results from the ECA and NCS studies suggest that mental disorder is more common among women, young persons, divorced or separated persons, unemployed persons, persons dependent on government financial support, and persons with lower socioeconomic status. Some evidence also implicates racial or ethnic status and urban-rural residence as possible correlates of mental disorder, although these data are more equivocal. Some exceptions to these general conclusions are noteworthy. In particular, severe cognitive impairment, a proxy for dementia of the Alzheimer's type, is more common among older persons. It should be noted that most of the prevalence rates reported here do not reflect adjustment for other correlates of mental disorder.

Correlates of Mental Disorder in Children and Adolescents

No studies comparable to the ECA or NCS have been conducted to assess the prevalence or correlates of mental disorder in children and adolescents. As a result, little definitive information is available concerning the prevalence of mental disorders among U.S. youths. Preliminary data from the 1992 NIMH Cooperative Agreement for Methodologic Research for Multi-Site Epidemiologic Surveys of Mental Disorders in Child and Adolescent Populations suggest that 3.2 percent of children aged 9–17 have a severe mental disorder (National Advisory Mental Health Council, 1993). In general, however, few studies have been conducted and comparison across those studies is hampered by differences with respect to the definition and measurement of mental disorder, the age groups studied, and the use of small, often nonrepresentative, samples.

Four studies were identified that appeared to reflected recent developments in the epidemiological study of mental illness. These developments include refinement of case identification procedures, sophisticated sampling strategies, and the use of well-validated instruments. Following a description of these studies, we summarize major findings.

Bird et al. (1988) conducted a two-stage epidemiologic survey on a probability sample (N = 843) of Puerto Rican children between the ages of 4 and 16 years. During the first stage, parents and teachers were interviewed using a symptom scale (Achenbach and Edelbrock, 1983, 1986) to identify children with a high likelihood of maladjustment. During the second stage, a Spanish-language version of the NIMH Diagnostic Interview Schedule for Children (DISC) was administered to high-risk children and their parents as well as a sample of low-risk children.

Kashani et al. (1987) studied a sample of 150 adolescents, aged 14–16, randomly drawn from persons attending public schools in Columbia, Missouri. During home assessments, the adolescent and one parent were administered a psychiatric assessment that included the Diagnostic Interview for Children and Adolescents and the Diagnostic Interview for Children and Adolescents—Parent Version (Herjanic and Reich, 1982). Persons were considered to have a disorder if they met DSM-III criteria and were judged to be both functionally impaired and in need of treatment.

Cohen et al. (1987) employed a multistage probability sample of households in two counties in upstate New York. Participants included all age-appropriate children from an earlier study who were available for follow-up. The final sample consisted of 775 children between the ages of 9 and 19. Cases were defined using DSM-III-R criteria and the DISC (Costello et al., 1984). Parallel forms of the DISC were used to interview parents and children. All children who met DSM-III-R criteria and who scored at least two standard deviations above the mean on the DISC were judged to have a definite diagnosis.

Garrison et al. (1992) conducted a two-stage study of unipolar mood disorder in adolescents residing within a single school district in South Carolina. A self-report inventory of depressive symptoms was administered to 3,283 adolescents as an initial screen to identify persons with probable depressive disorder. In stage two, 488 mother-child pairs were interviewed using the Schedule for Schizophrenia and Affective Disorders in School Age Children (Chambers et al., 1985). To receive a definitive diagnosis, adolescents had to meet DSM-III criteria and have significant functional impairment.

Prevalence estimates derived from these studies vary considerably. Moreover, these estimates are typically rather high, ranging from 15–25 percent. Most of these estimates are not restricted to severe mental disorders, however, and reflect the prevalence of all mental illness. Not surprisingly, definitions of mental illness that incorporate functional status as a criterion generally provide estimates toward the lower end of the range.

Perhaps because of the relatively small sample sizes, few correlates of mental illness in children and adolescents have been identified. For example, Kashani et al. (1987)

reported that overall prevalence rates were not related to gender, socioeconomic status, or parental marital status. They did report, however, that anxiety and mood disorders were more common in girls. In their study of adolescents, however, Garrison et al. (1992) reported no gender difference in one-year prevalence estimates for mood disorders. Furthermore, prevalence was not found to vary as a function of race or socioeconomic status. Some evidence suggests that parental marital status is related to adolescent mental illness prevalence. Adolescents not residing with two parents experienced higher rates of major depression and dysthymia as well as nonaffective disorders more generally. Cohen et al. (1987) provided no information concerning the sociodemographic correlates of disorder.

In summary, too few studies have been conducted to support definitive conclusions regarding the prevalence and correlates of mental disorder in children and adolescents. To the extent that general statements can be made, these studies suggest that the prevalence and correlates of disorder in children may be similar to those found for adults.

ANALYSES OF FACTORS PREDICTING NEED FOR COMMUNITY MENTAL HEALTH SERVICES

In this section, we report results of an empirical analysis we conducted to identify factors predicting need for community mental health services. This analysis uses data from the only two population-based epidemiologic studies of mental disorders in the United States: (1) the ECA, a survey of 17,803 household residents in the early 1980s representing the adult (18 and older) populations in five U.S. sites; and (2) the NCS, a recently completed national probability survey of 8,098 persons aged 15 to 54. We start by considering the definition of the population in need of community mental health services provided by the Block Grant program, as intended by the legislation. We then describe the development of our operational definitions of the population in need of services using available survey data. Finally, we summarize analytic methods, results of these analyses, and conclusions regarding factors predicting population need for community mental health services.

Definition of Population in Need of Community Mental Health Services

The ADAMHA Reorganization Act of 1992 mandated that the Secretary of Health develop definitions of populations in need for the states to use in planning and providing services under the Community Mental Health Services Block Grant program. Under this act, the Block Grant program funds are to be used for the provision of comprehensive community mental health services to adults with serious mental illnesses and to children with serious emotional disturbances. The Center for Mental Health Services provided definitions of "seriously mentally ill adults" and "seriously emotionally disturbed children" in a May 20, 1993, bulletin, thereby defining the population to be targeted by mental health Block Grant services. Adults with serious mental illnesses are defined as persons:

- age 18 and over,
- who currently or at any time during the past year
- had diagnosable mental, behavioral, or emotional disorders of sufficient duration to meet diagnostic criteria specified with DSM-III-R[2]
- resulting in functional impairment that substantially interferes with or limits one or more major life activities.

Children with serious emotional disturbances are defined as persons:

- from birth up to age 18,
- who currently or at any time during the past year
- had diagnosable mental, behavioral, or emotional disorders of sufficient duration to meet diagnostic criteria specified with DSM-III-R[3]
- resulting in functional impairment that substantially interferes with or limits their roles or functioning in family, school, or community activities.

It is clear from these definitions that the Block Grant funds are designated to serve those who have mental disorders at the severe end of the spectrum and not to target mild disorders or persons who may be at risk of developing future mental disorders. Those with developmental disorders are also excluded, even though these disorders are often severely impairing, because other programs are specifically designed to provide services to them. Similarly, persons with substance use disorders are excluded because of the specific Block Grant allocations for persons with these problems, although persons dually diagnosed with both serious mental disorders and substance use disorders are included in the mental health services target population. Those with Alzheimer's disease are specifically included because mental health services are needed to "deal with the psychiatric sequelae of this disabling disorder," even though such persons may receive long-term nursing home care through other provisions of OBRA.

While it is widely acknowledged that the mental health services Block Grant program provides services largely to the uninsured poor, no criteria relating to individuals' abilities to pay for services are included in the definitions (for example, indigence or lack of private health insurance). Nor is service of individuals by other federal health care financing programs such as Medicaid or Medicare considered reason for excluding these individuals from the target population of the Mental Health Block Grant.

---

[2] DSM-III-R stands for Diagnostic and Statistical Manual, Version III-Revised. It is the most recent diagnostic criteria published by the American Psychiatric Association.

[3] Developmental and substance use disorders are specifically excluded, but attention deficit disorder is specifically included.

Operational Definitions of Population in Need of Community Mental Health Services Based on Survey Measures

To analyze the ECA and NCS survey data and identify factors predicting need for community mental health services, we first had to determine which members of the survey population correspond to the populations in need of mental health services as defined by the ADAMHA Reorganization Act. That is, we had to operationalize those definitions in terms of the survey measures. In keeping with the criteria in the previous section, our operational definitions took into account recency, diagnostic criteria, and level of functional impairment.

Adults with Serious Mental Illness. The population-based data that are available include adults but not children (although the NCS included persons aged 15–17). Thus, our analysis was restricted to adults aged 18 or older and focused on indicators of serious mental illness.

Presence of Mental Illness in the Past Year. Both surveys collected information to identify persons who had mental disorders in the past year, so we focus on this prevalence period, consistent with the intent of the Block Grant program. In addition, we examined definitions using a more restrictive timeframe—persons with disorders in the past month—to test the sensitivity of the findings to a definition more heavily weighted with persistent and chronic problems. A past-month prevalence period overrepresents persons with long-lasting problems relative to a past-year prevalence period.

DSM-III Diagnoses. Both surveys used standardized diagnostic interviews that ascertained diagnoses according to accepted psychiatric criteria. The ECA used DSM-III criteria, the most current criteria of the American Psychiatric Association available at that time, and the NCS used the more recent DSM-III-R criteria. For the diagnoses that we focus on here, DSM-III and DSM-III-R criteria are very similar, the most significant difference being that fewer symptoms are required to meet criteria for major depression in the revised (III-R) criteria. The diagnostic interview protocols were also different across the two studies (the ECA study relied on the Diagnostic Interview Schedule, while the NCS employed the Composite International Diagnostic Interview), but were similar in that they covered the same set of major diagnoses.

Functional Impairment. The requirement that the mental disorder result in substantial functional impairment is the most vague and difficult component of the definition to operationalize, given the importance of social context in the definition of functional impairment, and the knowledge of sequential progression required to infer a link between a mental disorder and functional limitations. The field has not yet developed methods for assessing level of functional impairment associated with a disorder that are suitable for research purposes. Thus, while many of the diagnoses assessed as part of the ECA and NCS surveys by definition required specific indications of functional impairment, independent measures of dysfunction as a result of mental disorder were not included.

As a substitute for a direct measure of functional impairment associated with mental disorder, our definition of the population in need of services included only those who met criteria for the mental disorders that are considered the most severely impairing. These included schizophrenia, major depression, bipolar affective disorder, and panic disorder. Although neither survey determined the diagnosis of Alzheimer's disease, which also results in severe dysfunction, the ECA survey included an assessment of cognitive functioning, which we used to identify persons with severe cognitive impairment. These persons were therefore included in our definition of the population in need of mental health services as a proxy for Alzheimer's disease.[4]

Additional Severity Criteria. To restrict the definition to the most persistent, and by implication most impairing, cases of major depression and panic disorder, we imposed additional severity criteria. (A diagnosis of schizophrenia or bipolar affective disorder was considered sufficiently severe without additional criteria.) These additional criteria required at least two lifetime episodes of major depression, at least two years of chronic major depression, or multiple panic attacks (ten or more in NCS, and attacks in at least six different weeks in ECA).

Summary. Table 3.1 summarizes these operational definitions of the adult population with serious mental illness. Using two different time periods (the past year and the past month) and including or excluding the additional severity criteria described above resulted in four alternative definitions for each of the surveys. Table 3.2 gives the estimated prevalence of serious mental illness in the adult population determined by applying each of the definitions. In the ECA study, estimates of serious mental illness ranged from nearly 5 percent using the least restrictive definition to 2.5 percent using the most restrictive definition. Rates of serious mental illness were higher in the NCS study, ranging from 11.4 percent using the least restrictive definition to 5.4 percent using the most restrictive. The differences across the two

Table 3.1

Operational Definitions of Adults with Serious Mental Illness

Definition 1: Serious Mental Illness in the Past Year
—Met diagnostic criteria for schizophrenia, bipolar affective disorder, major depression, or panic disorder; *and* experienced episode of illness in past year
—*Or* had severe cognitive impairment (ECA only)

Definition 2: Serious Mental Illness in the Past Month
—Met diagnostic criteria for schizophrenia, bipolar affective disorder, major depression, or panic disorder; *and* experienced episode of illness in past month
—*Or* had severe cognitive impairment (ECA only)

Definition 3: Serious Mental Illness with Additional Severity Criteria in the Past Year
—Met diagnostic criteria for schizophrenia, bipolar affective disorder, two or more episodes of major depression (two years or more), or multiple episodes of panic disorder (six or more in ECA; ten or more in NCS); *and* experienced episode of illness in past year
—*Or* had severe cognitive impairment (ECA only)

Definition 4: Serious Mental Illness with Additional Severity Criteria in the Past Month
—Met diagnostic criteria for schizophrenia, bipolar affective disorder, two or more episodes of major depression (two years or more), or multiple episodes of panic disorder (six or more in ECA; ten or more in NCS); *and* experienced episode of illness in past month
—*Or* had severe cognitive impairment (ECA only)

---

[4]In the NCS survey, Alzheimer's disease would have been extremely rare, since the study population was under age 55. Therefore, no cognitive functioning assessment was included in the survey.

Table 3.2

Percentage of Persons with Serious Mental Illness in Adult Household Population

Data Source	Past Year		Past Month	
	SMI	SMI with Added Severity Criteria	SMI	SMI with Added Severity Criteria
ECA	4.9	4.0	3.1	2.5
NCS	11.4	10.4	5.8	5.4

studies are due to higher rates of major depression in the NCS than in the ECA, which is probably a result of differences in assessment approaches employed.

Analysis Methods

To identify the most important predictors of serious mental illness among adults, we conducted logistic regression analyses using both the ECA and NCS survey data. Table 3.3 shows the variables that were included in our examination of predictors. They included individual-level demographic variables available in the survey data as well as a number of census tract characteristics (linked to individual records) to reflect regional and demographic variations at the community level.

We next fit a separate logistic regression model for each indicator of need for treatment from both the ECA and NCS datasets. Each model uses a subset of the predictor variables described in Table 3.3 to estimate the likelihood that any individual in the population needs treatment.

Each model was fit in a similar fashion. A main effects model was fit using the entire candidate list of predictor variables given in Table 3.3. We then used backwards deletion to reduce the model to include only significant predictors. Some predictor variables were completely dropped from the model; others remained in the model but were transformed. For example, the categories of educational attainment were often collapsed into one or two categories when the probability of need did not differ significantly across two or more groups of the finer classification scheme.

Possible interactions between the main effects that remained in the model were investigated. We constructed a candidate list of potentially important interactions by running a Classification Tree analysis (Breiman et al., 1984). The most significant interactions were then added to the logistic regression model. Again, we used backwards deletion to remove insignificant interactions.

The best fitting models often contained many predictor variables, some of which were statistically significant but not important to the model's predictive power. It is important to note that the primary goal of this model-building process is prediction, rather than estimation and interpretation of risk factors where it is important to sort out the independent effects of correlated variables. When prediction is the goal, it is appropriate to allow a variable or a combination of variables to serve as a proxy for other predictors. Thus, we placed a premium on maximizing variance-accounted-for and model parsimony. Other variables included in the models were not available for

Table 3.3
Variables Examined as Predictors of Serious Mental Illness

Epidemiological Catchment Area Study (ECA)

Individual-level variables	
Gender	Male; female
Marital status	Married; widowed or divorced or separated; never married
Age	18–24; 25–34; 35–44; 45–54; 55–64; 65+
Number in household	Living alone; not living alone
Education	0–8; 9–11; 12 (including people with fewer than 12 years of education who have a high school diploma or a General Equivalency Diploma); 13–15 (including people with 16 or more years of education who do not have a college degree); 16+
Race	Hispanic origin; white; black; other
Veteran status	Veteran; not a veteran
Welfare	Respondent is currently receiving welfare; respondent is not currently receiving welfare
Unemployment compensation	Respondent is currently receiving unemployment compensation; respondent is not currently receiving unemployment compensation
Disability	Respondent is currently receiving disability payments; respondent is not currently receiving disability payments
Site	New Haven, CT; Baltimore, MD; St. Louis, MO; Durham County, NC; Los Angeles, CA
Census tract variables	
Age	% distribution of age categories in the Census tract
Race	% distribution of racial categories in the Census tract
Marital status	% distribution of marital categories in the Census tract
Number in household	% single occupancy; % female householder living with own children under 18 years of age with no husband present
Urbanicity	In an urban area; in a rural area; in neither an urban nor a rural area
Rent	Median gross rent
Property value	Median value of owner-occupied housing

National Comorbidity Survey (NCS)

Individual-level variables	
Gender	Male; female
Marital status	Married; widowed or divorced or separated; never married
Age	15–18; 19–24; 25–54
Number in household	Living alone; not living alone
Household composition	Single parent family; not single parent family
Education	0–8; 9–11; 12; 13–15; 16; 17 or more

Table 3.3 (continued)

Race	White; black; other
Hispanic origin	Hispanic origin; not Hispanic
Income	$0–$19K; $20K–$34K; $35K–$69K; $70K or more
Work status	Currently working; not currently working
Disability	Respondent reported currently work disabled; not currently disabled
Census region	Northeast; Midwest, South; West
Urbanicity of residence	Metropolitan area; urban area; rural area
Census tract variables	
Age	% distribution of age categories in the Census tract
Race	% distribution of racial categories in the Census tract
Education	% distribution of education categories in the Census tract
Household density	% of households with more than 1 person per room
Number in household	% single occupancy; % single parent households
Employment	% of males 16 or older in labor force; % of males 16 or older unemployed
Poverty	% of persons living below poverty line; % of households receiving public assistance income

the next stage of analysis where we predict state-level rates. Therefore, the best-fitting models were reduced even further to produce implementable predictive models. These implementable models are given in Tables 3.4 and 3.5.

Very few of the tract-level variables achieved significance in the final models. Among the NCS models, the only significant tract-level predictor was poverty, which related negatively to past-month serious mental illness at the $p = .006$ level. Among the ECA models, no tract-level variables achieved significance at the $p = .01$ level although single occupancy was nearly significant in the past-month serious mental illness model. Tract-level variables were therefore excluded from the implementable models.

Although the implementable models often contain many fewer predictor variables than the best-fitting models, the loss in fit was typically small. The relative R-square between the best and implementable models is typically very high, above 0.7 in all cases.[5]

---

[5]The relative R^2 is the ratio of the R^2 for the implementable model to the R^2 for the best fitting model The R^2 for any individual model is defined to be

$$R^2 = 1 - L_p/L_0$$

where L_0 and L_p denote the log-likelihoods for the models containing only the intercept and the model containing the intercept plus the covariates (Hosmer and Lemeshow, 1989).

Table 3.4

Final Models: Factors Predicting Serious Mental Illness in ECA Study

	Odds Ratios (and 95% Confidence Intervals)			
	Past-Year Definitions		Past-Month Definitions	
Predictors	SMI	SMI with Added Severity Criteria	SMI	SMI with Added Severity Criteria
Receiving disability or welfare income				
No	1.0	1.0	1.0	1.0
Yes	2.0 (1.7–2.3)	1.9 (1.6–2.3)	2.3 (1.9–2.7)	2.1 (1.8–2.6)
Gender				
Male	0.6 (0.6–0.7)	0.7 (0.6–0.8)	0.7 (0.6–0.9)	0.8 (0.7–0.9)
Female	1.0	1.0	1.0	1.0
Marital status				
Currently married	0.5 (0.4–0.6)	0.6 (0.5–0.7)	0.7 (0.6–0.8)	0.7 (0.6–0.8)
Never married	0.7 (0.6–0.9)	0.8 (0.6–0.9)	1.0	1.0
Disrupted marriage	1.0	1.0		
Education				
High school graduate	0.6 (0.5–0.7)	0.5 (0.4–0.6)	0.5 (0.4–0.6)	0.4 (0.4–0.5)
Non-high school graduate	1.0	1.0	1.0	1.0
Race/ethnicity				
Black, non-Hispanic		1.5 (1.1–1.9)	1.4 (1.2–1.6)	1.7 (1.3–2.3)
White, non-Hispanic		1.4 (1.1–1.8)	1.0	1.3 (1.0–1.7)
Hispanic and other		1.0		1.0
Age				
18–24 and over 44	1.0	1.0		
25–44	1.5 (1.3–1.7)	1.4 (1.2–1.6)		
18–24			1.0	1.0
25 and over			1.6 (1.2–2.0)	1.6 (1.2.–2.1)

Results

Tables 3.4 and 3.5 show the final reduced regression models predicting serious mental illness among adults, using each of the four alternative definitions of serious mental illness. Table 3.4 shows models based on ECA data; Table 3.5 shows models derived from NCS data. As these tables indicate, four demographic predictors are common across all definitions of serious mental illness and across the two datasets—serious mental illness is higher among women, the unmarried or separated, those who are disabled or receiving welfare, and those without a high school diploma. Age

Table 3.5

Final Models: Factors Predicting Serious Mental Illness in NCS Study

	Odds Ratio (and 95% Confidence Intervals)			
	Past-Year Definitions		Past-Month Definitions	
Predictors	SMI	SMI with Added Severity Criteria	SMI	SMI with Added Severity Criteria
Gender				
Male	1.0	1.0	1.0	1.0
Female	2.0 (1.7–2.3)	1.9 (1.6–2.2)	1.9 (1.5–2.3)	2.4 (1.8–3.1)
Marital status				
Currently married	1.0	1.0	1.0	1.0
Single or disrupted marriage	1.8 (1.5–2.1)	2.0 (1.6–2.3)	2.1 (1.7–2.7)	3.8 (2.6–5.5)
Education				
8 years or less	1.5 (1.2–1.9)		2.3 (1.3–4.0)	
9–11 years			1.8 (1.2–2.5)	
12–15 years	1.3 (1.1–1.6)		1.6 (1.2–2.1)	
16 or more years	1.0		1.0	
Work disability				
No		1.0	1.0	1.0
Yes		2.3 (1.4–3.5)	3.4 (2.1–5.5)	3.6 (2.2–5.9)
Household composition				
Living alone	1.4 (1.1–1.7)			
Other	1.0			
Sex by marital status interaction				
Females, not currently married				0.4 (0.3–0.7)

is a consistent predictor across all definitions of serious mental illness in the analyses of ECA data, with persons 25–44 at greater risk than those younger, but does not emerge as a predictor in the NCS data. Racial background is a predictor in some final ECA models, but not in the NCS study, and its effect is not robust enough to be identified as a predictor across all definitions of serious mental illness. In the NCS study, two additional factors were identified as significant predictors in models for at least one but not all definitions of serious mental illness. These factors included living alone and the interaction of gender with marital status (suggesting that among women, the positive benefit of marriage is reduced). Community-level variables, including urbanicity and region of the country, were not predictive of rates of serious mental illness.

Overall, these findings are consistent with prior literature on specific mental disorders, which has consistently reported higher rates of mental illness among women, younger adults, the divorced or separated, and those who are economically disadvantaged.

STATE-LEVEL ESTIMATES OF NEEDS FOR COMMUNITY MENTAL HEALTH SERVICES

This section presents the results of simulations to estimate state-level rates of serious mental illness among adults, based on the final predictive models described above. The results of these simulations are used to derive alternative measures of need for community mental health services[6] that are subsequently compared with the index of need generated by the current mental health Block Grant formula in Chapter Seven.

To produce state-level estimates of need for mental health services, we used the method of indirect estimation, a method that is growing in popularity in applications of this type. For a more comprehensive discussion of the application of indirect estimation to federal programs, see Federal Committee on Statistical Methodology (1993) and the references there. Indirect estimation is also known by several other names: synthetic estimation, small area estimation, and model-based estimation. We favor the term indirect estimation since it underscores the contrast with direct estimation.

Direct estimation is typically accomplished by directly measuring a characteristic, for example with a questionnaire, on the population of interest. If the population is randomly sampled or a census, it is a straightforward process to calculate the rate of the characteristic (e.g., severe mental illness) in the population or in a subpopulation. The drawback to direct estimation is that a sample of adequate size must be available for every subpopulation (states in our case) to produce stable estimates.

In contrast, indirect estimation typically models the characteristic as a function of its correlates on a smaller dataset (or one of more limited geographic extent). This model is then applied to a larger or geographically extended dataset to produce estimates. In our case, we used the ECA and NCS datasets to build logistic regression models predicting mental health. We then used the larger Public Use Micro-Sample (PUMS) from the 1990 Census to produce individual-level estimates of the probability of mental illness. These estimates were then aggregated to the state level to produce state incidence rates. This strategy was necessary since neither the ECA nor the

---

[6]This section does not consider state variations in rates of serious emotional disturbance among children, since epidemiologic data on children are too limited to estimate variations by state. In Chapter Seven, however, when alternative indices of need for mental health services are compared to the current index, an estimate of the number of children in need is included in the estimate of the population in need by assuming that a constant rate of 3.2 percent of a state's population of persons under 18 years of age are in need of treatment. This rate is drawn from a recent report of the National Advisory Mental Health Council (1993) and is based on preliminary data from a 1992 National Institute of Mental Health study of mental disorders in children and adolescents indicating that 3.2 percent of children 9–17 years of age have a severe mental disorder during any six-month period.

NCS were of adequate sample size or geographic breadth to permit the use of direct estimation. In addition, the PUMS could not be used on its own since it had no direct measure of mental health.

Our indirect estimation method takes the logistic regressions developed in the previous section of this report and uses them to estimate the probability of the various mental illness definitions for each person in the PUMS. These probabilities are then summed to the state level to get an expected number of persons at need.

$$\text{PIN} = \sum p_i \quad \text{where} \quad p_i = \frac{1}{1 + e^{-x\beta}}$$

PIN is the estimated population in need, β is from the logistic regressions, and x is the PUMS data.

The PUMS data provide individual-level correlates for a random sample of respondents to the 1990 Census. The estimates presented here are based on the 1 percent PUMS sample. This yields a sample of at least 2,000 persons for each state (substantially more for larger states). One challenge in the implementation of this method is developing a model for which comparable correlates are available in the PUMS data. The predictor variables that appear in our final models for both the ECA and the NCS analyses (presented in Tables 3.4 and 3.5) are all readily available in the PUMS data.[7]

Table 3.6 presents descriptive statistics and correlations for the eight different needs estimators. This table illustrates a very interesting pattern of results. While we find that the magnitude of our estimates of treatment need vary dramatically depending on the data source and operational definition of need, we observe very small differences across states in prevalence rates (rates of need per 100 population), irrespective of which needs measure is selected. It is important to note that two features of the model and dataset affect variability in the state-level rate estimates. First, the variable must be statistically significant to be included into the final model. Second, the variable must have a significantly different distribution from state to state. For example, gender may be a significant predictor at the individual level but may have little effect at the state level since the rate of women in the total population varies little from state to state.

Table 3.6 also shows that, no matter which definition of mental health need is selected, state differences in estimated need are, on the whole, remarkably consistent. This can be seen by examining the unweighted correlations of state rates of need between alternative needs estimators. These correlations are very high (r >

---

[7]Although conceptually simple, this type of indirect estimation can be computationally onerous. The 1 percent PUMS dataset contains over two million individual-level records. In Appendix B, we discuss simplified, more implementable methods of calculating state-level estimates. We also explore the effects of alternative model specifications and weighting schemes in that appendix. In particular, we look at model specifications that include tract-level aggregates as well as individual-level explanatory variables.

Table 3.6

Predicted Prevalence of Serious Mental Illness for States: Summary Statistics and Correlation Coefficients for Eight Alternative Definitions of Need for Treatment

	NCS				ECA			
	Less Severe		More Severe		Less Severe		More Severe	
	1 Month	1 Year	1 Month	1 Year	1 Month	1 Year	1 Month	1 Year
Summary statistics								
Mean	10.95	17.49	9.44	17.73	3.51	5.46	3.18	4.64
Std. dev.	0.63	0.31	0.44	0.62	0.40	0.28	0.39	0.36
Minimum	9.55	16.98	8.62	16.50	2.94	5.00	2.42	3.58
Maximum	12.99	18.45	11.35	20.52	4.92	6.26	4.43	5.54
Correlations								
NCS definitions								
Less severe								
1 year	0.2874							
More severe								
1 month	0.9690	0.3706						
More severe								
1 year	0.9430	0.3977	0.9831					
ECA definitions								
Less severe								
1 month	0.9044	0.0095	0.9076	0.9077				
Less severe								
1 year	0.8801	0.0389	0.8789	0.8674	0.9537			
More severe								
1 month	0.9233	0.0271	0.9021	0.8992	0.9776	0.9250		
More severe								
1 year	0.9057	0.0643	0.8690	0.8624	0.9198	0.9061	0.9759	

0.86), with the exception of the less severe one-year NCS definition (0.0 to 0.40). It is encouraging that the estimates are so similar, showing that alternative definitions of need give similar results. Although high correlations are encouraging, they are not a perfect measure of the interchangeability of two alternatives. The ultimate comparison is the effect on the formula discussed in Chapter Seven.

Because alternative definitions of need provide a similar picture of state variations in need, and to eliminate redundancy in subsequent analyses, we chose to narrow our focus to two sets of state-level estimates of rates of serious mental illness: those based on the ECA-derived predictions of more severe serious mental illness in the past year, and those based on NCS-derived predictions of less severe serious mental illness in the past month. Figures 3.1 and 3.2 provide maps of the estimated rates of serious mental illness obtained under each of the these two alternative prediction models. Neither of these models predicts large differences in population rates from state to state. The maps do, nonetheless, reveal a national pattern of higher rates in southeastern states and lower rates in northwestern states.

We also examined the relationship between state rates and three state characteristics. These characteristics were poverty rate, population size, and urbanicity. Urbanicity was defined as the percentage of the state's population living in Metropolitan Statistical Areas (MSAs). Neither population size or urbanicity were strongly correlated with mental illness rates (both were below $r = .20$). Poverty showed a strong correlation ($r = .63$).

38 The Substance Abuse and Mental Health Services Block Grant Allotment Formula

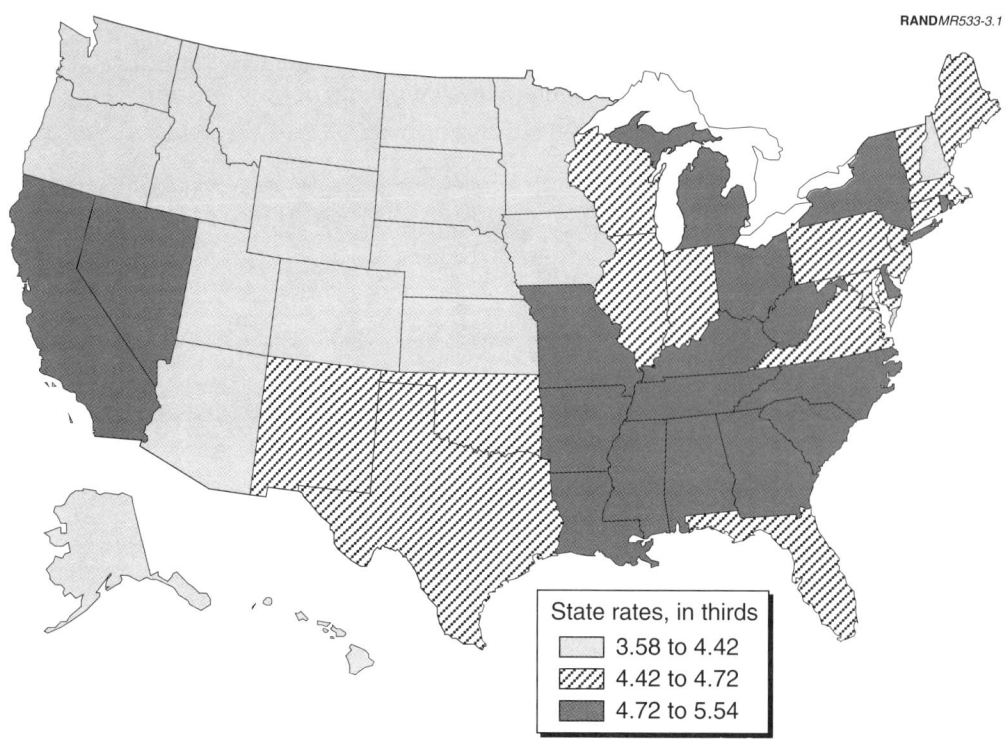

Figure 3.1—One-Year Severe Rates of Mental Illness, by State, ECA Data

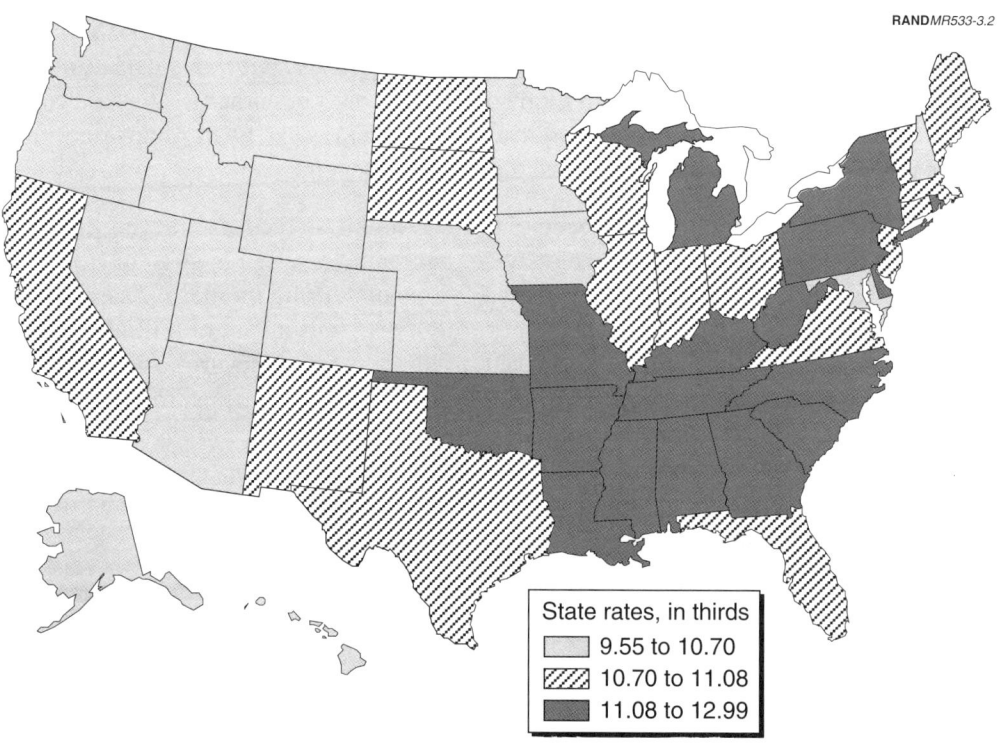

Figure 3.2—30-Day Rates of Less Severe Mental Illness, by State, NCS Data

Chapter Four

POPULATION IN NEED OF SUBSTANCE ABUSE PREVENTION AND TREATMENT

The substance abuse Block Grants are designed to assist states in providing both treatment and prevention services. The populations in need of such services differ dramatically in composition. In this chapter, we investigate the factors that can be used to predict the two populations in need. In Chapter Seven, we will propose a method for combining these populations in alternative measures of population need for substance abuse services and will compare the results of doing so with results generated by the SA Block Grant formula as currently defined.

In the first section, we describe the correlates of substance abuse found in previous studies. Next, we report the results of the analyses of the NHSDA that we conducted to estimate the importance of these correlates. We also describe the correlates for predicting those in need of prevention services. The third section presents the results of our estimates of each state's population in need of treatment and those in need of prevention. Because the NHSDA was not designed to provide information on drug abuse at the state level, but only for the nation as a whole, we used indirect estimation techniques to predict rates of treatment and prevention need for each state, based on the sociodemographic correlates of need.

OVERVIEW

In our analysis of the 1991 NHSDA, we defined the population in need of substance abuse treatment as persons with recent drug or alcohol dependence, as defined by the DSM-III-R. We also examined the population with drug dependence only because those with alcohol dependence so heavily influence the former definition. In defining need for prevention services, we used two approaches to reflect differential risk among youth for developing substance abuse problems: weighting the state's youth population by the estimated prevalence of (1) substance use among youth in that state and (2) substance dependence among adults in that state.

With regard to treatment needs, our logistic regression analysis identified the following predictors: males, white non-Hispanics, persons who are separated or unmarried, those aged 18–44, high school and college dropouts, and residents of the Western U.S. Many of these predictors are consistent with the literature. However, while higher rates of dependence among whites is consistent with the alcohol literature, the literature on drug use and abuse shows mixed results for race and ethnicity.

With regard to the need for prevention services, predictors of any substance use (alcohol, drugs, or tobacco) among youth include being an older adolescent, having lower family income, not attending school full-time, living alone, and working. Predictors of any substance dependence among adults include age (older adults had lower rates), being a veteran, and the household receiving welfare.

State-level rates of need (per 100 persons) for substance abuse treatment and prevention services, which we determined using the method of indirect estimation, were negatively correlated with urbanicity. State-level estimates of population rates with needs for treatment differ from those with needs for prevention. State-level estimates of need for treatment versus need for prevention were examined separately in this chapter, but are later combined as described in Chapter Seven to develop alternative measures of population need for services.

SUBSTANCE ABUSE LITERATURE REVIEW

This literature review is intended to provide insight into the sociodemographic factors that may explain cross-state variations in alcohol and drug dependence. The results of this review have informed our own analysis of needs for substance abuse services based on the NHSDA, presented subsequently. Existing literature focuses on seven variables: age, sex, race/ethnicity, geographic residence, education, employment, and marital status. Here we summarize published findings regarding the main effects of these factors. Although other factors such as religious affiliation or average income in the community may also be important predictors of substance abuse, they are unavailable in nationally representative databases; they cannot therefore be used to measure cross-state variations as a basis for determining Block Grant allocations.

We include literature relevant to substance dependence (including abuse, heavy use, and problem use) to identify factors associated with need for treatment. For a number of reasons it might make sense to focus on predictors of all substance dependence—alcohol and drug—jointly. First, the formula neither calculates separate measures of need for alcohol and drug treatment, nor allocates money separately for the two services. Second, many people who depend on one type of substance also have problems with the other. Nonetheless, since existing literature does not report sociodemographic predictors of such broadly defined substance dependence, we discuss predictors of alcohol dependence first, followed by predictors of drug dependence.

Literature deriving from three databases is particularly relevant to our review of factors predicting substance dependence: the ECA study, the 1988 National Health Interview Survey (NHIS) alcohol supplement, and the NHSDA. In addition, our review is augmented with findings from a number of services conducted by the Alcohol Research Group (ARG) at the University of California at Berkeley.

While our review of the literature presented below suggests factors associated with needs for substance abuse prevention and treatment services, the literature does not provide direct guidance regarding factors to include in the Block Grant formula's population needs component for a number of reasons. First, as noted above, the literature addresses alcohol and drug dependence separately, rather than jointly. Second, most of the literature has examined one or a small subset of the social demographic and geographic factors that may be associated with substance abuse treatment needs, rather than examining these factors comprehensively in a multivariate model. Finally, the literature does not provide guidance regarding the population in need of prevention services—how to operationally define persons with those needs or what factors are correlated with such need. Consequently, we review the literature to provide overall guidance and a context for interpreting results of later analyses, but mainly rely on this study's analysis, directly designed to identify factors related to need for substance abuse service, to evaluate the appropriateness of the measures of population needs for services included in the current Block Grant formula.

Predictors of Alcohol Abuse

Rates of alcohol dependence vary depending on the survey used, the year it was conducted, and, of course, on the definition of dependence including the time frame chosen to tally symptoms. The ECA, conducted during the early and mid-1980s, shows a one-year prevalence rate of 6.8 percent for the general population (Helzer, Burnam, and McEvoy, 1991), while the 1988 NHIS yields a figure of 8.6 percent (Grant et al., 1992).

Age. Of all the demographic predictors used to refine those estimates, age is the most widely reported and yields the most consistent findings. Studies based on the NHSDA (Norton and Colliver, 1988; Kopstein and Gfroerer, 1990), the ECA (Helzer, 1987; Helzer, Burnam, and McEvoy, 1991), the NHIS (Grant, 1992; Grant et al., 1992), and a nationally representative survey conducted by the ARG at Berkeley (Hilton, 1987; Herd, 1990) all show that youths, defined alternatively as 18–24, 18–25, or 18–29, have a higher frequency of heavy drinking and drinking-related problems than people in older age groups. Two analyses of NHIS data that examine the effect of age without controlling for other variables (Grant, 1992; Grant et al., 1992) show that people 18–29 are about twice as likely as the general population over 18 years of age to meet DSM-III-R criteria for alcohol abuse or dependence: 12 percent compared with 6 percent, respectively.

Gender. Gender is another variable whose reported effects are consistent across studies and databases. Men are more likely than women to drink heavily and to have alcohol-related problems according to data from the NHSDA (Norton and Colliver, 1988; Kopstein and Gfroerer, 1990), the ECA (Helzer, 1988; Helzer, Burnam, and McEvoy, 1991), and various studies conducted by the ARG (Hilton, 1987, 1988; Treno, Parker, and Holder, 1993). NHIS data from 1988 show that while over 9 percent of men suffer from alcohol abuse or dependence, just 3 percent of women have similar alcohol problems (Grant, 1992). ECA data show that 11.9 percent of men met DSM-III criteria for abuse or dependence during the year before the survey, while women had a rate of only 2.2 percent, making men 5.5 times as likely to experience alcohol problems as women (Helzer, Burnam, and McEvoy, 1991). The male/female ratio is similar when based on one-month prevalence data.

Race/Ethnicity. Conclusions vary regarding the significance of race/ethnicity, since most studies do not present its independent effect, or use local or regional data, or focus on only one gender or ethnic group. The one study that reports the independent effects of race on alcohol consumption (Grant, 1992) shows that whites are 1.5 times as likely as non-whites to meet standards for alcohol abuse or dependence: 6.5 percent compared with 4.3 percent.

Geographic Residence. Research on the relationship between alcohol consumption and geographic residence, including urbanicity, is spotty. ECA data generally show that living in an urban area increases the probabilities of heavy drinking, but the reverse is true in one of the five sites, namely, Durham, North Carolina, and the four rural counties surrounding it (Blazer et al., 1987). Looking at regional differences, Cahalan (1972) concluded that people who lived in "drier" areas[1] were more likely to abstain, but if they did drink they were more likely to have alcohol problems than drinkers in "wetter" regions. More recent data (Herd, 1990) show that traditional patterns of "dry" (South and Midwest) versus "wet" (Northeast and Pacific Coast) regions still apply for white males but not for all population subgroups.

Education. Little research has been done on the effects of education on drinking patterns. ECA data (Helzer, Burnam, and McEvoy, 1991) show that starting without completing a program of study (for example, starting but not completing college with a degree—or starting but not completing high school) is associated with higher rates of abuse or dependence, implying a "bumpy" relationship between years of education and alcohol abuse.

Employment. The relationship between employment and alcohol consumption has been studied in terms of employment status, occupation, and income. Data from the NHSDA (Kopstein and Gfroerer, 1990) show that unemployed respondents have a higher rate of heavy drinking (7.9 percent) than employed respondents, but that people employed full time (6.4 percent) have a higher rate than those employed part time (5.6 percent). The same study shows that among men in eight industries, those employed in construction have the highest rate of heavy drinking, followed by those in retail trade and then repair services; men in wholesale trade and finance have the lowest rates. NHIS data (Harford et al., 1992) indicate that average daily alcohol consumption and rates of DSM-III-R alcohol abuse or dependence are higher among blue collar than white collar workers. The reported relationship between income and alcohol is not entirely consistent. NHSDA data (Kopstein and Gfroerer, 1990) show that men with annual incomes below $12,000 are almost twice as likely to drink heavily as those who earn $30,000 or more. However, ECA data show that receiving welfare payments does not significantly affect rates of alcohol abuse or dependence.

Marital Status. The ECA (Blazer et al., 1987; Helzer, Burnam, and McEvoy, 1991) shows that people with disrupted marriages (separated or divorced) have the highest

---

[1] The study identifies wetter regions of the United States to include New England, the Middle Atlantic, the East North Central, and the Pacific states. The drier regions include the South Atlantic, the East South Central, the West South Central, the West North Central, and the Mountain states.

rates of lifetime prevalence, followed by those who never married. People in stable marriages are least likely to drink excessively.

Predictors of Drug Abuse

Some unique issues arise in presenting the literature on drug abuse. First, much alcohol literature reports abuse or dependence. Although some drug studies do measure abuse or dependence, a majority report rates for all illicit drug *use* regardless of consequences, making comparisons across studies and datasets more difficult. From a treatment perspective, rates of dependence are more appropriate, while from a prevention perspective, use is more relevant. Since the Block Grant has dual objectives, both types of rates are presented here, but care should be taken not to compare the two. Second, the literature on drug use/dependence is complicated by the separate study of various drugs. For example, cocaine and marijuana are frequently studied independently of other drugs. Since the Block Grant formula does not distinguish between types of drug use, this review is mostly limited to analyses of all illicit[2] drug use combined. Third, this review is simplified, though limited, by the fact that there are only two major sources of national data on drug abuse—the NHSDA and the ECA—as opposed to four for alcohol.

The one-year prevalence rate of drug abuse or dependence was 2.7 percent according to the ECA (Anthony and Helzer, 1991), while the lifetime rate was 6.2 percent. According to the NHSDA (Hughes, 1992), the 1991 prevalence rate of any illicit drug use during the previous month was also 6.2 percent. Marijuana dominates these figures on drug use and dependence (Kandel, 1991). Lifetime prevalence rates based on the 1990 NHSDA show that 37 percent of the population had used an illicit drug at some time; however, the rate for marijuana use was 33 percent, while the next most frequently used drug—cocaine—had only been used by 11 percent of the population. ECA data (Anthony and Helzer, 1991; Kandel, 1991) indicate that of the 6.2 percent of the population who had abused or been dependent upon drugs at some point in their lives, over 70 percent had had problems with marijuana, while just over one-quarter had had difficulties with stimulants, the next most troublesome drug category.

Age. Drug problems are concentrated among the young. NHSDA data (Hughes, 1992) show that the six-month prevalence rate for drug use peaks at 15.4 percent among 18- to 25-year-olds, followed by 8.9 percent among 26- to 34-year-olds. The same pattern also appears for any drug use, marijuana use, and cocaine use during the past month and during the past year (Gill and Michaels, 1991). ECA data show that annual prevalence rates of drug use and related problems are higher among 18- to 29-year-olds than among 30- to 44-year-olds in each of the five sites.

Gender. Men are almost three times as likely as women to have reported drug abuse or dependence during a one-year period according to the ECA: 4.1 percent com-

---

[2]Although the Block Grant legislation considers the use of alcohol by youths under 18 years of age to be "illicit," the substance abuse literature excludes all alcohol use from that analytic category.

pared with 1.4 percent (Anthony and Helzer, 1991). NHSDA data show less dramatic gender differences when use rather than dependence is measured—16.4 percent of men vs. 12.0 percent of women reported having used an illicit drug during the past year (Gill and Michaels, 1991).

Race/Ethnicity. NHSDA data by race/ethnicity show that blacks are most likely to have used an illicit drug in the last year (9.4 percent), while whites are least likely (5.8 percent), and Hispanics fall in between (6.4 percent) (Hughes, 1992). These results do not hold true across all geographic areas, however. Perhaps because of its geographic limitations, or perhaps due to the difference between drug use and drug dependence, ECA data show no significant racial differences in either one-month, one-year, or lifetime prevalence rates of drug abuse or dependence (Anthony and Helzer, 1991).

Geographic Residence. Geographic residence does influence drug use, as the Block Grant formula recognizes; however, geographic variations are not neatly described by a rural/metropolitan dichotomy. One study of NHSDA data (Hughes, 1992) presents a fairly extensive analysis of illicit drug use in several cities, other large MSAs, small MSAs, and non-MSAs. It shows that MSAs have higher rates of past-month illicit drug use than non-MSAs, but it is unclear whether there is any difference between large and small MSAs. The greatest differences are found among the individual cities. Miami ties the non-MSAs for the lowest reported rate of 5.4 percent, while the highest rate—8.5 percent—is in Los Angeles. Chicago and Washington, D.C., also have lower rates, while Denver and New York are on the high end. ECA data show that the six-month prevalence rate in Los Angeles (2.4 percent) is exceeded only by that in Baltimore (2.6 percent), which is double the rate in Piedmont, North Carolina (1.3 percent) (Burnam et al., 1987).

Education. Educational attainment, according to ECA data (Anthony and Helzer, 1991), has a curvilinear relationship to drug abuse or dependence. Overall, education seems to be positively associated with drug problems. However, people who finish the educational programs they begin have lower rates of abuse than those who do not finish the same programs. People who have started, but not finished, college have the highest rates of any educational category.

Employment. Results concerning the effects of employment status on drug use and dependence are mixed. According to the ECA (Anthony and Helzer, 1991), working for pay versus not working for pay has no effect on either (1) lifetime prevalence of drug abuse or dependence, (2) one-year prevalence based on most recent use, or (3) one-year prevalence based on most recent problem. NHSDA data, however, indicate that although full- versus part-time employment makes little difference, unemployed people are about twice as likely to have used an illicit drug during the past month (Kopstein and Gfroerer, 1990).

The NHSDA and the ECA yield mostly compatible results regarding occupation. ECA data show that skilled and unskilled labor and people with farm/rural occupations have higher rates of drug use and drug problems in the previous year, while people in service, sales/support, and management/professional occupations have lower rates (Anthony and Helzer, 1991). Likewise, of eight occupational categories selected from the 1985 NHSDA, people in production/craft occupations and operatives have the highest rates of past-month use of both marijuana and cocaine. In contrast to the ECA data, however, people with farming occupations (along with homemakers) have the lowest rates (Gill and Michaels, 1991).

Marital Status. Having a stable marriage is associated with a lower lifetime prevalence of drug abuse and dependence, according to ECA data, and those who were never married but had lived together as if married had the highest lifetime prevalence (Anthony and Helzer, 1991).

ANALYSES OF FACTORS PREDICTING NEED FOR SUBSTANCE ABUSE PREVENTION AND TREATMENT SERVICES

This section reports results of empirical analyses we conducted to identify factors predicting an individual's need for substance abuse treatment services and factors predicting an individual's need for primary prevention services. The analyses are based upon the 1991 NHSDA, a national probability survey of 32,594 household residents aged 12 and older. In addition to the large sample size and national coverage of this survey, its inclusion of a wide range of questions regarding use of and dependence on both alcohol and drugs makes it uniquely suitable for the present analysis.

While the NHSDA is the best existing dataset for describing substance abuse in the nation, it has limitations that make it uninformative for understanding certain types of drug abusing populations. Precisely because it is a household sample, the NHSDA omits institutional populations. The most important omission is prisons, since surveys of inmates suggest that half or more were using illicit drugs when they were incarcerated. An interesting conceptual question is whether prison inmates should be regarded as "needing treatment" during the period they are imprisoned and unable to gain regular access to illicit drugs. Our analysis does not include need for treatment among the prison population, which in 1991 totaled about 800,000 persons nationwide. The question of whether adding information about substance abuse treatment needs in the prison sample would substantially change estimates of state level needs for treatment, however, is worthy of further research. Another limitation of household surveys is that they are vulnerable to higher rates of nonresponse among persons whose heavy use of drugs or criminal involvement makes them harder to contact. Thus, the NHSDA is not used to generate estimates of heroin dependence—both because the rate of heroin dependence in the general population is low and consequently difficult to reliably estimate, and because heroin users tend to be concentrated among socially marginal and difficult to reach populations that are likely to be underrepresented in household surveys. To the extent that cocaine dependence has become concentrated among socially marginal individuals, our confidence in the accuracy of the NHSDA to provide estimates of the size of that population is lessened. Currently, cocaine dependence is quite prevalent in the NHSDA sample, and so the household survey probably does a reasonably good job of representing cocaine users for the nation as a whole, but state-level estimates may be more vulnerable to differential nonresponse among those dependent on cocaine. We return to a consideration of these limitations of the NHSDA sample when describing results of our analyses estimating state-level rates of need for treatment services.

This section now turns to issues in defining need for substance abuse treatment and prevention services and then describes the operational definitions of such needs developed for our analysis of NHSDA data. It then reports the methods, results, and conclusions of these analyses to identify factors predicting need for substance abuse treatment and prevention services.

Definitions of Population in Need of Substance Abuse Treatment and Prevention Services

The target population in need of Block Grant substance abuse treatment and prevention services, unlike that for community mental health services, has not been explicitly defined by the Secretary of Health and Human Services (nor was there a legislative mandate that a specific definition of the target population be provided). It is clear from the legislation, however, that the population to be targeted for primary prevention (that is, deterrence of initial use of substances) is distinct from the population targeted for treatment (those who have developed problems typically associated with prolonged and heavy substance use). The relative proportion of funds to be targeted to those in need of treatment versus those in need of prevention is not specified, although the states are mandated to spend a minimum of 20 percent of their funds for primary prevention services.

In the absence of more specific guidance regarding the definition of the populations in need of treatment and prevention services, we queried staff of SAMHSA's Center for Substance Abuse Treatment and Center for Substance Abuse Prevention for their views regarding the target population. For the population in need of treatment, those with DSM-III-R diagnoses of alcohol or drug dependence were considered clearly in need, irrespective of the type of drug abused. For example, staff did not distinguish those dependent only upon marijuana, a drug associated with relatively minor social and health problems, from those dependent upon more harmful drugs such as cocaine or heroin; all were considered clearly in need of treatment. Nor did they suggest that some types of substance dependence (e.g., cocaine) be weighted more heavily than others (e.g., alcohol). Beyond those with diagnoses of substance dependence, there was no consistent view among the SAMHSA staff of who else should be included in the definition of the population in need of treatment, such as youth, heavy users, or those whose use is associated with specific types of problems (e.g., driving under the influence).

As with mental health treatment services, it is clear that in practice the Block Grant program provides substance abuse treatment services largely to the uninsured poor. However, no explicit requirements relating to ability to pay for services have been suggested to delineate the population in need of substance abuse treatment services.

The SAMHSA staff appear to conceive the population targeted for prevention services broadly. They suggest that prevention interventions might be appropriately targeted to individuals at risk of initiating substance use who have not yet done so (for example, through school-based programs that instruct adolescents to resist drug use), those who have used substances but not yet developed problems with them (for example, through early intervention with adolescents who have used drugs), or entire communities (for example, through advertising campaigns). Overall, however, there is a clear emphasis on youth under the age of 21, since initiation of substance use typically occurs during adolescence. Furthermore, the SAMHSA staff considered prevention of tobacco use, as well as alcohol and drug use, part of the mandate of substance abuse prevention services (even though persons with tobacco dependence are not included in the definition of the population in need of treatment).

Operational Definitions of Populations in Need of Substance Abuse Treatment and Prevention Services Based on Survey Measures

Our central operational definition of persons in need of substance abuse treatment was a measure that approximated DSM-III-R criteria for substance dependence. While the NHSDA included questions that covered many of the DSM-III-R criteria, the survey was not explicitly designed to assess these diagnoses, and so it was necessary to construct a proxy measure that replicated the DSM-III-R criteria as closely as possible.[3] Table 4.1 summarizes this measure, which is based on problems reported with drugs or alcohol over the past year. In addition, we examined a measure for dependence on drugs but not on alcohol, also shown in Table 4.1, because predictors of need for drug treatment may differ from those for alcohol treatment needs, and the measure of need for any substance abuse treatment largely reflects need for alcohol treatment (since dependence on alcohol is much more common in the household population than dependence on drugs). Table 4.2 shows the estimated percentage of the national household population aged 12 and older in need of substance abuse treatment, determined using each of these definitions. In Appendix B, we consider two other definitions of populations in need that include an alternative operational definition of dependence, and a definition of need that includes not only dependent users, but nondependent heavy users.

Conceptually, the development of operational definitions of the population in need of prevention services was more difficult, because of the broad range of interventions and their targets that are included in this category. Given the emphasis, however, on primary prevention among youth, we focused on the population aged 12 to 20. We

---

[3]DSM-III-R requires that three of the following nine criteria be met: (1) substance often taken in larger amounts or over a longer period that the person intended; (2) persistent desire or one or more unsuccessful efforts to cut down or control substance use; (3) a great deal of time spent in activities necessary to get the substance, in taking the substance, or in recovering from its effects; (4) frequent intoxication or withdrawal symptoms when expected to fulfill major role obligations at work, school, or home, or when substance use is physically hazardous; (5) important social, occupational, or recreational activities given up or reduced because of substance use; (6) continued substance use despite knowledge of having a persistent or recurrent social, psychological, or physical problem that is caused or exacerbated by the use of the substance; (7) marked tolerance: need for markedly increased amounts of the substance to achieve intoxication or desired effect, or markedly diminished effect with continued use of the same amount; (8) characteristic withdrawal symptoms; (9) substance often taken to relieve or avoid withdrawal symptoms. The NHSDA included items that fully or partially assessed eight of these nine criteria, with information collected specifically for alcohol and each type of drug. DSM-III-R also requires that some symptoms of the disturbance persist for at least one month or occur repeatedly over a longer period of time. We were unable to operationalize this duration requirement with the NHSDA data.

Table 4.1

Operational Definitions of Persons Needing Substance Abuse Treatment Services

Definition 1: Dependence (DSM-III-R criteria)
— Experienced three or more of the following problems with a specific type of drug or alcohol in the past year:
1. Tried to cut down on use, or unable to cut down (A-2)
2. Needed greater quantities to achieve the same effect (A-7)
3. Used a substance daily for two or more consecutive weeks (A-1, A-2)
4. Felt dependent on substance (A-6)
5. Felt sick due to substance use (A-8)
6. Psychological problems due to substance use (i.e., depression, loneliness, nervousness, feeling upset, suspiciousness, or concentration difficulties) (A-6)
7. Social problems due to substance use (arguments, problems at work or school, problems harder to handle due to substance use) (A-4, A-5)
8. Substance use contributed to physical health problems (i.e., substance use precipitated medical emergencies) (A-6)

Definition 2: Dependence on a drug, but not on alcohol
— Experienced three or more of the problems listed above with a specific type of drug but not with alcohol in the past year

Table 4.2

Percentage of Persons with Substance Dependence in Household Population

Drug or Alcohol Dependence	Drug Dependence Only
6.8	1.7

then considered two approaches to defining need for prevention services among this population. The simplest approach is to consider all youth, irrespective of their characteristics or living environments, as the target of prevention services. Under this approach, state-level need for prevention services is directly proportional to the size of the state's youth population. More complex approaches recognize that some youth are at higher risk than others for developing problems related to substance use, and that these higher-risk youth have a greater need for prevention services. We suggest two ways that level of risk could be included in a definition of relative need for prevention services: weighting the size of the state's youth population by the estimated prevalence of substance use among youth in that state, or by the estimated prevalence of substance dependence among adults in that state. Thus we use NHSDA data to examine predictors of both substance use among youth and substance dependence among adults to develop weights that can later be applied to the youth population (Chapter Seven). Table 4.3 shows the definitions of these risk indicators. The definition of dependence among adults when used to assess risk for youth differs slightly from that used to measure need for substance abuse treatment in that the former includes adults dependent on tobacco (measured as daily smoking). The national prevalence of these risk indicators in the household population over 12 is 44.5 percent for substance use among youth and 30.4 percent for substance dependence among adults.

Table 4.3

Operational Definitions of Risks to Youth for
Developing Substance Use Problems

Definition 1:	Any substance use among youth
	Among persons aged 12–20, percentage using any substance (alcohol, drugs, or tobacco) in the past month
Definition 2:	Substance dependence among adults
	Among adults aged 21 or older, percentage dependent on any substance (alcohol, drugs, or tobacco) in the past year

After developing operational definitions of substance abuse "treatment" need and "prevention" need, we then have the issue of how the two types of service needs should be combined to produce an integrated definition of need for substance abuse prevention and treatment services. To resolve this issue, we cannot turn to empirical findings, as the two types of needs are so different in nature that simply summing the number of persons with each type of need makes no sense. To combine the two separate need definitions into a single definition, we must arrive at some basis for valuing or weighting one type of need relative to the other. There is no explicit policy guidance from SAMHSA or Congress on the issue of how to weight treatment relative to prevention needs. States have flexibility to allocate funds to prevention or treatment services as they see fit, with the legislatively imposed constraint that at least 20 percent of the Block Grant funds for SA services must be spent on prevention services. Rather than selecting a single definition of combined treatment and prevention needs, we instead created two definitions of combined SA service needs that we believed would bound the choices of most states regarding the balance of prevention and treatment needs. In our first definition, we set prevention need at 20 percent and treatment need at 80 percent of total SA service need, reflecting the minimum emphasis that states can give to prevention. In our second definition, prevention and treatment need were weighted equally, contributing 50-50 to total SA service need, a likely upper bound for the emphasis that states would give to prevention relative to treatment. These combined SA service need definitions were used in the final stage of analyses, reported in Chapter Seven, where we compared the current SA Block Grant formula in Chapter Seven with a formula that used our alternative population need measures.

Analysis Methods

To identify the most important predictors of an individual's need for substance abuse treatment or need for substance abuse prevention, we conducted logistic regression analyses using 1991 NHSDA data. Logistic regression models the probability that an individual is in need of treatment services on the basis of the observed rate of need in the sample. Table 4.4 shows the variables we examined as predictors. They included individual-level demographic variables available in the survey data.

Table 4.4
Variables Examined as Predictors of Need for Substance Abuse Treatment and
Prevention Services, National Household Survey of Drug Abuse

Individual-level variables	
Gender	Male; female
Marital status	Married; widowed, or divorced or separated; never married
Age	12–17; 18–24; 25–34; 35–44; 45–54; 55–64; 65+
Number in household	Living alone; not living alone
Education	0–8; 9–11; 12 (including people with fewer than 12 years of education who have a high school diploma or a GED); 13–15; 16+
Work status	Working full-time or holding two jobs; working part-time; not working
Student	Full-time student; not a full-time student
Veteran status	Veteran; not a veteran
Health insurance	Has medical insurance; has no medical insurance
Race	Hispanic origin; white; black; other
Population density	MSA with a population of 1 million or more; MSA with 250,000–999,999; MSA with less than 250,000; not in a MSA and not in a rural area; not in a MSA and in a rural area
Region	Northwest; North Central; South; West
Welfare	Respondent or any household member has received welfare during the last month; no household member has received welfare during the last month
Income	Annual total family income, not including food stamps
Census tract variables	
Gender by marital status	Percent of females currently married
	Percent of females separated, divorced, or widowed
	Percent of females never married
	Percent of males currently married
	Percent of males separated, divorced, or widowed
	Percent of males never married
Age	Percent under 18 years
	Percent 19 to 24 years
	Percent 25 to 34 years
	Percent 35 to 44 years
	Percent 45 to 54 years
	Percent 55 to 64 years
	Percent 65 years or older
Household composition	Percent living alone
	Percent female headed household with no spouse and children under 18
Education (persons over 18)	Percent 0 to 8 years of school
	Percent 9 to 12 years of school
	Percent high school graduates
	Percent attended college, no degree
	Percent associate degree
	Percent bachelor's, graduate, or professional degree
Work status	Percent females 16 years or older in labor force
	Percent males 16 years or older in labor force
Race	Percent Hispanic origin
	Percent white (non-Hispanic)
	Percent black (non-Hispanic)
	Percent other race (non-Hispanic)
Poverty	Percent of families below poverty line
Public assistance	Percent households with public assistance income
Disabilities	Percent persons 16 to 64 with a work disability
Housing	Percent housing units owner-occupied
	Percent housing units rented
	Median value owner-occupied housing units
	Median rent for rental units

Each model was fit using a model-fitting procedure analogous to that used in Chapter Three. A main-effects model was fit using the entire candidate list of predictor variables given in Table 4.4. We then used backwards deletion to simplify the model. Through this process, some of the predictor variables in Table 4.4 were completely dropped from the model; others remained in the model but were transformed. For example, six categories of age were often collapsed into three or four when the likelihood of need did not differ significantly across two or more groups using the finer classification scheme.

We then explored the effects of interactions between the remaining predictors. All two-way interactions between the main effects (or the most significant effects) were included in the model. Backwards deletion was again used to remove insignificant terms.

This procedure produced the best-fitting model for each outcome variable. The best-fitting models were reduced even further to include only those variables available for the purposes of subsequent prediction of state-level needs. These final models appear in Tables 4.5 and 4.6.

There did not tend to be large differences between the predictive power of the best-fitting and the implementable models. For our estimates of drug or alcohol dependence, the relative R^2 comparing the two models was .90, and the correlation between the two models' predictions of the probability of dependence was very high ($r = .95$).[4] For our estimates of any substance use among youth, the relative R^2 for comparing the best-fitting to the implementable model was .96, and the correlation of the two models' predicted probabilities of use was extremely high ($r = .98$).[5]

Results

Table 4.5 shows the final reduced regression models for predicting an individual's need for drug treatment and for predicting individual need for drug or alcohol treatment. For both measures of need, five demographic variables were highly predictive: males, those who were separated or unmarried, those aged 18 to 44, those with low educational attainment (high school dropouts or high school graduates who did not finish college), and those living in the Western states had a higher probability of

---

[4]The relative R^2 is the ratio of the R^2 for the implementable model to the R^2 for the best fitting model. The R^2 for any individual model is defined to be

$$R^2 = 1 - L_p/L_0$$

where L_0 and L_p denote the log-likelihoods for the models containing only the intercept, and the model containing the intercept plus the covariates (Hosmer and Lemeshow, 1989).

The variables deleted from the best-fitting model were: percent of one-person households; percent of housing units rented; percent of families living below the poverty level; percent of households with public assistance income; median value of owner-occupied housing units; interactions of gender with percent of one-person households and with percent of families living below the poverty level; and an interaction of MSA with percent of housing units rented.

[5]The variables deleted from the best-fitting model were: percent of residents age 19 to 24; percent of one-person households; percent of persons aged 16 to 64 with a work disability; percent of males separated, divorced, or widowed; percent of housing units rented, percent of residents over age 18 with 0 to 8 years of school; and median value of owner-occupied housing units.

Table 4.5

Final Models: Factors Predicting Drug or Alcohol Dependence or Drug Dependence Alone

	Odds Ratios (and 95% Confidence Intervals)	
Predictors	Drug or Alcohol Dependence	Drug Dependence
Gender		
Female	1.0	1.0
Male	1.8 (1.7–2.0)	1.5 (1.3–1.8)
Race		
White, non-Hispanic	1.4 (1.3–1.5)	0.7 (0.3–1.5)
Other	1.0	1.0
Marital status		
Currently married	1.0	1.0
Separated or not married	1.7 (1.6–1.9)	1.9 (1.5–2.4)
Age		
12–17	1.0	3.5 (2.0–6.1)
18–44	2.2 (1.9–2.5)	
45–64	1.5 (1.2–1.8)	1.0
65 or older	0.7 (0.5–1.0)	
Education		
0–8 years and a student	1.0	0.2 (0.1–0.3)
0–8 years, not a student		2.8 (2.2–3.5)
9–11 years	2.5 (2.1–2.9)	1.0
High school and a student	1.9 (1.6–2.2)	
High school, not a student		1.9 (1.6–2.3)
College graduate	1.2 (1.0–1.5)	1.0
Welfare status		
Welfare recipient		1.8 (1.4–2.3)
Not welfare recipient		1.0
Population density		
In MSA	0.7 (0.6–0.8)	
Not in MSA	1.0	
Geographic region		
Mid-Atlantic/East Central[a]	1.0	0.7 (0.6–0.9)
West[b]	1.6 (1.4–1.7)	1.4 (1.2–1.7)
Other	1.0	1.0
Age by race interactions		
12–44 years and white		2.8 (1.2–6.6)
Other		1.0
Number of children in household		0.7 (0.7–0.8)

[a]Includes: AL, IL, IN, KY, MI, MS, NJ, NY, OH, PA, TN, and WI.
[b]Includes: AK, AZ, CA, CO, HI, ID, MT, NM, NV, OR, UT, WA, and WY.

needing treatment for dependence. Also, white non-Hispanics under age 44 were more likely to need treatment under either definition and older white non-Hispanics were more likely to need treatment under the definition that includes both drug and alcohol dependence.

People from families that receive welfare are more likely to be drug dependent, but they do not have a significantly greater likelihood of being drug or alcohol dependent. Also, those living in metropolitan areas are less likely to need drug or alcohol treatment but metropolitan status is not a significant predictor of need for drug treatment.

Table 4.6

Final Models: Factors Predicting Risks for Developing Substance Use Problems

Predictors	Odds Ratios (and 95% Confidence Intervals)	
	Any Substance Use Among Youth	Any Substance Dependence Among Adults
Gender		
Female	1.0	1.0
Male	1.4 (1.3–1.5)	1.5 (1.4–1.6)
Race		
White, non-Hispanic	1.9 (1.7–2.0)	1.8 (1.6–1.9)
Black, non-Hispanic	1.0	1.4 (1.2–1.5)
Other		1.0
Age		
Continuous age		
90th percentile	55.8 (30.7, 80.9)	
10th percentile	1.0	
Continuous age squared		
90th percentile	0.2 (0.1, 0.2)	
10th percentile	1.0	
18–54 years		3.3 (2.9–3.8)
55–64 years		2.3 (1.9–2.7)
65 and older		1.0
Family income		
Continuous income (log)		
90th percentile	0.9 (0.9–1.0)	
10th percentile	1.0	
Student		
Full-time student	0.7 (0.7–0.8)	
Not full-time student	1.0	
Number in household		
Living alone	1.0	
Not living alone	0.6 (0.4–0.8)	
Work status		
Working full- or part-time	1.0	
Not working	0.8 (0.7–0.8)	
Veteran status		
Veteran		1.3 (1.2–1.5)
Not a veteran		1.0
Household receives welfare		
No		1.0
Yes		1.5 (1.3–1.7)

Many of the predictors identified in these models are consistent with both the alcohol and drug dependence literature, including relationships with gender, age, marital status, and education. Employment was not a contributing predictor, as reported in previous studies based on the NHSDA, but its effects may be partly captured by the welfare variable. The higher prevalence of dependence among whites relative to other major racial/ethnic groups is consistent with the alcohol literature but not with the drug literature. The finding of higher need in the Western region of the United States is also consistent with alcohol epidemiology, since that area of the country has relatively high per capita levels of alcohol consumption.

A surprising finding is that being in a nonmetropolitan relative to a metropolitan area predicts higher rates of substance dependence.[6] Because living in a nonmetropolitan area does not significantly contribute to the prediction of treatment need for drug dependence, but does contribute to the prediction of treatment need for substance dependence, these results indicate that rates of alcohol dependence, but not drug dependence, tend to be higher in nonmetropolitan relative to metropolitan areas, other sociodemographic factors being equal. This is consistent with some of the previous literature on alcohol use and dependence, where the evidence on urban/rural differences in prevalence has been mixed.

The fact that we did not find drug dependence to be higher in metropolitan relative to nonmetropolitan areas, however, concerns us, since past research has found drug use to be higher in metropolitan areas, and large urban areas in particular are believed by experts to have the most serious problems with illicit drugs. There are several possible explanations for the absence of a relationship between metropolitan areas and illicit drug dependence in our analyses. First, we examined the effect of living in a metropolitan area as a partial effect in a multivariate model, after taking into account the effects of other predictors, including gender, race, marital status, age, education, welfare status, geographic region, and number of children in the household. Many of these variables (for example, welfare status) may capture some of the association between urbanicity and illicit drug use. Second, we were unable to distinguish between highly urban metropolitan areas and those metropolitan areas that are less urban in the NHSDA data. It is possible that the higher rates of drug dependence in highly urban areas are obscured by lower rates of drug dependence in smaller cities. In addition, as mentioned previously, the NHSDA data are based on a household sample and thus have the limitations of excluding the prison population and underrepresenting socially marginal individuals such as heavy and criminally involved drug users. It is likely that these omitted and underrepresented groups are substantially more urban than the NHSDA sample generally. Thus, these analyses may understate the extent to which drug dependence is concentrated in urban populations.

Turning now to results relevant to need for SA prevention services, Table 4.6 shows final models for predicting two alternative indicators of social/environmental risk for

---

[6]There are several different indicators of urban status used in the literature. Here, we distinguish between residents of metropolitan and nonmetropolitan areas, using the Census Bureau designation of Metropolitan Statistical Areas. While distinguishing between inner-city or highly urbanized and other, more suburban, metropolitan areas might have improved the predictive utility of this model, we were unable to do so because information to distinguish highly urbanized areas from their larger MSAs was not available to us from the NHSDA. Within the constraints of the available data, however, we found that the relationship of residing in a metropolitan area to lower treatment need is robust. It is not an effect that is restricted to the six oversampled large MSAs included in the 1991 NHSDA. The results are also consistent across alternative specifications of metropolitan area: That is, results are similar across large and smaller metropolitan areas (MSAs) and across rural and nonrural nonmetropolitan areas. The effect of residing in a metropolitan area is also similar whether data are weighted or unweighted in the multivariate modeling. It is important to note, however, that the metropolitan status effect is a partial effect; that is, it represents the predictive effect of residing in a metropolitan area after controlling for other covariates (such as age, gender, ethnicity, marital status, and education) included in the model. The simple main effect of residing in a metropolitan area is not as strong as the partial effect. Without controlling for other covariates, the estimated rate of SA treatment need in nonmetropolitan areas (6.9 percent) is only slightly higher than the rate of SA treatment need in metropolitan areas (6.6 percent).

youth to develop substance abuse problems. The first model predicts an index of prevalence of any substance use among youth and the second an index of the prevalence of any substance dependence among adults. These indicators were examined because we expect that youth in states with higher rates of substance using youth and higher rates of substance dependent adults are at higher risk for developing substance use problems and therefore have higher needs for prevention services. Because the indicators focus on two very different ways to operationalize risk, the models are quite dissimilar, with the exception of males and white non-Hispanics having higher estimated need across both indicators. For the measure of any substance use (alcohol, drugs, or tobacco) among youth, being an older adolescent, having lower family income, not attending school full-time, living alone, and working were predictive factors. Predictors of any substance dependence among adults (including alcohol, drugs, or tobacco) included age (older adults had lower rates), being a veteran, and the household's receiving welfare.

STATE-LEVEL ESTIMATES OF NEED FOR SUBSTANCE ABUSE PREVENTION AND TREATMENT SERVICES

This section presents the results of simulations to estimate state-level rates of need for substance abuse treatment among adults and prevention needs among adolescents, based on the final predictive models described above. The results of these simulations are used to derive alternative indexes of need for treatment and prevention services that are subsequently compared to the index of need generated by the current substance abuse Block Grant formula in Chapter Seven. Our indirect estimation method takes the logistic regressions developed above and uses them to estimate the probability of the various substance abuse and prevention need definitions for each person in the Census PUMS. These probabilities are then summed to the state level to get an expected number of persons at need.

$$\text{PIN} = \sum p_i \quad \text{where} \quad p_i = \frac{1}{1 + e^{-x\beta}}.$$

PIN is the estimated population in need, β is from the logistic regressions, and x is the individual-level PUMS data.

The PUMS data provide individual level correlates for a random sample of respondents to the 1990 Census. The estimates presented here are based on the 1 percent PUMS sample. This yields a sample of at least 2,000 persons for each state (substantially more for larger states). One challenge in the implementation of this method is developing a model for which comparable correlates are available in the PUMS data. Most of the predictor variables that appear in our final models for the NHSDA analysis (presented in Table 4.5) are available in the PUMS data.[7] The ex-

---

[7]Although conceptually simple, this type of indirect estimation can be computationally onerous. The 1 percent PUMS dataset contains over two million individual-level records. In Appendix B we discuss simplified, more implementable methods of calculating state level estimates. We also explore the effects of al-

ception was the population density variable; for it, we substituted the PUMS MSA variable.

Table 4.7 presents some descriptive statistics and correlations for the estimated state-level rates (per 100 persons) of treatment and prevention needs. There is a fairly large range of rates of persons needing service from state to state, in contrast to the mental health needs in Chapter Three. It is important to note that two features of the model and dataset affect variability in the state-level rate estimates. First, the variable must be statistically significant to be included into the final model. Second, the variable must have significantly different distribution from state to state. For example, gender may be a significant predictor at the individual level but may have little effect at the state level since the rate of women in the total population varies little from state to state.

The models for drug or alcohol abuse treatment needs and for drug abuse treatment need give state-level rate estimates that are highly correlated (see Table 4.7). The state-level rate estimates given by the models for prevention needs are poorly correlated, both with each other and with the results of the treatment needs models.

Estimated need rates differ across treatment and prevention domains and also vary depending on the definition of need selected. Figures 4.1 and 4.2 are maps of the estimated rates (per 100 population) using models predicting need for treatment using different definitions of treatment need. Figure 4.1 shows results for treatment need defined as alcohol or drug dependence, while Figure 4.2 shows results for treatment need defined as drug dependence only. While treatment need predictions broadly correspond with available epidemiologic literature on alcohol problems, showing that Western states tend to have high per capita levels of alcohol consumption (the literature on state variations in drug problems is unfortunately limited), there are

Table 4.7

Prevalence of Substance Dependence for States: Summary Statistics and Correlation Coefficients

	Treatment Needs Indicators		Prevention Needs Indicators	
	Drug or Alcohol Dependence	Drug Dependence Only	Substance Use Among Youth	Dependence Among Adults
Summary statistics				
Mean	7.72	1.73	44.36	24.80
Std. dev.	1.70	0.43	2.19	1.05
Minimum	5.61	1.10	38.09	20.61
Maximum	11.94	2.71	49.27	26.86
Correlations				
Treatment needs indicators				
Drug dependence only	0.8402			
Prevention needs indicators				
Substance use among youth	–0.2339	–0.0981		
Dependence among adults	0.2649	0.1419	0.2172	

ternative model specifications and weighting schemes in that appendix. In particular, we look at model specifications that include tract-level aggregates as individual-level explanatory variables.

Population in Need of Substance Abuse Prevention and Treatment 57

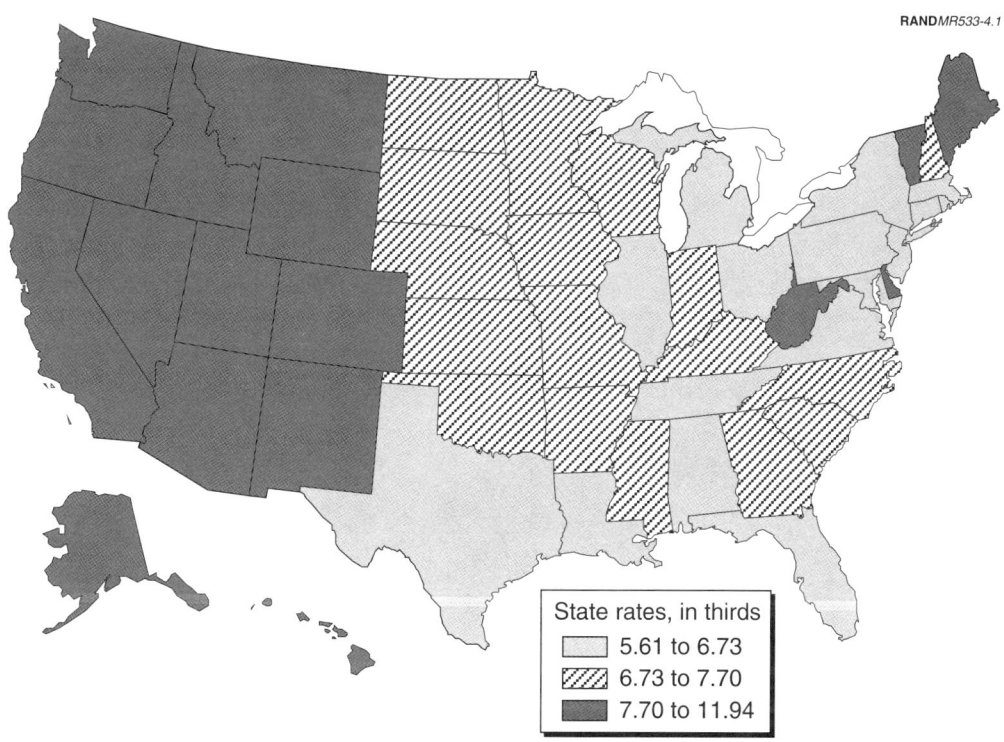

Figure 4.1—Percentage of Population Meeting RAND Criteria for Drug or Alcohol
Dependence, by State, NHSDA Data

some notable problems. Utah, estimated by our models to have high rates of substance abuse problems because it is located in the Western region of the United States and has a youthful population largely of white non-Hispanic racial background, has very low per capita alcohol consumption, and thus the simulation probably overestimated need for substance abuse treatment for this state. Florida, a state with an older and sizable Hispanic population, is estimated by our models to have low rates of substance abuse problems but has moderately high rates of per capital alcohol consumption. Thus, we may have underestimated need for treatment for Florida.

This points to one of the limitations of the data upon which we base our simulation models. In a nationally representative study such as the NHSDA, data are too sparse to directly estimate state-level variations, thus grosser measures such as Census region must serve our purposes. Furthermore, specific states are not identified on data that are available for public use. Even for larger states in which sample sizes would be adequate to make more direct estimates, this information is unavailable. As a consequence of these characteristics of the NHSDA study, our simulations are unlikely to reflect important idiosyncrasies related to need for services that may differentiate a particular state from the more general profile, especially if the state is small and therefore sparsely represented in the available survey data. The simulations do, however, provide a much more comprehensive and rigorous prediction of state-level variations in population needs than does the current formula, and thus should be a

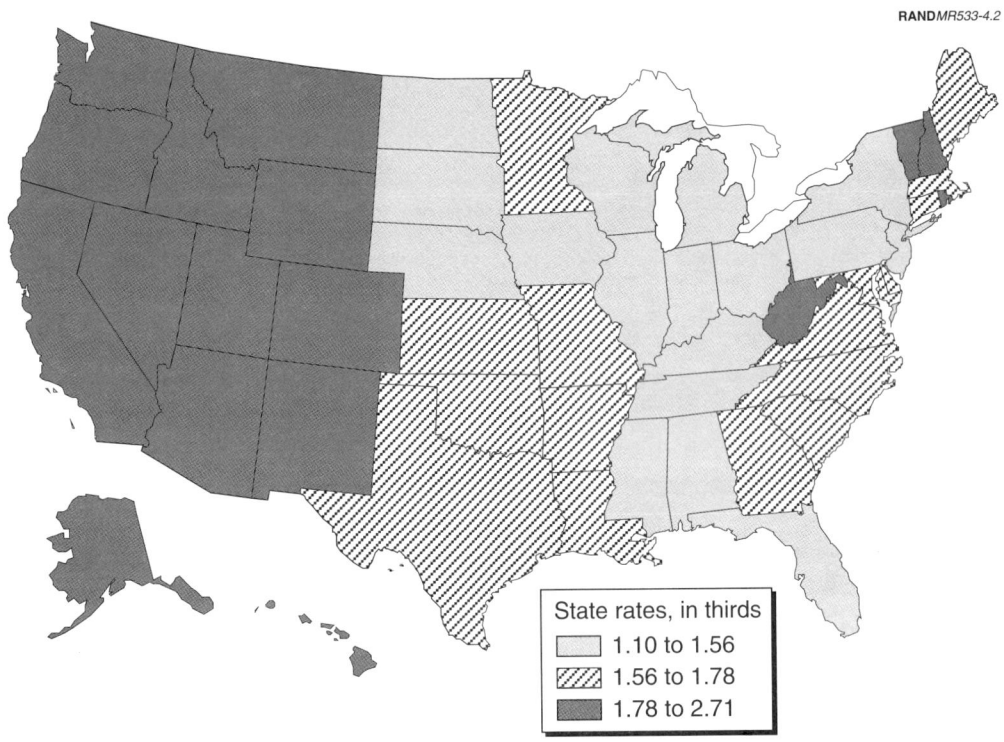

Figure 4.2—Percentage of Population Meeting RAND Criteria for Drug Dependence Only, by State, NHSDA Data

much closer approximation to true variations in needs. Furthermore, the predictions make full use of the best available epidemiologic data. To improve upon state-level estimates, a new national study would have to be mounted that would be specially designed to obtain stable state-level prevalence estimates. Given the expense of this type of study, it is unlikely that such an effort will be undertaken.

We examined the relationship of state-level estimates of population rates of need for prevention and treatment (rates per 100 population) with three major state characteristics: state population size, state poverty level, and state urbanicity. Estimated rates of need for prevention were not strongly associated with population or poverty (correlations were less than .20), but were negatively correlated with poverty (r = –.42). State-level rates of need for alcohol or drug treatment tended to be higher for less urbanized states (correlation with urbanicity of –.44), and for smaller states (correlation with population size of –.30). Treatment need had no significant correlation with poverty.

Chapter Five
COST OF SERVICE INDICATORS

Even if all states had the same populations in need of substance abuse and mental health services, their expenditure needs could differ sharply due to cost differences. For example, Pope (1990) computed a cost of service index (COSI) that ranged from 0.77 to 1.52—indicating that, to serve the same number of people, the most costly state would have to spend twice as much as the least costly state. The equity concepts outlined in Chapter Two imply that grant allocations should take such differences into account.

Although well motivated by equity considerations, cost adjustments have only recently been added to the SA and MH Block Grant formulas. The current COSI was newly developed in the study cited above and was first included in the SA and MH grant allocation formula by the legislation of 1992. So far, the cost adjustment has not affected actual SA and MH services grant awards because they remain subject to stringent hold-harmless provisions. However, initial factor estimates suggest that the COS adjustment could substantially alter future grant allocations. Looking ahead, policymakers might be concerned about the sheer magnitude of the changes—and about whether they will truly represent an improvement in equity.

This chapter evaluates the current methodology for estimating COS factors. We begin by laying out specific criteria for judging whether cost factors fairly represent cost differences among states.[1] Next, we describe the COS measurement methodology currently mandated by the SA and MH services legislation, explaining that it uses a set of weights to combine measures of wages and rents into an overall COSI. Then the chapter evaluates each of those components of the COS factors.

OVERVIEW

Equity in COS measurement is a legitimate concern because the current methodology does not measure actual spending rates. Instead, the COS formula applies standardized weights to broadly defined measures of wages and rents. This makes the COSI *independent* of actual spending and hence does not create undesired incentives

---

[1] Throughout this chapter, "state" means any of the 50 states or the District of Columbia; hence, we refer to 51 states. The current SA and MH services formula does not use cost factors to determine grants to Guam, Puerto Rico, the Virgin Islands, or the Trust Territories, and we lack data with which to evaluate cost measurement for those places.

for states to modify their spending simply to influence their grant awards. However, the use of a standardized formula leaves open the question as to whether the wage and rent measures and, ultimately, the overall COSI fairly represent cost differences among states. In particular, questions can be raised about whether the wage measures accurately represent current interstate cost differences for SA and MH service-related workers, about whether standardized weights properly account for differences between urban and rural settings in the delivery of SA and MH services, and about whether a single formula can properly represent interstate cost differences for both SA and MH services.

Initially, we considered potential improvements in the wage and rent indexes within the current COSI formula (i.e., without changing its current weights). The criteria for judging the wage and rent indexes are whether they are *proportional* to wage and rent variations among states, *timely* in terms of reflecting wage and rent variations at the time grant funds would be used, and *relevant* to the specific types of labor and facilities used in providing SA and MH services.

We cannot propose practical improvements in the methodology for estimating rents because alternative data sources do not exist for all or even most states, but we are able to update the estimates from Pope's 1980 data to 1990. We find that rent changes over the decade were not uniform across states, which suggests that the rent index is perishable. However, updating the index more than once per decade may not be warranted because the updating process is difficult and time-consuming and rent variations contribute relatively little to determining the overall COSI with its current weights.

We were able to use 1990 Census data to compare alternative wage indexes based on median or mean wages in manufacturing, nonmanufacturing, or SA and MH service-related occupations and industries.[2] In theory, the means of SA and MH service-related wages should provide the best index in terms of proportionality and relevance. However, only median manufacturing wages are regularly updated between Census years by the Bureau of Labor Statistics, forcing a tradeoff between timeliness and other criteria when choosing among the alternative wage measures. It is impossible to generalize about whether the tradeoff favors the use of median manufacturing wages because that depends on whether interstate wage patterns are changing rapidly, which happened between 1980 and 1990 but may be less dramatic in other decades.

Notably, that tradeoff would be far less important if the COSI formula did not rely on a fixed and arbitrary set of weights. If, instead, the weights were also updated to reflect the degree to which wages and rents account for actual SA and MH services spending patterns, the results would be far less sensitive to subtle differences in the way wages and rents are measured. Moreover, the weights could be adjusted to ac-

---

[2]Throughout this chapter, all wage calculations from the 1990 Census use the 5 percent PUMS sample from the 1990 Census. Workers in mining industries are always excluded from the sample. We included wage and self-employment income of full-time, employed-for-pay workers over age 18, setting negative values to zero before summing; hourly earnings are the ratios of such income to reported hours worked in the previous year.

count for systematic differences in the mix of labor and facilities used to provide SA and MH services and interstate differences in the clienteles receiving those services.

Accordingly, this chapter suggests an alternative methodology that would improve the COS formula's fairness while preserving the independence of the COSI. Based on data from the NDATUS and the NRPMHS, the proposed methodology applies regression analysis to estimate relationships between actual SA and MH services spending and the costs of labor and facilities, then uses the regression results to predict what spending patterns would be if all states used the same (i.e., standardized) combination of labor and facilities to provide SA and MH services, and finally converts those standardized predictions into an index of interstate cost variation. We refer to this as an "experience-based" methodology because it derives its weights directly from evidence on actual SA and MH services cost experience.

The regression analysis (summarized below and detailed in Appendix C) indicates that the extent to which wages and rents influence overall cost variation differs between SA and MH services.[3] This finding is not surprising because SA services are much more likely to be provided on an outpatient basis and hence to require a different mix of labor and facilities than MH services. Accordingly, the chapter develops separate COSIs for the two types of services.

The regression analysis also indicates that expenditure patterns differ systematically according to the urbanicity of the population being served.[4] Specifically, states with a larger share of clients in metropolitan (urban and suburban) areas tend to spend less on both SA and MH services per client, other things (such as wages and rents) held constant. Though health economists would not be surprised to learn that more dispersed populations make it more costly to provide SA and MH services in rural areas, this study does not prove that the urbanicity variation in SA or MH costs is attributable to differences in production costs. But even if states are simply willing to spend more on their rural beneficiaries, the regression shows that the spending difference is systematic across the states. Accordingly, the COSIs developed in this chapter recognize interstate differences in urbanicity as well as labor and facilities costs.

The alternative COS methodology described below is neither difficult nor costly to apply. Our work was hampered by lack of access to the Census 20 percent household sample, by late arrival of the NRPMHS data, and by the short time frame of this study—but these limitations could be overcome with a very modest amount of addi-

---

[3]Interstate cost variation may also differ between substance abuse treatment and prevention services, but we were unable to obtain and analyze prevention cost data within the time frame of this study. Like the existing COSI methodology, our alternative indexes consider only sources of interstate variation in treatment costs.

[4]Although the SA and MH services legislation specifically refers to "urbanized" areas in the context of measuring population in need, it makes no reference to urbanicity with regard to the cost index. To the extent that costs do differ by setting—which is strongly indicated by our analysis—an ideal cost index would define urbanicity in the same way it is defined for population in need. The alternative indexes proposed here and in Chapter Four both measure urbanicity based on the population distribution between MSAs and non-MSA counties because that was the best available proxy for urbanized population in both analyses.

tional analysis. The methodology illustrated below could be readily implemented in time for the next scheduled update of the COS factors in the SA and MH services formula, and regularly updated thereafter.

EVALUATION CRITERIA

In this study, the key criterion for evaluating the SA and MH services cost of service factor is *equity*. The current COS policy imposes restrictions on the COS factor values, apparently in an attempt to prevent their introduction from causing sudden changes in the grant allocations. Due to that concern, we provide some information on the extent to which using either the current or alternative COS methodology would affect the grant awards. But our principal objective is to judge whether the COS factor itself, before phase-in adjustments or other policy modifications, fairly represents interstate differences in expenditure needs due to differences in the costs of providing services.

Furthermore, this analysis focuses on the *methodology* used to develop the index. We gain insight into the implications of alternative methods by comparing particular results, but our objective is to judge whether the methods themselves will produce fair measures in repeated annual applications of the formula.

The overall equity criterion implies that the COS factor should possess certain basic properties:

- *Relevance:* The factor should measure costs for the types of services the Block Grants are intended to fund.

- *Timeliness:* The factor should measure interstate cost differences at (approximately) the time the grant funds will be used.

- *Proportionality:* The factor should vary among states in proportion to cost differences, so that if the cost in state A is twice as high as in state B, the index is twice as high.

- *Sensitivity to circumstances:* The factor should account for interstate differences in the circumstances under which services are provided, such as differences (if any) in delivering services to urban versus rural clients.

- *Independence:* The factor should be independent of the discretionary spending decisions of individual states.

A measurement approach that would satisfy most of these criteria would be to measure actual SA and MH services expenditures per beneficiary. If reliable evidence on those expenditures is available (a question we address later in this chapter), the evidence presumably would pertain to relevant services, reflect proportional cost differences, and account for interstate differences in delivery circumstances.

However, using actual expenditures would violate the independence criterion: If cost factors are estimated using actual outlays, the grant formula would reward a state for providing more or higher-quality services per beneficiary, or for using especially expensive (or inefficient) providers. But creating incentives for states to pay more for services would contradict a basic tenet of the SA and MH services Block Grant program.

A methodology that satisfies the independence criterion is to estimate the cost of providing a *standardized* level of services using a *standardized* mix of resources. According to this approach, if all of the relevant resources (e.g., counselors and office space) cost twice as much in a given state, then so will the standard level of services. If only some resources cost more, then the COS difference depends on how much those resources contribute to the overall cost of services. Thus, the standardized-cost method constructs COS estimates by measuring each state's resource prices and summing the prices using a standard set of contribution weights.

Though it certainly meets the independence criterion, this approach may yield measures that suffer by other criteria. In particular, standardized weights may not recognize possible differences in the mix of resources necessary to deliver care under different circumstances. Because current SA and MH services policy (described next) mandates the use of the standardized cost approach, our analysis pays particular attention to how well alternative weighting methodologies could represent SA and MH services cost differences.

THE CURRENT COS MEASURE

Public Law 102-321 mandates that the factor used to measure interstate differences in costs of services

> shall be determined according to the methodology described in the report entitled "Adjusting the Alcohol, Drug Abuse and Mental Health Services Block Grant Allocations for Poverty Populations and Cost of Service," dated March 30, 1990, and prepared by Health Economics Research....

The same language applies to both the substance abuse and mental health grants.

The specified Health Economics Research (HER) report is the Pope study cited earlier. It applied the standardized-cost approach by estimating separate resource price indexes for wages (here denoted by w), rents (r), and "supplies, drugs, and miscellaneous" (m). The report used data from the 1980 Census of Population and Housing to estimate the labor and rental indexes but explicitly assumed that the costs of all other resources are equal (m = 1) for all states. Finally, the report computed an overall COSI by applying resource weights based on the composition of office-practice expenses reported by self-employed physicians in a 1987 survey:

$$\text{COSI} = 0.75w + 0.15r + 0.10m. \tag{5.1}$$

The Alcohol, Drug Abuse and Mental Health Administration Reorganization Act requires this methodology but does not require the actual HER index values to be used. New index values were to be prepared by October 1, 1993, and they "shall remain in effect through fiscal year 1994, and shall be recalculated every third fiscal year thereafter." It is not clear whether legislators intended the updates to include new weights or just the labor and rent indexes, but the values SAMHSA implemented for FY 1994 use the original HER weights.

In addition, the law explicitly constrains the COSI values that may be used in the grant formula: A state's cost factor may not be less than 0.9 or more than 1.1.[5] We refer to this as the "constrained" COSI and will evaluate it after examining the unconstrained COSI estimates.

ISSUES IN MEASURING RESOURCE PRICES

Under the standardized-cost methodology, the first step is to identify the resources used in providing relevant services. Like the HER report, we group these resources into labor and nonlabor categories. For example, the labor resources for treating substance abuse and mental health patients include health and social-service professionals and administrators, while nonlabor resources include medical and office supplies and equipment, as well as office space.

Our evaluation of resource price measures focuses on the first three of our equity criteria: relevance, timeliness, and proportionality. All of the price measures we considered satisfy the independence criterion because they are based on statewide prices for resources that are used for many purposes besides SA and MH services delivery. Sensitivity to delivery circumstances is a matter we take up in evaluating COS weights, later in this chapter.

Wages

Labor cost is currently the principal determinant of variation in the overall SA and MH services COSI. The wage index not only has the highest weight but varies considerably among states, ranging from a low of 0.745 to a high of 1.636 in measures based on the 1980 Census. In the original HER report, variation in the wage index alone accounted for better than 90 percent of the interstate variation in the overall COS.

Still, the choice of a labor cost measure would be less significant if only a single measure were available, or if alternative measures yielded nearly identical indexes. But that is not the case. The HER report used an index of nonmanufacturing wages, but the current implementation of the formula uses manufacturing wages instead. We developed still other measures, finding that they alter the range and distribution of the index and even produce different state rankings.

Proportionality. According to the equity criterion, the wage index should vary in proportion to interstate differences in what SA and MH services providers would have to pay their professional and support staffs. If wages were uniform within states, such differences would be relatively easy to ascertain. In practice, however, wages vary considerably within as well as among states. This raises the question of

---

[5]We interpret this to mean that COSI values below 0.9 should be replaced by 0.9, and values greater than 1.1 should be replaced by 1.1 before using them in the grant formula.

how to generate a state-level summary statistic that properly represents the comparative wages states would have to pay.

The HER report measured a state's labor cost using the median hourly wage. By definition, half of the state's workers earn less than that, and half earn more. The median is sensitive to the number of people earning low or high wages but not to just how high the lowest or highest wages might be.

The median is a common measure of state wages because the usual objective is to judge whether, in general, one state's workforce is "better off" than another's. However, the objective for COS measurement is to evaluate how much, on average, providers would have to be paid to supply services to SA and MH services beneficiaries. For that purpose, the mean is arguably a better indicator.[6] The traditional argument against using the mean as an overall wage indicator—i.e., that it is sensitive to extreme values—does not carry over to the current context in which a large data sample (the Census 20 percent sample) can be used and the objective is to estimate the expected cost of labor services.[7]

The choice between the median and the mean would have little effect on interstate wage indexes if the ratio of mean to median wages were more or less constant across states. To determine if that is the case, we compared indexes based on the means and medians of nonmanufacturing wages using a 5 percent population sample from the 1990 Census.[8] We found that using the mean instead of the median often—but not always—increases the index values in low-wage states and reduces them in high-wage states.

To illustrate how this would affect grant allocations, we also computed the percentage difference between the mean and median indexes. Holding other variables in the grant formula constant, increasing a state's cost index by, say, 10 percent implies that the grant award would increase by a factor of 0.1.[9] Therefore, whenever we consider changing a measure used in constructing the cost index, we can get some informa-

---

[6]The mean is an unbiased estimator of the expected value of wages for a provider selected at random from the population. In small samples, statisticians would argue that a different statistic (the Stein estimator) would be more precise, but it is complicated to use and probably unnecessary if the analysis uses the Census' full 20 percent sample of detailed wage data. If providers for SA and MH services were not drawn from the entire population of providers, then the mean should be computed by sampling the relevant portion of the provider population, but we have no basis on which to select such a sample.

[7]As a technical matter, an index based on the mean of wages is also simpler to compute (correctly) from a sample of wages. To compute the index, one needs a measure of the nationwide wage. The nationwide median should proceed by using sampling weights to compute the number of individuals represented by each wage observation in the sample, sorting the observed wages from lowest to highest, and then "moving up" the sorted list until the number of individuals represented sums to half the national population. (Our study used this method.) In contrast, the nationwide mean is simply the mean of the population-weighted state means.

[8]Sampling weights used in constructing each index cause the averages of the indexes to differ from 1.0. Since that would cause apparent differences that would not affect the distribution of grant funding, we rescaled each index to have an average of 1.0. Rescaling to eliminate irrelevant differences among indexes is done consistently in all of this study's index comparisons.

[9]This is true even though the grants must sum to the same total amount. That is because all of the indexes presented in this chapter are scaled to have a mean of 1.0, which means that the sum of their values over the 50 states and Washington, D.C., always equals 51. Whenever one index value increases by (say) 10 percent, other index values decline by enough to offset the effect on the sum of all grants.

tion about the potential effect on grant awards (other things equal) by looking at the percentage change in the measure. Figure 5.1 shows the percentage differences with states sorted so that the median index increases from left to right.

Of course, because the COSI weights the labor index by a factor less than one, the effect on the overall cost index is smaller than the percentages shown in the figure. Furthermore, the legislation imposes both a floor and a ceiling on the COSI, rendering it insensitive to changes in the wage index for many low- and high-wage states. Nonetheless, as a result of the effects illustrated in the figure, we find that several states could experience changes of up to 5 percent in their grant awards if the current index were replaced by one based on mean wages.

Relevance. Because wages differ widely among industries and occupations, a wage index that covers a broad spectrum of jobs may be a poor indicator of labor costs for SA and MH service providers. Recognizing that, the HER report restricted attention to nonmanufacturing workers. Indeed, as Figure 5.2 indicates, 1990 wage indexes[10] for manufacturing and nonmanufacturing workers are markedly different.

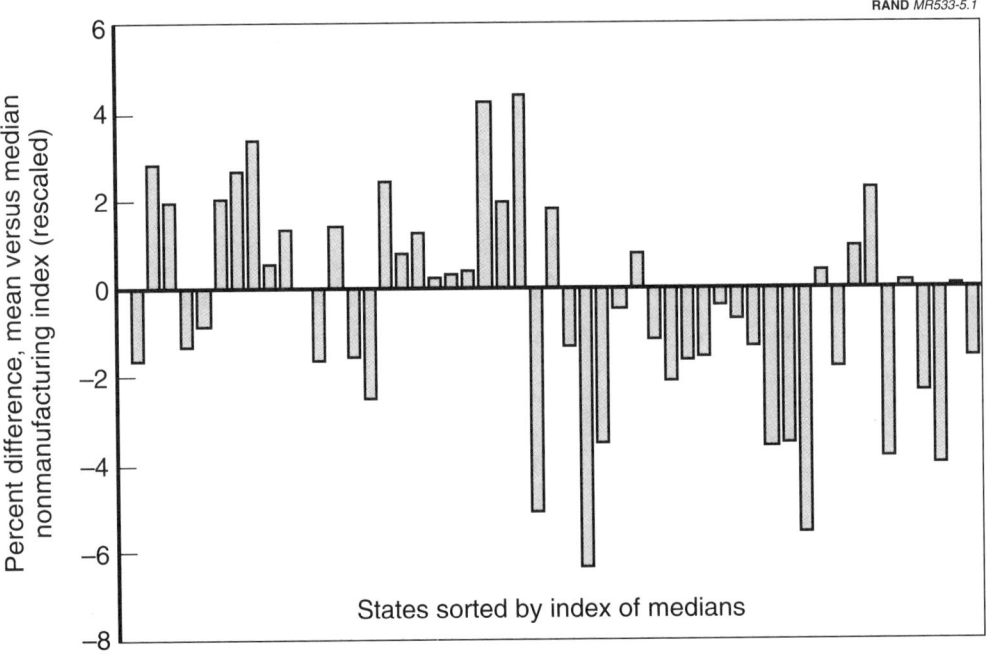

Figure 5.1—Percentage Differences Between (Rescaled) Mean and Median Nonmanufacturing Wage Indexes for 1990

---

[10] Here and in the remainder of this section, indexes are based on mean wages unless otherwise indicated. Median indexes of manufacturing and nonmanufacturing wages also show marked differences, similar in magnitude and distribution to those illustrated here.

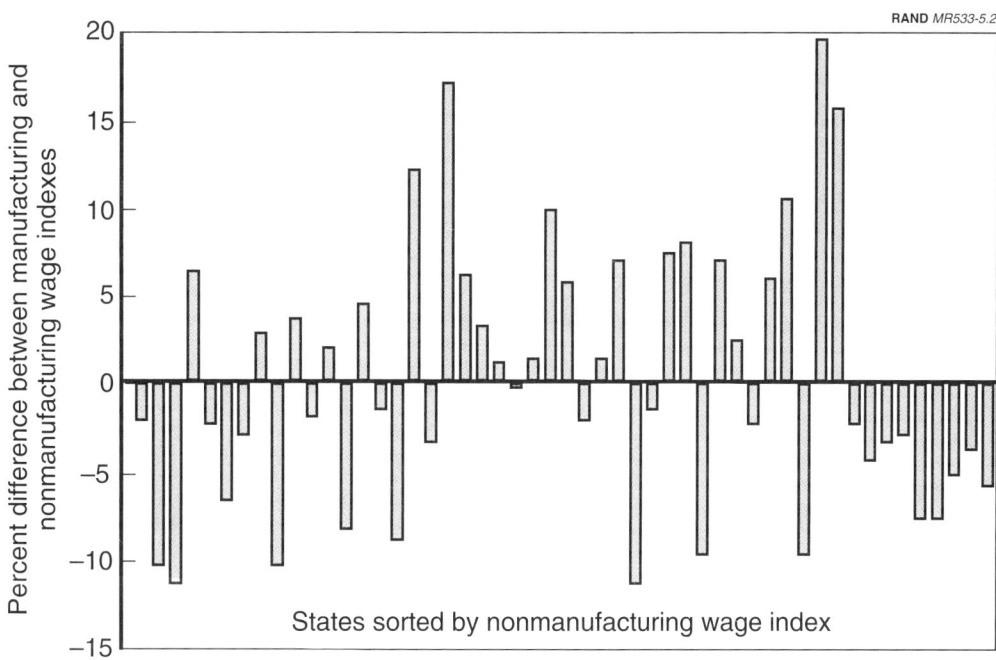

Figure 5.2—Percentage Differences Between (Rescaled) Indexes of Manufacturing and Nonmanufacturing Wages

However, nonmanufacturing industries still include many workers who are not relevant to the provision of SA and MH services. The Bureau of the Census can estimate state-level mean wages for quite detailed industry and occupational categories using its 20 percent population sample. The particular industry and occupational groups we would consider most relevant to SA and MH treatment services are:[11]

- Occupations: Physicians including psychiatrists; registered nurses; psychologists; and social workers and counselors (Census occupation codes 084, 095, 167, and 174).[12]

- Industries: Offices and clinics of doctors of medicine; offices and clinics of other health practitioners; hospitals; nursing and personal care facilities; and miscellaneous health and allied services (Census industry codes 812, 830, 831, 832, and 840).

To determine whether indexes based on selected worker categories would differ from the nonmanufacturing wage index, we computed mean state wages using the 5 per-

---

[11] Both the NDATUS and the NRPMHS list similar occupational titles for the staffs of their service organizations, and we used those titles to select the occupational and industry categories listed here. Since we did not have time to analyze data concerning prevention activities, we did not attempt to define prevention-related occupations or industries.

[12] To select this list of occupational codes, we compared the Treatment Unit Staff job titles used in the NDATUS database with the occupational categories in the *Alphabetic Index of Industries and Occupations* for the 1990 Census.

cent population sample the Bureau of the Census makes available to outside parties.[13] That sample proved to be too small to calculate reliable wage estimates in all states at the detailed occupation and industry level. Therefore, we used data from somewhat larger worker categories than those listed above—"SA and MH services-related industries" (industry codes 812–893) and "SA and MH services-related occupations (occupation codes 084–106 and 166–177)—to develop alternative wage indexes for all states.

Figure 5.3 shows that wage indexes for workers in SA and MH services-related occupations and industries are distinctly different from indexes for all nonmanufacturing workers. More often than not, states with below-average nonmanufacturing wages would have a higher index using SA and MH services-related wages, and states with above-average manufacturing wages would have lower SA and MH services-related values. Again using the percentage differences between measures as a partial indicator of effects on grant awards, we found that the SA and MH services-related index differs from the nonmanufacturing index by 5 percent or more in half of all states. Half of those states would experience increases, and half would experience decreases in their cost indexes if the nonmanufacturing (mean) wage index were replaced by the SA and MH services-related one in the current COSI formula.

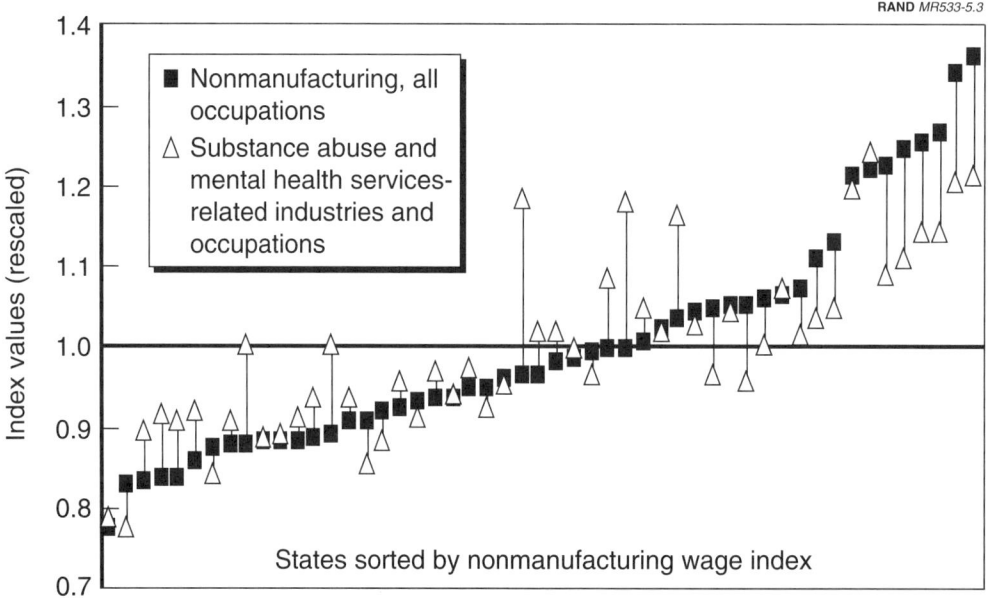

Figure 5.3—1990 (Rescaled) Indexes of All Nonmanufacturing Wages Versus Wages in SA and MH Services-Related Industries and Occupations

---

[13]The 20 percent sample is not released for external use to protect respondent confidentiality. The time frame for this study allowed us to examine wage differences by occupation and industry using the 5 percent sample but did not provide sufficient time to request corresponding calculations from the Census Bureau.

Figure 5.4 tells more of the related-wage story. It shows the numbers of states that fall into various ranges of the index values. Only about half the states have indexes between 0.9 and 1.1 using the nonmanufacturing wage, whereas almost two-thirds of them do according to the SA and MH services-related index. Overall, states appear to have more similar labor costs for SA and MH services-related workers than the nonmanufacturing wage index suggests. This is not too surprising: The nonmanufacturing wage varies because of differences in occupational mix as well as wage differences within occupations, whereas the SA and MH services-related index restricts attention to wage variations within a small group of occupations.[14]

Timeliness. Ideally, the wage index should reflect interstate wage differences at (or near) the time services funded by grant awards will be provided. If wages moved up or down over time in the same way across states, then even fairly old wage data might be good indicators of current and future wage differences, but that is not always the case.

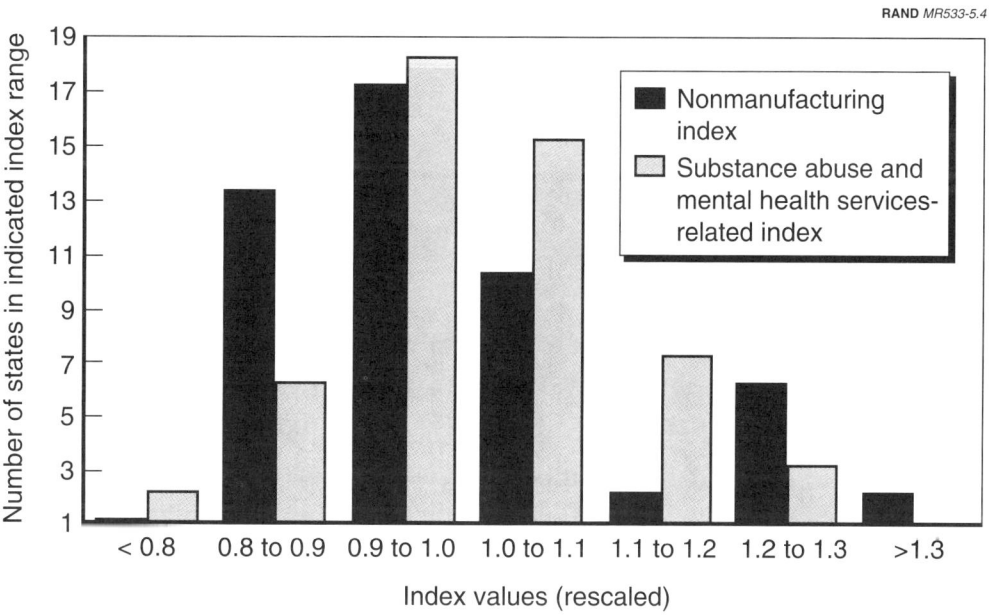

Figure 5.4—Numbers of States with Alternative Index Values

---

[14]Having determined that selecting relevant occupations and industries would substantially affect the indexes, we attempted to judge whether the indexes would be similar for individual occupations. Our small Census sample could generate usable occupational indexes only for 10 to 20 of the largest states. Unfortunately, the indexes for those states appeared to differ substantially among the specific health-related occupations we examined. Consequently, it appears that additional research, not only to take advantage of the larger Census sample but also to build a COSI using more detailed labor categories, would be warranted.

For example, the 1990 median nonmanufacturing index values we calculated differ from the 1980 HER wage index values by –20 percent to +20 percent;[15] the wage indexes of 15 states changed by more than 10 percent and, as Figure 5.5 shows, the state rankings (where 1 indicates the lowest index value) changed dramatically over that period. When wage patterns change as much as they did in the past decade, the cost of service index—and hence the grant awards to states—can show quite different distributions depending on which vintage of wage data is used.

Unfortunately, estimates of SA and MH services-related wages or even all nonmanufacturing wages are difficult to update between Census years. The Bureau of Labor Statistics regularly updates state-level wage data between Census years only by collecting payroll data for manufacturing workers.[16] Therefore, when the wage indexes are to be updated between Census years, the choice between manufacturing and alternative wage measures represents a tradeoff between relevance and timeliness. Furthermore, the nature of the tradeoff changes from one updating cycle

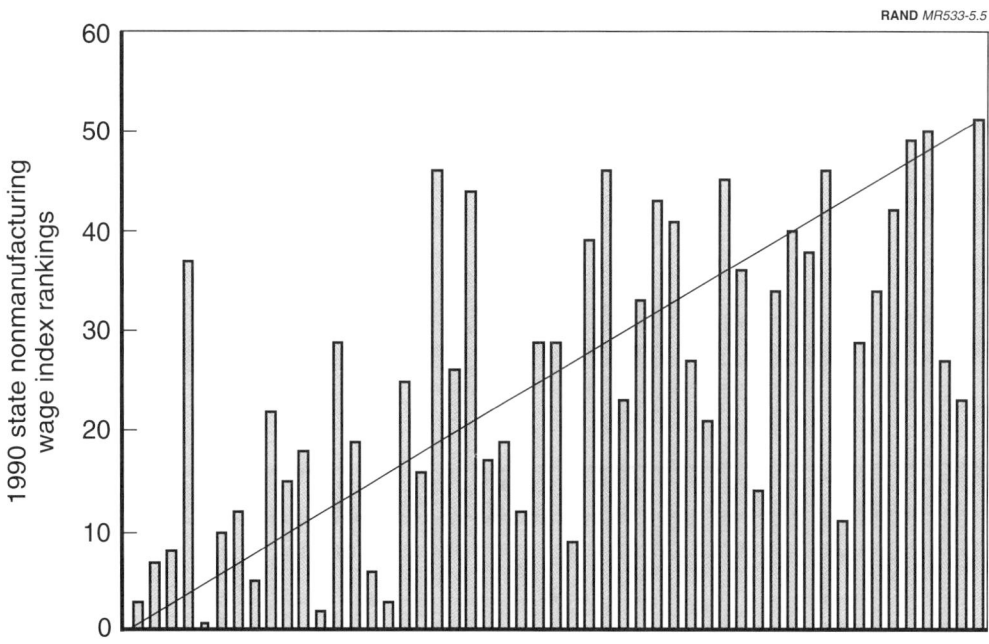

Figure 5.5—State Wage Index Rankings, 1990 Versus 1980 Median Nonmanufacturing Wages

---

[15]As noted above, our calculations applied specific procedures to the 5 percent PUMS sample from the 1990 Census. The HER report indicates that it used a 20 percent sample from the 1980 Census but does not describe how the wage rates were computed. Because the short-term nature of this study prevented us from recomputing our own indexes from the 1980 Census, the comparisons between the HER index and the one we computed may reflect some differences in estimation methodology as well as in sample size.

[16]Two frequently updated data sources, the U.S. Bureau of Labor Statistics (BLS) Area Wage Surveys and the Current Population Survey, do not sample widely enough to generate reliable state-level wage indexes.

to another, with timeliness becoming a greater consideration later in each decade and especially when labor markets are experiencing rapid structural change.

One option we considered would be to adjust the Census wage estimates based on wage trends revealed by other sources. For example, the BLS develops Employment Cost Indexes (ECIs) that track rates of wage change by region and industry. If wage trends for relevant occupations and industries are similar among states within a region, an ECI might be used to adjust the SA and MH services wages between Census years. The research necessary to develop this methodology could not be conducted during the current study but could easily be accomplished in time to support the next scheduled SA and MH services cost of service update.

Summary. The proportionality and relevance criteria suggest that wage indexes should be based on mean rather than median wages and should reflect SA and MH services-related occupations and industries. Census data could be used to generate specific wage data for the occupations most pertinent to providing SA and MH services. However, Census measures may not properly represent interstate wage differences for services to be provided between Census years. Above, we described how additional research could develop methods for updating Census-based wage measures to account for wage trends in the current COSI formula. Below, however, we will suggest that the choice among wage measures would be less critical to achieving equity if the proposed experience-based formula were used instead.

Rents

Although the HER study included office rental as a source of interstate cost differences, rents played a relatively small role in setting the overall HER cost index. The rent index varied about as much as the wage index (from a low of 0.679 to a high of 1.396) but was given a much lower weight (0.10 versus 0.75) in the COSI formula. By itself, the rent index accounted for less than 10 percent of the interstate variation in the HER cost of service index.

That is fortunate because rents are difficult to measure appropriately. At present, there are no national data available on commercial office rents. The HER report measured them by proxy, using the "fair market rents" (FMRs) for residential structures[17] reported by the Department of Housing and Urban Development (HUD). This is also the only source of rental cost data we could find that covers rents in all the states.

With respect to our evaluation criteria, it is obvious that residential rents are independent of actual SA and MH service office rental expenditures by states. Nonetheless, interstate differences in average residential rents may be a fair indicator of commercial rent variation. Local housing rents may reflect amenity values that have less relevance for commercial uses, but average statewide residential rents presum-

---

[17]FMRs are reported for residential units of varying size. The HER index uses FMRs for four-bedroom units, arguing that larger units are likely to be more representative of the type of office space used for SA and MH services.

ably vary with general land values and construction costs—factors that also influence statewide average commercial values. Furthermore, our analysis of SA and MH services survey data (described below) shows that an FMR-based rental index is an effective predictor of actual SA and MH services spending differences among states. In short, there is no evidence to suggest that the FMR-based rental index is inadequate with respect to relevance, proportionality,[18] sensitivity, or independence criteria.

The only remaining fairness criterion is timeliness. FMRs are updated annually,[19] making it possible to update the COS rental indexes as well. If rents change rapidly over time and in markedly different ways across states, it could be argued that the rent index should be updated frequently. To judge that, we compared the HER rent index, which was based on 1980 FMRs and population weights from the 1980 Census, with an index we developed from 1990 FMRs and the 1990 Census. The newer rent index (given in Appendix C) differs from the older one by less than 10 percent in most states. Given the small weights attached to rents by the HER formula, such rent changes would have quite small effects on the allocation of Block Grant funds. However, six states experienced more dramatic rent changes over the decade, and the HER rent index appears out of date for them.

Although the 1990 rent index appears more representative of current costs than the 1980-based HER index, it remains unclear whether updating future rent indexes between Census years would be warranted. Updating is a time-consuming process because HUD's rental market areas (MSAs and non-MSA counties) do not precisely match the geographic areas used by the Census. (For example, an FMR might be stated for the "Los-Angeles-Riverside-San Bernardino" market area, whereas the Census reports population statistics for Los Angeles-Long Beach and several other MSAs in the vicinity.) Furthermore, the indexes could be updated between Census years only by applying "old" population weights to recent FMRs, which would improve the measures only for states whose population distributions are fairly stable over time. In short, updating the rent index following each Census appear warranted, but the benefit of inter-Censal updates is arguable.

Prices of Miscellaneous Resources

The HER report assumed that the prices of resources other than labor and office space do not vary among states. The explicit justification was that most drugs, medical supplies, and equipment items can be purchased at established prices from national suppliers. Beyond that, however, there are practical reasons for omitting price indexes for miscellaneous resources: There are no readily available measures of local prices for these products. And, since data from private physician practices (AMA

---

[18]A potential concern about proportionality derives from the fact that FMRs are designed to reflect rents at the 45th percentile (i.e., the dollar amount below which 45 percent of the rental housing units rent). FMRs might be distributed differently from average rents, just as median wages are distributed differently from mean wages. But since FMR-based rent indexes are helpful predictors of actual SA and MH services funding, we infer that the rent indexes are reasonably proportional.

[19]HUD calculates FMRs for base years from data collected for the decennial Census of Population and Housing. Estimates for intermediate years are adjusted with data collected by post-Census Annual Housing Surveys as well as telephone surveys of statistically random samples of rental housing units.

Center for Health Policy Research, 1990) suggest that such items contribute relatively little to total costs, it seems unlikely that investments to gather detailed pricing data would be warranted by improvements in measuring the overall COSI.

While this argument has merit, there remains some reason for concern about the equitability of assuming that "other" resource prices are constant. Even for nationally sold products, distribution and delivery charges vary from place to place, and suppliers may offer discounts for volume purchases; thus, the constant-price assumption may neglect some price variations that penalize buyers in remote locations or benefit buyers in high-volume markets. And some miscellaneous costs—e.g., for client or provider transportation, or for replacement of perishable drugs—may differ systematically for services provided in different delivery settings.

Without gathering data on local prices for selected supplies, equipment, and drugs, it is still possible to account for some systematic differences in the "miscellaneous" portion of SA and MH services costs. If there are such differences, we would expect them to be apparent in the spending patterns of SA and MH services providers. To test that, we used the urban-rural mix of SA and MH services clients as an explanatory variable in our analysis of actual spending patterns. As described in the next section, we found that it indeed seems to account for systematic cost differences among states.

Implications of Revising the Price Measures

To illustrate the practical implications of revising the wage and rent indexes within the existing formula, we constructed two overall COSIs. We will call one the "Current COSI" because it corresponds to the one computed for grant awards in FY94. For that year, SAMHSA used the HER formula weights and the HER study's rent index (based on 1980 Census and FMR data) but updated the wage index. Our Current COSI also updates only the wage index but does so using mean nonmanufacturing wages instead of the median manufacturing wages we understand SAMHSA used; our version also differs because we have not constrained the index. In contrast, the second COSI applies the HER formula to the revised wage and rent measures described above (mean wages in SA and MH services-related jobs, and rents computed from 1990 data). To compare them properly, we scaled each of the indexes to have a mean of 1.0.

Figure 5.6 shows the percentage difference between the two COSIs and sorts the states according to their Current COSI. The figure shows that revised rent and wage measures would raise the COSI for most of the states with low or intermediate values under the Current index and would reduce the COSI for most states whose Current COSI values are high. Only two of the differences are greater than 10 percent, both of those pertain to sparsely populated states, and both of them would involve increases in the grant awards. If all else in the grant formulas remained unchanged, the percentage differences shown in the figure would translate directly into percentage differences in grant awards if the cost index were not constrained.

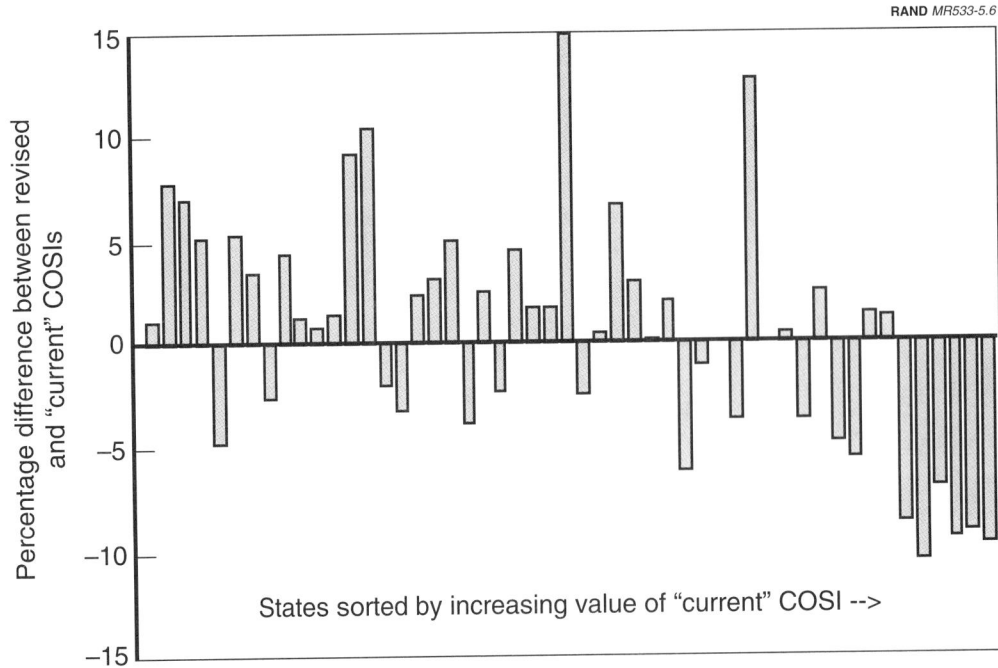

Figure 5.6—Percentage Effects of Using Revised Wage and Rent Measures in the Current Formula

WEIGHTS FOR COMBINING RESOURCE PRICES

The current COSI methodology uses wage and rent index values that vary from state to state but multiplies them by a single set of weights representing the labor and facilities requirements for a standard level of services. In effect, the current COSI methodology postulates that SA and MH services providers in different states could provide the same level of services per client if they used the same amount of resources per client—the same amount for substance abuse and mental health clients and for urban and rural clients.

To see if those hypotheses are reasonable, this study examined data on the actual provision of SA and MH services from the 1991 NDATUS and the 1992 NRPMHS. Those surveys collect information from reporting units (i.e., treatment and other service organizations) in all states; they include data on funding from all sources, professional and administrative staffing, and numbers of clients. In addition, the NDATUS also categorizes clients by urban, suburban, or rural status, while the NRPMHS includes its reporting units' expenditures.

Survey data are subject to a variety of reporting errors, especially missing values. In particular, the NDATUS does not account for the full amount of federal Block Grant funding. For our purposes, however, it was not essential for the surveys to provide complete data for every SA and MH services organization in the nation. Instead, we needed an adequate *sample* of reporting units with complete funding, client-load, and staffing data in each state. Better than two-thirds of the NDATUS records met the completeness criteria, including at least half of the reporting units in every state. The NRPMHS database had been evaluated and edited before we received it, and we were able to use nearly all of its records.

After selecting complete records, we computed state-level averages[20] of funding per client, staffing per client, and other variables, and reviewed those measures for evidence of extreme values or other anomalies. Using the NRPMHS, we also confirmed our hypothesis that state-level funding closely approximates expenditures.[21] Judging by these reviews and by the strength of the statistical relationships we later observed, we believe that the cleaned data adequately support the findings summarized here and detailed in Appendix C. The appendix discussion also indicates that we believe the provider samples in the data are reasonably representative of all providers in each state, so that we infer that the interstate variations in observed spending and labor utilization are proportional and relevant to the actual differences for SA and MH services. And if these surveys continue to be repeated every year or two, the analyses performed here could be updated regularly to assure their timeliness.

Resourcing Patterns Observed in SA and MH Services Survey Data

The surveys corroborate our expectations that substance abuse and mental health services use a different level and mix of resources. Mental health funding per client (nationwide average, $7,917) exceeds substance abuse funding per client ($5,805) by 36 percent. Mental health staffing per client (0.150) also exceeds the substance abuse (paid) staffing rate (0.134) by about 12 percent. Utilization of space and facilities also appears to differ, with mental health units delivering a substantial amount of services to inpatient and rest-home clients and often serving a much larger number of clients per unit (664 versus 97 for substance abuse).

The data also show considerable differences in the interstate patterns of substance abuse and mental health funding. To illustrate this point, we converted observed funding per client into an index (i.e., we divided each state's value by the nationwide average). Figure 5.7 compares the resulting values, showing that the mental health pattern bears no resemblance to the substance abuse pattern. We would *not* recommend using this index as a COSI for allocating funds, however, because the measures are explicitly derived from actual state behavior. As we explain below, standardizing the rates of resource utilization across states makes the interstate patterns for SA and MH services cost indexes much more similar than the actual funding rates suggest.

---

[20]These are weighted averages of the per-client variables where the weights are the reporting-unit's share of the total clients covered by each state's final sample of reporting units.

[21]When aggregated over all sampled units in each state, funding and expenditures proved to be quite similar, differing by only about 3 percent on average, and by less than 5 percent in two-thirds of the states; where the differences were much larger, the funding data appeared to be more consistent with client loads and staffing than the expenditure data. In addition, Appendix C provides a theoretical justification for using funding per client as the dependent variable in our regression analysis.

76 The Substance Abuse and Mental Health Services Block Grant Allotment Formula

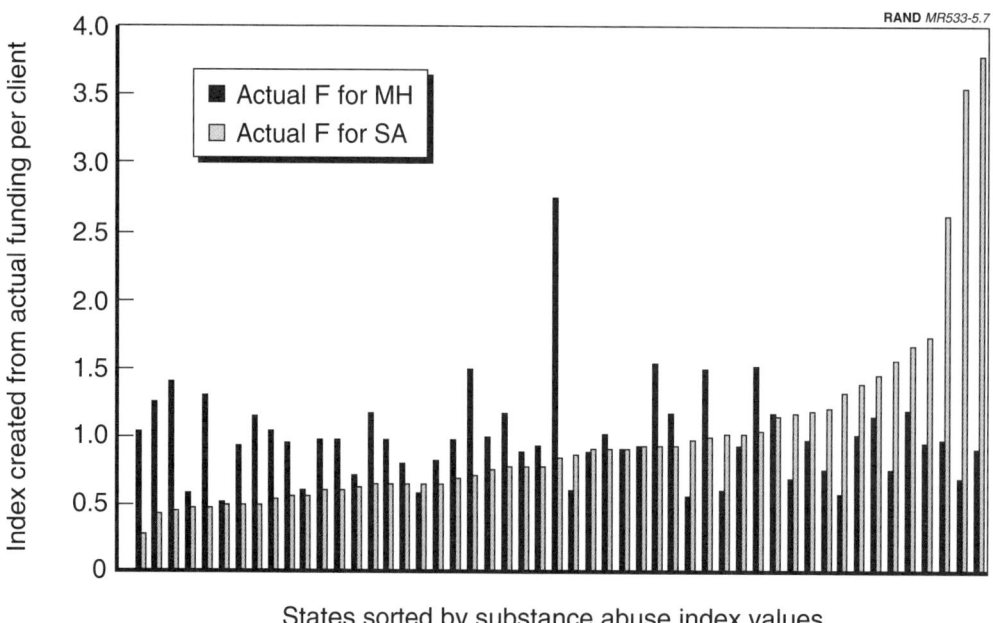

Figure 5.7—Index Comparison of Reported Funding per Client, Substance Abuse Versus
Mental Health Services

To learn more about the sources of cost variation, and to test the hypothesis that costs differ between urban and rural settings, we combined the survey data with our 1990 wage and rent indexes. We then used regression analysis to estimate relationships between funding per client (a proxy for spending per client) and resource costs. The analyses summarized here are detailed in Appendix C.

Both the substance abuse and mental health regressions included proxy variables for the portion of each state's caseloads served in urban settings. For substance abuse, this was represented by the NDATUS-reported share of clients described as "urban" and/or "suburban."[22] Because the NRPMHS did not report client urbanicity, the mental health regressions used the share of each state's overall population residing in MSAs as reported in the 1990 Census 5 percent sample.

Urbanicity could influence costs in several ways: It could serve as a proxy for differences in the prices and usage of miscellaneous resources, or it might help account for otherwise unmeasured differences in the types, usage, or prices of labor or space resources. A regression specification that allows urbanicity to affect costs in all these ways is:

$$F = a(U) + b(wL) + c(wL*U) + d(rS) + e(rS*U) + \varepsilon, \qquad (5.2)$$

---

[22]In some analyses, we used just the NDATUS "urban" client share instead of including "suburban" clients to see if a measure more closely aligned with "urbanized" population would be a better predictor of costs. It was not. Therefore, the results reported here use the NDATUS urbanicity measure that is most similar in definition to the MSA-based Census measures of population urbanicity. See footnote 4 of this chapter.

where

F = the statewide average funding per client
$a - e$ = parameters to be estimated
U = the urbanicity measure
w and r = our 1990 wage and rent indexes
L = the average staffing per client[23]
S = the number of reporting units per client (a proxy for space usage)
ε = unexplained differences between actual funding and the spending levels predicted by the equation.[24]

In practice, the terms in Equation (5.2) that include U (i.e., U, wL*U, and rS*U) are so highly correlated that a regression equation cannot distinguish among all three of them. Therefore, our estimating equations included various combinations of the variables, as well as some that replaced U with a simple constant term. The results reported here are from the equations that appeared to do the most reliable job of predicting funding per client while satisfying various statistical criteria. But other specifications also told essentially the same story: For both substance abuse and mental health services, increased urbanicity implies *lower* funding per client.

For substance abuse, the variables U, wL, and rS explained almost three-quarters of the interstate variation in funding per client,[25] lending credence to our view that funding is a reasonable proxy for expenditures and that the client and staffing data are reasonably accurate. Furthermore, the interpretation of the regression parameters seems sensible: If the number of clients is held constant, adding one full-time staff member increases costs by about $43,000, and adding one delivery organization (i.e., one reporting unit) also increases costs by about $43,000 per year. The coefficient on U, which might be interpreted as the overall effect of urbanicity on resource costs, is –1,878; other things equal, a client load that is, say, 50 percent urban costs about $188 *less* per client than a client load that is only 40 percent urban.

In our separate analysis of mental health services, the regression equation that met our statistical criteria turned out to have the same form and variables as the substance abuse regression and explained about 80 percent of the variation in mental health services funding per client.[26] As might be expected, the estimated costs of adding a staff member ($47,000) or adding a delivery organization ($807,000) are higher in the mental health regression than for substance abuse services. The mental health regression also indicated that costs per client are lower in urban settings, but the savings from a ten-point urbanicity increase (about $115 per client) are smaller than for substance abuse.

---

[23]For substance abuse, L was the statewide full-time-equivalent paid staff per client. Because the NRPMHS data did not provide a conversion formula for estimating full-time-equivalence, L for mental health services was the total statewide staffing per client.

[24]Although Equation 5.2 omits a constant term, we also tested that specification. That coefficient was not statistically significant in any of the specifications that included urbanicity.

[25]We dropped North Dakota from the analysis because its data included extreme values that seemed to influence the regression results excessively.

[26]The mental health regression omitted Washington, D.C., because its data included extreme values.

Researchers and other professionals familiar with health care delivery in urban and rural settings do not find these results surprising. Although land and labor costs are often lower in rural areas than in nearby cities and suburbs, smaller populations make it difficult to provide services efficiently in rural areas. Specialized staff and facilities may be underutilized at times, increasing overhead expenses per patient. Our findings from the NDATUS and NRPMHS data indicate that SA and MH services might also be subject to conditions that make them more costly in rural settings. But even if the urbanicity effect we observe simply reflects a willingness to spend more on rural clients, the evidence suggests that the effect is systematic and shared by states across the urbanicity spectrum.

Using SA and MH Services-Based Experience to Develop Standardized COSIs

Once the parameters of an equation like 5.2 have been estimated, it can be used to predict what spending per client would be for alternative levels of staffing, space usage, and client urbanicity. In particular, the equations can be used to project what each state's spending rates would be if it used a *standardized* level and mix of resources and applied *standardized* criteria to determine the urban-rural mix of its delivery settings—and those standardized COS measures can then be translated into COSIs for substance abuse and mental health services. Those COSIs would be "experience-based" in the sense that they derive from evidence on actual SA and MH services costs, but standardization also assures that the indexes would be independent of actual state spending decisions.

We performed those calculations separately for substance abuse and mental health. The first step was to substitute standardized values for L, S, and U in each estimated equation. For all states, we replaced the actual measures of L with the nationwide average staffing per client and we replaced S with the nationwide average ratio of delivery organizations to clients; as described above, these averages differ markedly between SA and MH services. Then for each state, we used the share of its population residing in MSAs (from the 1990 Census) to estimate the urbanicity of its population in need.[27] To convert predicted spending per client into an index, we divided each state's predicted cost by the nationwide average predicted cost.[28]

Although these experienced-based indexes reflect insights from observing actual SA and MH services behavior, standardization of the labor, space, and urbanicity measures assures that the indexes are truly *independent* of actual SA and MH services spending. For example, Figure 5.8 shows that the experience-based substance abuse index we computed differs considerably from the index of actual funding per client.

---

[27]This did not change the measure of U in the mental health equations, where the Census value was the only available measure of urbanicity. For the substance abuse analysis, we regressed the NDATUS client urbanicity measure on the Census measure and used those results to compute predicted client urbanicity values. Those predicted values replaced the NDATUS values in the standardized index computation.

[28]As elsewhere, nationwide averages were computed by weighting the states' cost estimates by their shares of total substance abuse or mental health clients. The indexes were also rescaled to have overall means of 1.0.

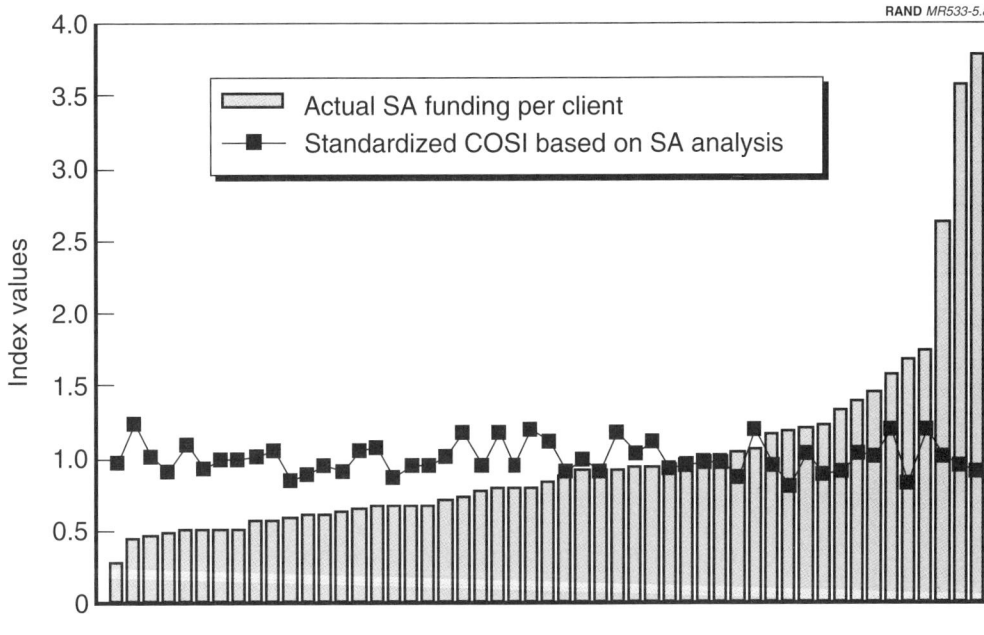

Figure 5.8—Comparison Between the Standardized Substance Abuse Cost Index and an Index Constructed from Actual Funding Data

A similarly constructed figure for mental health services would look much the same. In both cases, at least half of all states currently spend substantially less per client than the standardized indexes would imply, whereas less than a third of the states spend more.

Although we saw above that the difference between actual SA and MH services funding per client varies widely among states, standardizing each of the cost indexes substantially reduces those disparities. In Figure 5.9, the percentage difference between the two index values is quite small in all states, suggesting that the funding differences we observed above are largely attributable to the way states actually allocate resources between these two types of services.

Conclusions Regarding the Current Weights

We can use the experience-based cost indexes to judge how well the current weights reflect the average contributions of labor, facilities, and other resources to the overall cost of services per SA or MH services client. To do that, we regressed each of the experience-based COSI on our revised wage and rent indexes and compared the coefficients with the HER weights.

The experience-based indexes emphasize labor costs just as the HER weights do. But instead of assuming that labor accounts for 75 percent of costs, experience-based indexes raise the labor contribution to 80 percent for SA services and reduce it to 70 percent for MH services. Our SA index reduces the contribution of facilities from the

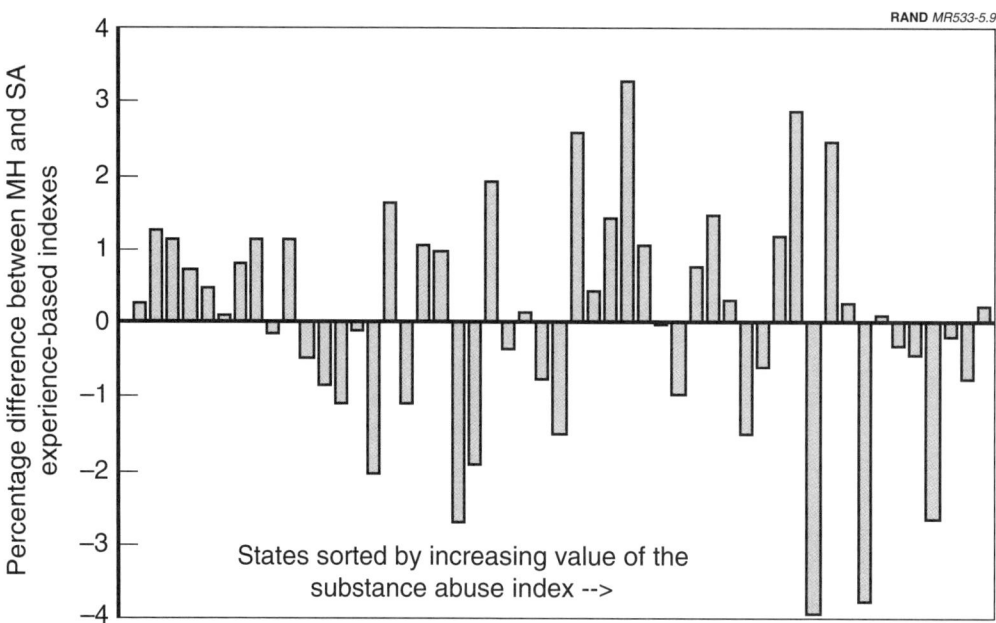

Figure 5.9—Percentage Differences Between the Experience-Based Indexes for Mental Health and Substance Abuse Services

15 percent assumed by the HER index to just 9 percent, but our MH services index increases the facilities share slightly, to 16 percent. These adjustments appear reasonable because some MH services clients are served in inpatient or residential settings that are relatively facility-intensive.

Beyond that, however, the experience-based indexes implicitly adjust the weights to account for interstate differences in the urbanicity of their populations needing services and in the standardized resourcing needs of substance abuse and mental health services. This makes the experience-based indexes more *relevant* to SA and MH services conditions and *sensitive* to interstate variations in service needs and settings. Moreover, because the experience-based predictions are based entirely on recent (1990 or later) data, they are more *timely* than indexes using the HER weights derived from 1987 data on physician practice costs. Thus, in addition to being *independent* of actual state behavior, the experience-based indexes are better suited to meeting this chapter's other equity criteria than the currently legislated methodology.

A further attribute of the experience-based methodology is that its COSIs are relatively robust with respect to alternative measures of wages. Stated in nontechnical terms, regression analysis computes coefficients that enable the explanatory variables to explain as much as possible of the interstate variance in spending. Unlike the current COSI methodology—which applies the same weights to any set of wage and rent indexes—regression analysis adjusts the coefficient estimates according to the variables used in the equation, thus tending to moderate the effect on the computed COSI. In regressions not reported here, we used alternative wage indexes in place of the mean SA and MH services-related wage index and, although the explanatory power of the regressions varied somewhat,[29] we observed very little effect on the standardized COSIs for SA or MH services.

OVERALL IMPLICATIONS OF IMPROVING THE COSI METHODOLOGY

This chapter has argued that improvements can be made in the wage and rent measures used to develop the COSI; that the COSI should also reflect population urbanicity and could reflect SA- and MH-specific differences in resource requirements; and that the parameters used to combine all these measures would be more relevant if derived from actual evidence on SA and MH services cost relationships. We now turn to the question of how improvements in the COSI (holding other measures in the grant formula constant) would affect the interstate allocation of the federal Block Grants.

To address this question, we compared the Current COSI[30] with each of the following alternative indexes:

- An index labeled "Revised HER" uses the rent index we updated to 1990 and the SA and MH services-related mean wage index but retains the HER weights.

- An index labeled "SA Alternative" uses the experience-based methodology described above to derive standardized costs from the regression results for substance abuse services. (The rent and wage measures are the same as in the Revised HER index, urbanicity is based on client urbanicity predicted from the 1990 Census measure of population urbanicity, and standardized labor and space utilization rates are nationwide averages from the NDATUS data.)

- An index labeled "MHS Alternative" also uses the experience-based methodology but applies it to the regression results for mental health services. (The rent and wage measures are the same as in the Revised HER index, urbanicity is based on 1990 Census data, and standardized labor and space utilization rates are nationwide averages from the NRPMHS data.)

Figure 5.10 illustrates the distributions of the four sets of index values across the United States. The four indexes generally agree that the highest cost states are in the far west and northeast and that the northern plains states tend to be among the least costly. The two HER indexes show very similar patterns of interstate cost variation, as we expect given their reliance on the same weights. Notably, the most readily apparent differences between the alternative indexes and the pair of HER indexes is that the former place fewer states below the 0.9 cutoff and more states above the

---

[29]Median wage indexes never performed as well as mean wage indexes covering the same categories of workers. For mental health services, the SA and MH services-related wage index produced a better fit (as measured by adjusted R-square) than did either the manufacturing or nonmanufacturing wage index. That was not true for substance abuse services, however, where manufacturing or nonmanufacturing wages have about the same predictive value.

[30]Recall that the Current index uses the HER study's rent index and weights and a wage index for mean nonmanufacturing wages we computed from the 1990 Census; because our wage index is not identical to the one used in the FY 1994 SAMHSA grant award formula, our illustration of the Current index differs from the one currently being implemented.

82 The Substance Abuse and Mental Health Services Block Grant Allotment Formula

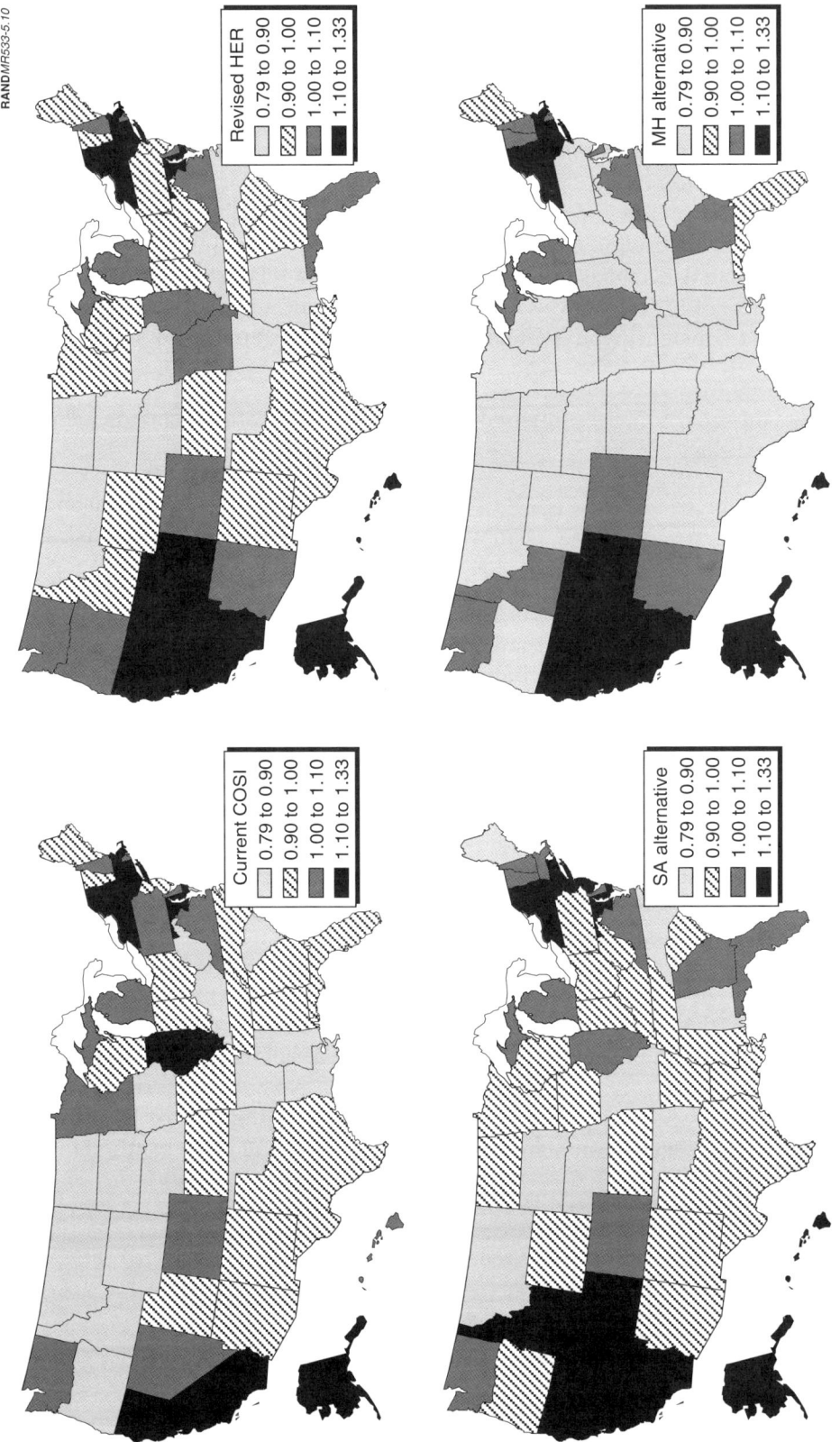

Figure 5.10—Current and Alternative Cost of Services Indexes

1.1 cutoff imposed by the COSI constraints. If the constraints were imposed, the states in light gray would move up in the index scale and the darkest-colored states would move down, making all four indexes look quite similar to one another in map figures like these. In effect, the constraints would eliminate much of the ability of the alternative methodology to discriminate among states based on the costliness of their services.

The crude index classifications in the map figures conceal the extent to which different indexes would affect the grant allocations for individual states. To reveal the more detailed effects, we compared each alternative with the Current one by computing the percentage differences between them for each state. (As we noted above, the percentage difference between two COSIs indicates the percentage effect on grant awards, other things equal.) For each alternative, we computed the percentage differences twice—once to compare the indexes when both the alternative and the Current COSI are unconstrained and again after applying the currently legislated constraints that prevent index values from falling below 0.9 or above 1.1.

Even if the indexes were unconstrained, any of the three alternatives would differ from the Current index by modest amounts (–10 to +10 percent) in at least three-quarters of the states. The largest changes would occur in Utah and Idaho, where any of the three alternatives would increase the index by 15–20 percent. Under any of the alternatives, the largest effects would all occur in the same set of states and would take the form of increases in the index values. That is, the alternative indexes tend to raise grant awards noticeably in a few states while spreading smaller percentage reductions across a large number of other states.

Constraining the index values would not be very effective at eliminating large swings in the index values. Utah and Idaho would still experience relatively large changes in their index values; their Current COSI values are close to 0.9 without the constraint and the alternative indexes do not move them much above 1.1, so the constraints have little effect on them. States that would experience intermediate-sized increases of 10–15 percent in the absence of constraints would instead experience noticeably smaller increases, but the states whose allocations would be reduced by the alternative indexes would find that the constraints moderate their losses only slightly or not at all.

The three alternative indexes differ from one another in some respects, most notably in how they would affect grant distributions between urban and rural states. To address that question, we computed the correlations between the Census measure of urbanicity and the percentage differences between the Current COSI and each of the three alternatives. The results appear in Table 5.1, where a negative coefficient implies that, compared to the Current index, an alternative index would tend to reallocate grants from urban to rural states.

In the table, all but one of the entries is statistically different from zero at better than 90 percent confidence. The sole exception is the Revised HER index after applying constraints. That is, all of the alternative indexes would tend to reallocate grants

Table 5.1

Simple Correlation Between Population Urbanicity and
Percentage Differences Between Current and
Alternative COSI Values

Alternative Index	Both Indexes Unconstrained	Both Indexes Constrained
Revised HER	–0.236	–0.045
SA alternative	–0.474	–0.406
MH alternative	–0.454	–0.334

from urban toward rural states, but constraining the Revised HER index would eliminate that effect.

The first entry in the table (–0.236) indicates that simply revising the wage and rent indexes in the HER formula would tend to reallocate grant awards from rural to urban states—but the correlations for the experience-based indexes are even stronger.[31] Even with constraints on the index values, both the SA and MH services alternatives would reallocate grants in favor of rural states (other things equal).

Of course, the index values in our comparisons are simply illustrative. The ultimate grant effects of improving the COSI methodology also depend on how other factors in the grant formula might be revised and hence cannot be fully assessed until Chapter Seven. Furthermore, the illustrated effects depend on measures that can change over time; in future years, updated analyses of Census, rent, and SA and MH services survey data could produce indexes that are distributed differently from the values displayed above. The fundamental benefits of improving the COSI methodology lie not in the effects on particular index values but in improving the estimates' inherent relevance, proportionality, and sensitivity to circumstances—characteristics that will contribute to the fairness of the cost of services indexes as they are reestimated and reapplied in future years.

---

[31]The correlations shown for the Revised HER index are significantly smaller than the correlations for the SA and MH services indexes with better than 99 percent confidence. However, the difference between the constrained SA and MH services correlations is significant with only 80 percent confidence, and the difference between the unconstrained SA and MH services correlations is not statistically significant.

Chapter Six
MEASURING STATES' FINANCING CAPACITY

The formula for allocating federal Block Grant monies is intended to effect an equitable distribution of federal resources among states for SA and MH services. To do so, it must distribute federal aid in such a way as to enable each state to provide a standard level of these services to its population in need. A state with a greater ability to raise revenues, all other things being equal, ought to require fewer federal funds to provide a standard level of services, and vice versa. Since these grants supplement states' internal allocations for treatment, it is desirable for equity-based grant formulas to account for each state's own revenue-raising abilities. Thus, fiscal measures are appropriate for inclusion in the formula.

To implement such measures in the formula, we must first produce estimates of each state's ability to fund services internally, i.e., estimates of its fiscal capacity. The economic literature offers a number of formulas for measuring fiscal capacity. PCPI was the measure initially included in the formula when fiscal capacity was introduced. Total taxable resources, a second measure developed by the U.S. Department of the Treasury, replaced PCPI in the SA and MH formulas in 1992. We also consider the representative tax system (RTS), a measure developed by the Advisory Commission on Intergovernmental Relations. RTS is not currently used in any U.S. grant allocation formula, though it has been recommended as an appropriate measure of a state's ability to raise revenues (ACIR, 1993).

In this section, we evaluate the appropriateness of including PCPI, TTR, and RTS in the SA and MH Block Grant allocation formulas as the measure of a state's fiscal capacity. First, we consider the theoretical basis for each measure, seeking an indicator that reliably captures the total ability of a state to finance public services internally from all types of potential resources (USGAO, 1992). We also analyze the empirical volatility of existing fiscal capacity measures. An indicator that is highly volatile may be error-prone, as fiscal capacity reflects state economic conditions that do not change dramatically from year to year. In addition, we consider the availability of these measures.

OVERVIEW

After analyzing the theoretical basis for alternative measures of fiscal capacity and investigating the availability, reliability, and volatility of available indicators, we conclude that the current measure of fiscal capacity included in the formula, TTR, is the least volatile and most reliable indicator of fiscal capacity currently available. TTR accurately captures a state's ability to raise revenues and is a relatively stable indicator, suggesting that it is not contaminated by large measurement errors. PCPI does not comprehensively reflect a state's ability to raise revenues, since it measures only residents' abilities to pay taxes and ignores tax exporting. RTS depends on a state's economic choices rather than actual capacity, since it is based on standardly defined tax bases; it is also a more volatile indicator than TTR. We also find that averaging TTR over the three most recent years for which it is available, as is currently recommended by the Alcohol, Drug Abuse, and Mental Health Administration Reorganization Act, does not significantly increase the stability of the estimator and may mask important changes in a state's economy.

WHY NOT USE ACTUAL FUNDS ALLOCATION?

If the grant formulas are intended to equalize the tax burden of providing a standard level of public services, why not simply include actual allocations for these services as the measure of each state's fiscal capacity? The reason for excluding such measures relates to incentives to spend and questions of equity. If states are "rewarded" for actually spending greater amounts, incentives for inefficient delivery of service arise. A state may find it advantageous to operate inefficiently if its high costs are compensated with increased Block Grant funds. In addition, fiscal measures are included in the Block Grant formula to promote equity as detailed in Chapter Two. The effect of including actual allocations as the measure of capacity to pay would be to favor states with greater resources, all other things being equal, as wealthier states will be able to allot greater internal resources to SA and MH services. Since this is clearly undesirable, we do not consider actual state expenditures on substance abuse and mental health services for inclusion in the formulas.

Another measure for possible inclusion in the Block Grant allocation formulas might account not only for a state's ability to raise funds through taxes but also for its success or failure in doing so. This concept is complex—the formula would need to concentrate resources in states that lack funds while at the same time not discouraging states from allocating internal resources to public treatment for fear of losing federal support. It might thus be desirable to include measures of a state's "fiscal effort" toward actually raising internal funds in addition to information on its potential capacity to do so. One measure of fiscal effort is termed "tax effort," which is defined as the ratio of a state's total tax collections to its potential total tax collections (as measured by the RTS index, discussed below). Another measure, state "fiscal blood pressure," is summarized by two statistics: the ratio of a state's current tax effort to its average tax effort, and the ratio of current effort to tax effort in a base year. This statistic has the advantage of accounting for taxation in a dynamic framework (ACIR, 1982).

However, it might be best not to include fiscal effort measures in the Block Grant formulas, as the purpose of the Block Grant program is *not* to stimulate state spending on substance abuse and mental health services but rather to help states provide a standard level of services to their population in need. Where federal funding *is* intended to stimulate state spending, programs typically require states to provide matching funds. Since federal spending on substance abuse and mental health services is generally much lower than state spending, matching requirements are likely to have little effect.

A STANDARDIZED MEASURE

Chapter Two discusses the specification of a generic grant allocation formula. A state's "expenditure need" is based on the difference between the cost of providing a standard level of benefits to its population in need of SA and MH services and the state's ability to pay for these services internally. A state's need score is defined as the product of its population in need, a factor that accounts for differences in state costs, and a measure of the state's need for federal funding per person (which varies inversely with fiscal capacity, all other things being equal).

Conveniently, it can be shown that fiscal capacity affects Block Grant allocations independent of population in need or cost considerations. Thus, while the fiscal capacity measure appears adjusted for cost of service and population in need in the formula legislation (ADAMHA Reorganization Act, 1992), by manipulating the formula algebraically we find that fiscal capacity does not interact multiplicatively with cost or population-in-need factors in determining grant allocations. Measures of capacity to pay enter the formula in the form $F_i/\bar{y}$, where F_i represents a state's fiscal capacity and $\bar{y}$ is the national fiscal capacity average per capita.[1] Thus, our analyses of alternative measures of fiscal capacity are based on examination of indicators in the form $F_i/\bar{y}$, since it is variation in this quantity (rather than in F_i itself) that is transmitted to the formula.

EVALUATION CRITERIA

In evaluating the alternative measures of fiscal capacity to determine their appropriateness for inclusion in the Block Grant formulas, we use three criteria: volatility, availability, and reliability.

Volatility

The appropriateness of any operationalization of revenue-raising ability depends on the measure's variability from year to year. If a measure of fiscal capacity is volatile, then we must consider whether the fluctuations reflect actual differences in state capacity or whether they represent measurement error. Since capacity reflects state economic conditions, which generally do not change dramatically from year to year, an estimate of capacity that is not reasonably stable indicates that a large degree of error is included. Thus, we seek an indicator that is reasonably stable over time. It is desirable that Block Grant allocations not change drastically from year to year due to errors of measurement of ability to pay, as this may causes service disruption and

---

[1] Mathematical proof of this can be found in Appendix A.

poor planning for service provision. Measures suspected to be error-prone may benefit from averaging values from recent years to smooth the effect of fluctuations.

Availability

Fiscal capacity estimates are derived from national income and product accounts data that reflect state finances. Measures that are used in computing fiscal capacity must exist for all geographic entities under consideration and must be readily available for use in calculating grant allocation formulas in a timely manner. Calculating fiscal measures based on data that do not become available until many years after the measurement date will necessarily introduce lags in the formula's ability to target aid to areas with low revenue-raising ability. Thus, preferred measures are those that are collected on a regular basis and that are widely disseminated in a timely manner.

Reliability

The indicator needs to accurately reflect states' relative capacities for raising funds. This implies that the data from which the indicators are calculated must be taken from well-defined and reliable sources. Generally, it is advisable to use data sources that are widely and publicly available and that are used for many accounting purposes. The greater utilization of data, the more likely that the procedure and definitions will be scrutinized for error. Measures that are generally used to measure state revenues and that are frequently analyzed are thus preferable to little known and underutilized measures.

ALTERNATIVE MEASURES OF FISCAL CAPACITY

The fiscal capacity indicator should be easily interpretable and should accurately reflect each state's revenue-raising ability. Since revenue-raising ability is conceptual, the appropriateness of any operationalization will be based on the degree to which an empirical measure accurately captures the elements of theoretical fiscal capacity. We consider the strengths and weaknesses of three measures below: personal income, total taxable resources, and the representative tax system.

Personal Income

The literature suggests a number a ways of gauging fiscal capacity. Historically, state personal income or PCPI has been used to measure a state's ability to raise tax revenues. This measure has been used in numerous federal grant funds allocation formulas, including Aid to Families with Dependent Children (AFDC) and Medicaid, among others. PCPI was the measure of fiscal capacity that was included when revenue-raising ability was first introduced into the SA and MH Block Grant allocation formulas.

Personal income measures state residents' ability to pay taxes, rather than a state's revenue-raising capacity. Personal income does not measure a state's ability to "export" taxes to nonresidents. Tax exportation refers to a state's ability to tax nonresidents and to collect taxes from outside its physical borders. Nevada, for example, has a relatively small population but is able to displace much of its revenue needs to visitors due to its large tourist trade. Thus, personal income does not effectively measure states' revenue-producing base (Kincaid, 1989). Personal income has also been criticized for its inability to capture income produced within a state but not realized there, such as corporate retained earnings and capital gains (USGAO, 1992).

Personal income does not truthfully measure a state's fiscal capacity, since it does not accurately capture the breadth of options available to states for raising revenues. Thus, we do not consider PCPI to be a valid measure of fiscal capacity and do not further evaluate it with respect to its volatility, reliability, or availability.

Total Taxable Resources

The Anti Drug Abuse Act of 1988 replaced PCPI with a new, more comprehensive measure of fiscal capacity known as total taxable resources (Carnevale and Fastrup, 1991). The TTR approach to measuring a state's fiscal capacity is based on an average of gross state product and personal income. TTR counts total product of a jurisdiction and then adds income received by residents but produced elsewhere (Institute for Health and Aging, 1986). By accounting for interstate transfers, TTR measures all income potentially subject to a state's taxing authority (USGAO, 1992). TTR is the fiscal capacity measure currently included in the SA and MH Block Grant formulas.

Since TTR includes both personal income and gross state product, it is a more comprehensive measure of a state's resources than simple measures of personal income. It is also a better measure because it reflects the ability of a state to export taxes.

The availability of TTR estimates depends on the agencies responsible for calculating personal income and gross state product (Bureau of Economic Analysis) producing these components promptly. This has proven problematic in the past; the most recent estimates of gross state product are from 1989. Thus, the U.S. General Accounting Office has produced annual TTR estimates for each year from 1989–1992 as the average of that year's personal income and the gross state product from 1989. For example, 1990 TTR is computed as the average of 1990 personal income and 1989 gross state product. Recent delays in producing gross state product data stem from procedural changes as well as a change in administration, which legislative staffers believe to be transitional. Thus, delays in obtaining gross state product are not likely to persist in future years, so current delays are not sufficient grounds for dismissal of TTR as a valid instrument for gauging fiscal capacity.

TTR is calculated as the average of personal income and gross state product, two well-known, often used measures. Thus, while TTR is a fairly new concept in fiscal capacity measurement, its components are traditional measures of state resources. Also, TTR is currently being considered for inclusion in other Block Grant allocation formulas. For example, a 1992 GAO report recommended that TTR replace PCPI in the maternal and child health services Block Grant formula (USGAO, 1992). As TTR is integrated into a greater number of allocations, its reliability is likely to increase.

Figure 6.1 shows the percentage change in each state's TTR indicator between 1986 and 1988. We analyze data from this particular time period because gross state product data are not available for 1990–1991, and, thus, TTR estimates for those years are calculated using gross state product data from 1989. Thus, any TTR variation for 1989–1991 is due to variation in personal income, since gross state product is entered identically in each year. Hence, we analyze data only from 1986–1988, so that the TTR estimates are based on full data availability.

TTR does not appear to change significantly over time. During 1986–1988, no state's TTR changed by more than 8 percent. In fact, only four states experienced a change in TTR that was greater than five percent. We also examined changes in the ranking of states' TTR over time in Figure 6.2, which displays TTR indicator rankings for 1988 when states are sorted according to the 1986 rankings. Differences between the 1986 and 1988 rankings can be observed where the 1988 rankings fall either above or below a line drawn at 45°, since this line represents states' ordered 1986 rankings. This figure indicates that ranking changed little during 1986–1988. Only 11 states experienced any change in rank of TTR with only one state changing rank by more than one place between 1986–1988. Thus, the TTR appears to be a stable indicator.

The current legislation recommends the use of the most recent three-year average of TTR for block grant allocations (Alcohol, Drug Abuse and Mental Health Reorganization Act, 1992). This averaging is done ostensibly to avoid large changes in allocations based on high variation from year to year. Figure 6.3 compares TTR in 1991 with the most recent three-year average available at this time (1989–1991).[2] We find

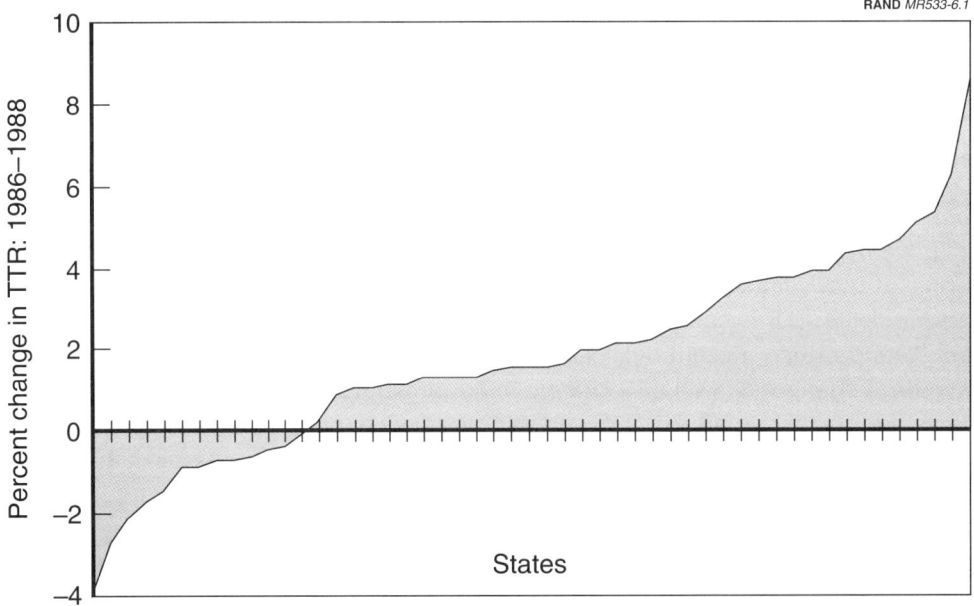

Figure 6.1—Percentage Change in States' Total Taxable Resources (TTR), 1986–1988

---

[2]1989, 1990, and 1991 are the only three consecutive years for which TTR estimates are currently available (ACIR, 1993).

Measuring States' Financing Capacity 91

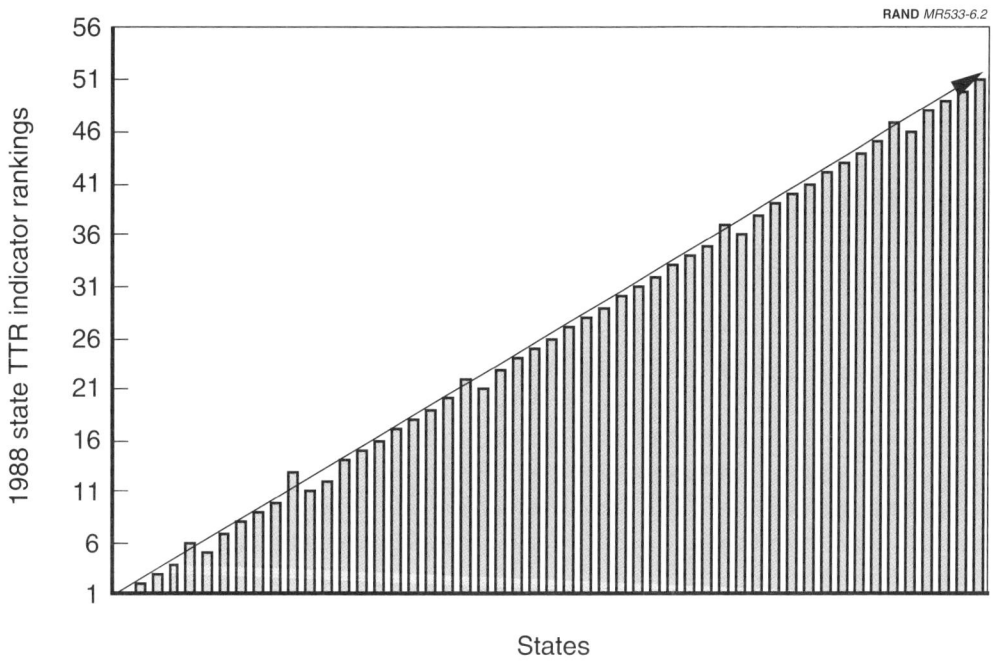

Figure 6.2—State TTR Rankings, 1988 (states sorted by 1986 rankings)

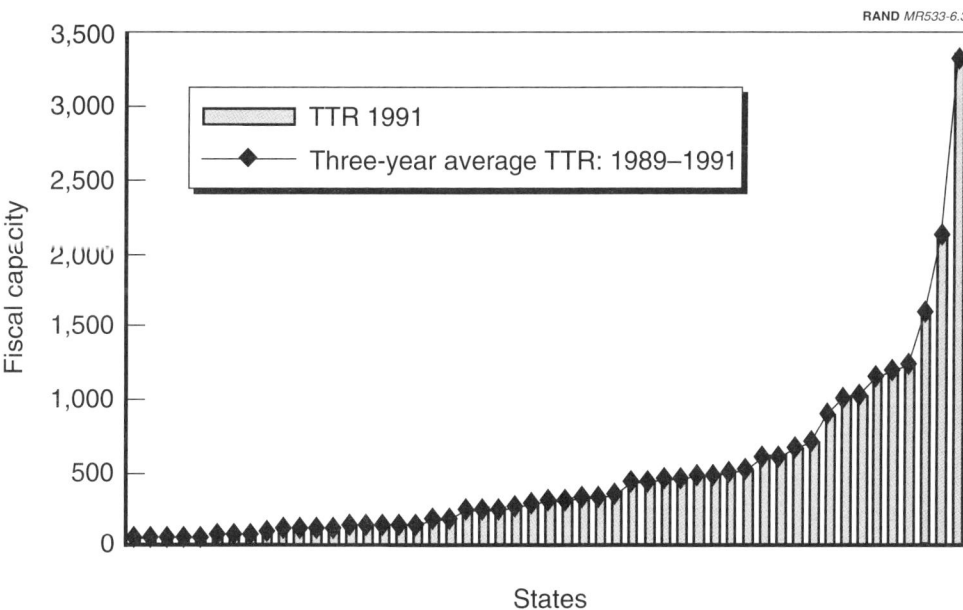

Figure 6.3—TTR 1991 Versus Three-Year Average TTR, 1989–1991

that there are virtually no significant differences between the TTR for a given year and the most recent three-year average. Given this, and the fact that averaging tends to understate the effect of real year-to-year economic changes, use of three-year averages of TTR does not appear to improve the measure conceptually. Instead, averaging is likely to mask real changes in a state's economy that are relevant to its ability to provide SA and MH services with internal funding.

The Representative Tax System (RTS)

Another measure of state fiscal capacity we consider is the RTS. RTS calculates the average tax rate over all states and then applies it to each state's particular tax base. Each state's tax base is calculated using a standard definition, since actual definitions vary considerably. This definition includes personal and corporate income, retail sales, and property tax bases, among other sources of tax revenue. RTS thus measures the amount of revenue per capita a state would collect if it used the national average tax rate and defined taxable revenues using this standardized formula (ACIR, 1990). Since RTS measures the size of states' current tax base, it thus reflects currently rather than potentially taxable resources.

However, RTS has been criticized for reflecting the economic choices of states rather than actual capacity. Since RTS is based on the relative sizes of states' tax bases, it necessarily reflects state residents' preferences for consumption and resource use in addition to fiscal capacity. For example, states whose residents channel their income into savings rather than consumption will have relatively lower fiscal capacity as measured by RTS than comparable states whose residents prefer to spend on taxable retail purchases (Barro, 1986).

While RTS is not currently used in fiscal equalization formulas in the United States, it has been adopted for use in Canada's program of federal-provincial equalization assistance. In addition, the Advisory Commission for Intergovernmental Relations recommends RTS as a fiscal capacity measure suitable for grant formulas (ACIR, 1993). Thus, we also consider RTS estimates as an alternative measure of fiscal capacity.

Figure 6.4 shows the percentage change between RTS estimates in 1986 and 1988, the two most recent years for which RTS estimates are available. Figure 6.5 graphs state RTS rankings in 1988 sorted according to 1986 rankings, similar to Figure 6.2 for TTR, above. RTS appears to be significantly more volatile than TTR: Between 1986 and 1988, 21 states experienced changes in RTS that were greater than 5 percent, whereas only four states' TTR changed by 5 percent or more between 1986 and 1988. Additionally, 19 states changed RTS ranking between 1986 and 1988, as evidenced in Figure 6.5, though no state changed rank by more than two places.

We cannot evaluate the effect of using three-year averages of RTS at this time, since estimates are not currently available for 1987, 1989, or 1990.

Measuring States' Financing Capacity 93

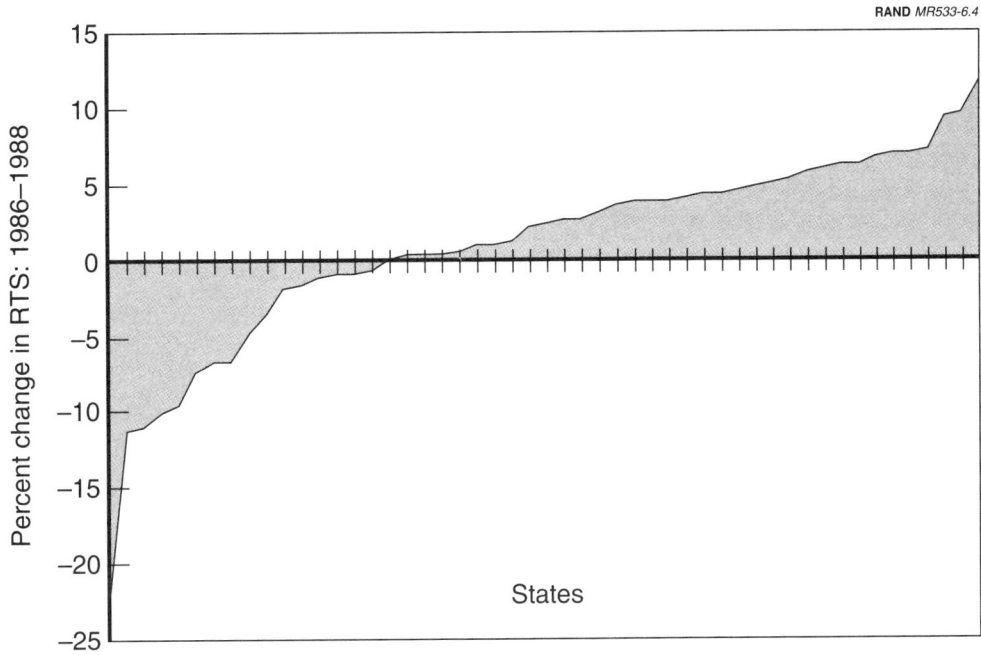

Figure 6.4—Percentage Change in States' RTS, 1986–1988

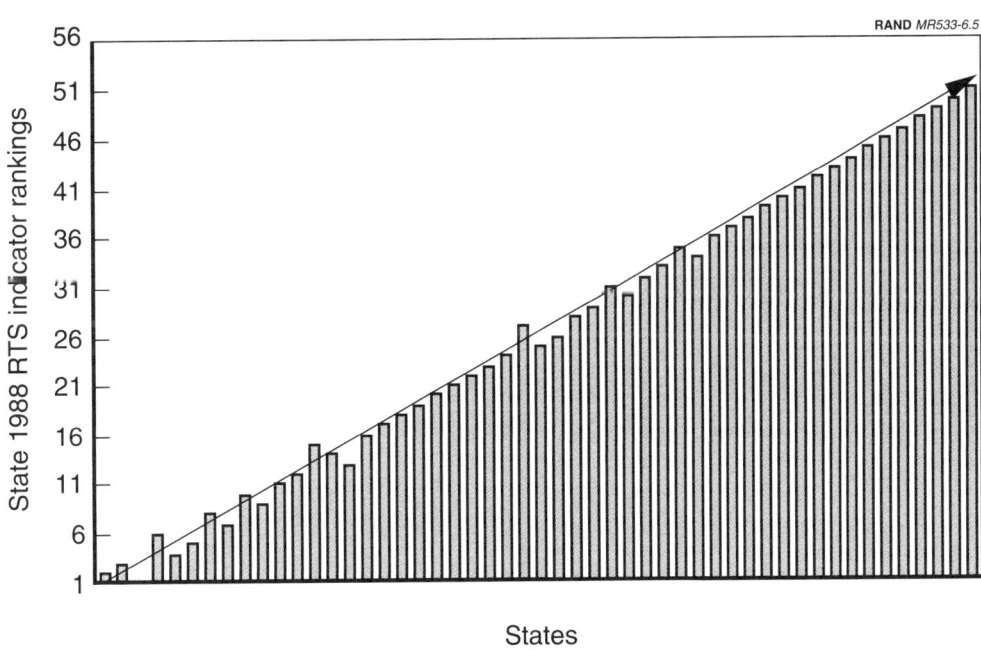

Figure 6.5—State RTS Rankings, 1988 (states sorted by 1986 rankings)

COMPARING INDICATORS—DOES IT MATTER?

Comparison of the appropriateness of including PCPI, TTR, and RTS indicators as the fiscal capacity measure in the SA and MH Block Grant allocation formulas suggests that TTR, the measure currently used, is the most suitable measure of states' abilities to fund services internally. PCPI measures residents' abilities to pay taxes but does not comprehensively account for states' abilities to raise revenue. RTS estimates have serious theoretical shortcomings and are more volatile than the measure currently used in the formula, TTR.

Figure 6.6 charts states' TTR and RTS estimates for 1991, with states sorted according to their 1991 TTR. It suggests that states' TTR and RTS estimates are not very different. This is encouraging, since both indicators are supposed to measure a state's fiscal capacity. However, variations in the RTS indicator are more extreme than those for TTR. RTS reflected a greater than 10 percent change in nine states between 1988 and 1991 while TTR changed by more than 10 percent in only three states. TTR thus produces a "smoother" estimate of fiscal capacity over time. The rate of change in the two indicators over time is markedly different: Changes in TTR are not mirrored in RTS. Thus, it appears that the choice of whether to use TTR or RTS is an important one.

TTR is the most readily obtainable indicator available to policymakers for measuring states' fiscal capacity. TTR is easily calculated as the average of gross state product and personal income, both of which are calculated annually by the U.S. General Accounting Office for use in making other fiscal decisions. RTS estimates are not

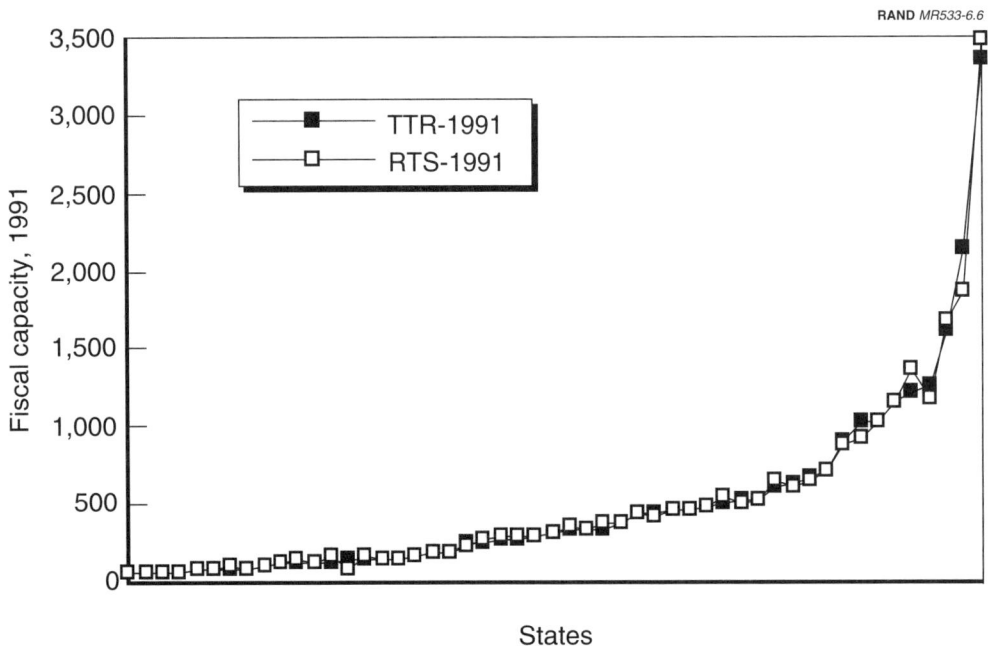

Figure 6.6—Fiscal Capacity, 1991, TTR and RTS

currently used in any other federal allocation formulas, and were not even officially calculated in 1987, 1989, or 1990. TTR also exhibits less year-to-year variation than does RTS, which helps smooth states' Block Grant allocations and thus aid in planning. In addition, we find that using three-year averages of TTR does not significantly change the estimates. Year-to-year differences in TTR are not so great as to require the use of averaging, and any such differences may represent meaningful changes in a state's revenue-raising ability.

Chapter Seven

EVALUATION OF THE EFFECTS OF ALTERNATIVE COMPONENT DEFINITIONS IN ALLOTMENT FORMULAS

Previous chapters dealt with individual components of the Block Grant formulas (population in need, cost of service, fiscal capacity), using new databases or more refined analyses to develop a series of alternative measures for each component. The alternative measures seem more appropriate than those currently contained in the formulas, either because the new data and analyses are more relevant to the substance abuse or mental health context (e.g., surveys of mental health service providers) or more comprehensive (e.g., the NCS data). However, the question remains as to how much difference using alternative measures would make to Block Grant allocations. This chapter addresses that question by examining the allocations produced by revising the component measures, singly and in concert, in the current Block Grant formula.

The issues to be addressed concern *fundamental* differences between the current allocations and those produced by alternative measures. In any year, the Block Grant legislation might apply hold-harmless provisions or minimums on state allocations, but those are devices for overriding the formula allocations and hence are not pertinent to this chapter's comparisons. In any year, total Block Grant funding might change, raising or lowering the dollar grants for all states under any version of the formula; for our purposes, however, the relevant comparisons are not among dollar amounts states would receive but among the states' *shares* of any given total funding. We pay particular attention to the overall proportion of total funding that would be shifted among states if the formula measures were changed—a basic indicator of the differences among alternatives—and to whether the shifts would favor states depending on whether they have large or small populations, are more or less urban,[1] or have larger or smaller shares of their population living in poverty—matters of particular interest to policymakers.

As a practical matter, of course, the numerical comparisons in this chapter reflect specific estimates of the current and alternative measures, and the specific grant allocations that derive from them. As the Block Grant formula is reapplied in future years, the component measures will be updated, their values will change, and so will

---

[1] In this chapter, urbanicity is defined as the percentage of a state's population living in MSAs. We refer to states with a higher percentage of their populations in MSAs as more "urban" and those with a lower percentage of their populations in MSAs as more "rural."

the state funding shares. Nonetheless, we believe these numerical comparisons convey valid information about the fundamental implications of changing the need, cost, and fiscal capacity measures. The observed allocation patterns with respect to population size, urbanicity, and poverty rates result from the inherent design of the component measures (e.g., urbanicity is a variable used in estimating populations in need) or from general demographic patterns that change slowly over time.[2]

This chapter focuses on a selected group of alternative measures. Based on criteria presented in earlier chapters, the selected measures are the ones we consider best suited to meeting the funding objectives of the Block Grants for SA and MH services. However, Appendix B applies this chapter's analysis to the other alternative measures that were developed in this study.

Following a brief overview of the chapter's findings, we explain the methodology we used to compare alternative component measures. Then, for each component of the Block Grant formula, we show the specific effects of using our "preferred" alternative measures in place of a current one, holding all other components in the formula constant. Finally, because population in need and cost of services jointly determine a state's expenditure need (see Chapter Two and Appendix A), we combine those two components to examine how alternative measures of expenditure need would affect the grant allocations.

OVERVIEW

Our preferred estimate of the population in need of mental health services (see Chapter Three) combines the adult needs predicted by the NCS model for serious mental illness in the past month (without additional severity criteria) and a crude estimate of youth needs based on 3.2 percent of a state's population under age 16. Substituting this estimate in the current Block Grant formula for mental health (replacing the current population need measure but leaving all other formula components unchanged) would shift 5 percent of total funding among the states and would favor states with higher poverty levels.

Among the alternatives considered in Chapter Four, our preferred estimate of population in need of substance abuse treatment uses the definition that includes both drug and alcohol dependence, and our preferred estimate for SA prevention uses the "risk" definition based on the relative rate of substance use among youth. The effect of these measures depends on the weights assigned to treatment relative to prevention needs when they are combined to allocate SA funding. If policymakers weight treatment needs four times as heavily as prevention needs, our preferred measures of population need would reallocate 18 percent of total substance abuse funding; alternatively, if policymakers weight prevention and treatment needs equally, the percentage of total SA funding that would be shifted falls somewhat to 13 percent. In either case, the shift of funding would favor smaller and more rural states.

---

[2] Furthermore, we took care to assure that our stated conclusions do not depend on small differences in the evaluation statistics and are not attributable to extreme component values for just one or two states.

Our preferred COSIs are the separate, experience-based SA and MH measures developed in Chapter Five. Although these indexes are quite different from the index based on the currently mandated COS methodology, retaining the constraints imposed by the Block Grant legislation (i.e., that each state's index value must lie between 0.9 and 1.1) would prevent the new indexes from having much effect on the Block Grant allocations: Replacing the current index would shift only 3 percent of total mental health funding and substance abuse funding among the states, with shifts toward states that have larger proportions of their populations living in rural areas. However, if Congress removed the constraints, the effects would be larger (shifting 7 percent of mental health funding, and 8 percent of substance abuse funding), and the favoring of more rural states would be diminished.

Chapter Six questioned the necessity of using a three-year average of total taxable revenue in the fiscal capacity index, but showed that using just the most recent year values would have little effect on the index. Not surprisingly, this chapter also finds that revising the index in that way would have little effect on the Block Grant allocations.

Replacing the current values for both population needs and costs with our preferred measures yields effects quite similar to replacing the population need measures alone, particularly if the cost index remains constrained. However, if the cost index constraints were removed, the shares of both mental health and substance abuse funding that would be shifted among the states would rise.

EVALUATION METHODOLOGY

Throughout this chapter, the basis of comparison is the Block Grant allocations that would derive from applying the currently legislated formula to our estimates of the currently mandated measures of population in need, costs of services, and fiscal capacity. Differences between our data sources and those used by SAMHSA might cause our estimates of the Current measures to differ somewhat from the values actually being implemented.[3] Furthermore, as noted above, we do not apply hold-harmless provisions or state minimums when calculating the Current formula allocations.

When considering alternative measures, we substitute them in the current formula, again without regard to hold-harmless provisions or state minimums. As Chapter Two explained, the current formula applies the "taxpayer equity" concept, and this analysis takes that concept as given. Changes in the basic formula that would arise under other equity concepts (e.g., beneficiary equity) are not evaluated here.

Our comparisons use the following indicators to assess how the alternative measures affect the Block Grant allocations:

_____
[3]For example, Chapter Five explained that our estimate of median nonmanufacturing wages was developed independently of the wage estimates SAMHSA currently uses.

- The overall percentage of total funding that would be reallocated among the states if the alternative(s) replaced the current measures. This is a basic indicator of how "different" an alternative allocation would be.

- The numbers of states whose allocation *shares* would rise or fall by various percentages. (For example, if a state that currently receives 5 percent of total funding would experience a 10 percent increase in its share, the new share would be 5.5 percent of total funding.) This metric is independent of the actual dollar amount of total funding, which can vary from year to year, yet it conveys information about how many states would gain or lose from the reallocation and whether the gains or losses would be large relative to the current allocations.

- The percentage of the U.S. population residing in states whose allocation shares would rise or fall by various percentages. This metric portrays whether the gains or losses from revising the formula component measures would be concentrated in states that are heavily or sparsely populated.

We also report three summary statistics aimed at identifying the attributes of states whose shares would increase or decrease if current component measures were revised:

- The simple correlation between state population size and the ratio of each state's share given by the preferred alternative component measure to that given by the current formula's component measure. If this correlation is positive, revising the component measure(s) in question tends to redistribute funds from smaller states to larger ones; a negative correlation indicates funds are shifted in the opposite direction.

- The simple correlation between the proportion of a state's population living in MSAs as measured by the 1990 Census,[4] and the ratio of each state's share given by the preferred alternative component measure to that given by the current formula's component measure. A positive correlation indicates that the alternative component measure(s) shift funding toward more urban states, whereas a negative correlation indicates that the shift is toward rural states.

- The simple correlation between the proportion of a state's population living in poverty, again as determined by the 1990 Census, and the ratio of each state's share given by the preferred alternative component measure to that given by the current formula's component measure. A positive correlation indicates that states with relatively large poverty populations tend to benefit from revising the component measures, but a negative correlation indicates that they tend to lose.

In principle, any of the simple correlation coefficients could show a large positive or negative value if just one or two states had extreme values for both the change in their allocation shares and their population, urbanicity, or poverty rates—but that was not the case for the statistics reported here. In these results, a noteworthy corre-

---

[4]We also computed correlations between the change in state shares and the Census measure of proportion of population living in "urbanized" areas. Correlations based on urbanized population do not contradict our MSA-based findings but are weaker than the values reported here.

lation (i.e., greater than 0.4 or smaller than –0.4) means that the funding shift would involve several (but generally not all) of the states at each end of the population size, urbanicity, or poverty scale in question. And where additional information seems warranted, we include graphs showing the numbers of affected states and the sizes of the gains or loses they would experience.

We have chosen not to present information state by state for changes in allocations that would occur if the formula were revised to incorporate our preferred alternative measures of formula components. Our reason for this omission is straightforward. The major objective of the study was not to develop an alternative formula but to evaluate the equity of the current formula by comparing it to empirically based alternatives. The comparison of the current formula to one using these alternative measures, then, is designed to provide a broad picture of the ways in which the current formula might be improved. If one were to develop a new formula based upon the conclusions of this study, component measures would be specified that would take into account the availability of updated data on relevant state characteristics over time. While a new formula based on this study's results would probably not differ greatly from the alternative measures used here, some simplification of measures to facilitate the implementation of the formula on an annual basis would be desirable. We would expect, then, that a new formula based upon the current study would generally change state allocations in the direction indicated in this chapter, but results for specific states could vary from our study findings. To avoid overinterpretation of findings for specific states, then, we have not presented our results by state names.

EFFECTS OF REVISING THE POPULATION NEEDS COMPONENT

Population Needs for Mental Health Services

Our estimators of need for community mental health services are the sum of two components: an adult needs estimate and a youth needs estimate. Chapter Three examined eight alternative definitions and state-level estimates of adult needs, four definitions for ECA-based models, and four definitions for NCS-based models. Because adequate epidemiologic data were not available for children, we took 3.2 percent of the state's population under 16, which the National Advisory Mental Health Council (1993) gives as the percentage of children with serious emotional disturbance.

Of the adult needs measures, we prefer the one based on the NCS model that predicts serious mental illness in the past month (without additional severity criteria) for several reasons. First, because the NCS models are derived from a national sample and one that is more recent than the ECA, we have greater confidence in these models when making indirect estimates of rates of serious mental illness for the states. Second, among the NCS-based models, three definitions resulted in similar state-level estimates of rates of serious mental illness, suggesting that a measure based on one of these three models is relatively robust. Third, among the three NCS-based measures that gave similar results, we favored the parsimony of the predictive model and relatively low overall prevalence in the population (since prevalence rates of serious mental illness as assessed in the NCS were generally high).

Table 7.1 summarizes how the preferred alternative measure for population need for mental health services changes state allocation shares relative to the current formula for mental health services. This table shows that the preferred alternative population needs index leads to a 5 percent shift in state allocations for mental health services, all else being equal. That is, if nothing else changed, 5 percent of the funds would be added or subtracted from state shares. Further, the shares of about 20 percent of the states (13) would change by more than 10 percent. The affected states contain 12 percent of the U.S. population.

Table 7.2 lists the correlations of several state characteristics with the ratio of shares given by the preferred population needs index to those given by the current index. Poverty has the strongest relationship, with a correlation of over 0.6. Figure 7.1 graphs these ratios ordered from states with lower percentages of their populations in poverty on the left to those with higher poverty percentages on the right.

Table 7.1

Effect on Mental Health Allocations of Changing Population Needs Index Only

	Preferred Alternative
Share of total allocation changed	5
Number of states with allocation changed by	
> 20% lower	1
10–20% lower	5
0–10% lower	20
0–10% higher	18
10–20% higher	6
> 20% higher	1
Percent of U.S. population in states with allocation changed by	
> 20% lower	0
10–20% lower	4
0–10% lower	41
0–10% higher	47
10–20% higher	8
> 20% higher	0

Table 7.2

Correlation of State Characteristics with Mental Health Allocations, Changing Population Needs Index Only

Correlation with	Change to Preferred Alternative
State population size	0.04
State percent of population in urban areas	−0.03
State percent of population in poverty	0.63

Evaluation of the Effects of Alternative Component Definitions in Allotment Formulas   103

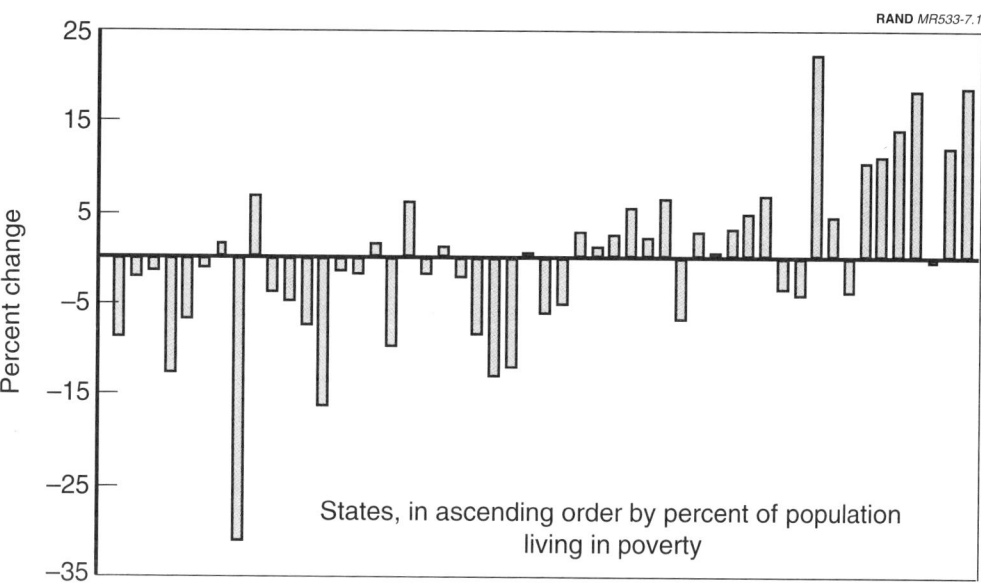

Figure 7.1—Percentage Change in the Mental Health Allocation Under the Preferred Alternative Measure of Population Need, by State

Population Needs for Substance Abuse Services

Our estimators of need for substance abuse services also depend on two components: treatment needs and prevention needs. Chapter Four directly estimated population in need of treatment using two alternative definitions of need, but estimating prevention needs is more complicated. We assume that prevention needs are proportional to the state's population aged 12 to 20, weighted by alternative measures of social environmental risk as described in detail in Chapter Four, but we do not know what the constant of proportionality should be and hence cannot convert our prevention needs estimates into the number of people who need prevention services. To resolve this issue, we converted both the treatment and prevention needs to indexes (the ratio of the state rate to the national rate). We then combined the two indexes with weights of 0.2 for prevention and 0.8 for treatment, or 0.5 for prevention and 0.5 for treatment. This produces combined need measures: The first sets the balance of treatment to prevention service needs at 4 to 1; the second sets them equal.

Among the two alternative definitions and state-level estimates of population need for substance abuse treatment examined in Chapter Four, we prefer the definition that includes both drug and alcohol dependence because it corresponds to the explicitly defined target population for substance abuse treatment services.

In Chapter Four, we also proposed two definitions of need for substance abuse prevention, one that weighted the number of youth in a state by a "risk" rate equivalent to the rate of substance use among youth, and one that weighted the number of youth by a "risk" rate equivalent to the rate of substance dependence among adults.

The first is an operationalization of the concept of primary prevention—preventing initiation of drug use among youth—and the second definition expresses the concept of secondary prevention—preventing the development of serious drug problems. Because the Block Grant legislation emphasizes primary prevention, we selected the first definition as our preferred alternative.

Table 7.3 summarizes how state shares change from the current substance abuse allocation formula under the preferred alternative measure of need for substance abuse services. This table shows that, with prevention need weighted at 20 percent of total need for substance abuse services, the preferred alternative leads to about an 18 percent change in allocations for substance abuse, all else being equal. That is, if nothing else changed, about 18 percent of the funds would be shifted among the states. Further, the shares of almost three-quarters (37/51) of the states would change by more than 10 percent. The affected states contain 65 percent of the U.S. population. If prevention need is weighted at 50 percent of total population need, the change from current formula allocations is somewhat less dramatic: About 13 percent of the allocation would be shifted, with 54 percent of the population in states with allocation shifts of more than 10 percent.

Table 7.4 lists the correlations of several state characteristics with the ratio of the share given by the preferred alternative formulation of population need to that given by the current formulation. Urbanicity and state population size have the largest correlations with the changes, in general. The negative correlation means that the preferred alternative population need index tended to increase allocation shares to smaller and more rural states under both the 20 percent and 50 percent prevention

Table 7.3

Effect on Substance Abuse Allocations of Changing Population Needs Index Only

	Preferred Alternative	
	20% for Prevention	50% for Prevention
Share of total allocation changed	18	13
Number of states with allocation changed by		
> 20% lower	6	4
10–20% lower	5	6
0–10% lower	8	5
0–10% higher	6	9
10–20% higher	4	5
> 20% higher	22	22
Percent of U.S. population in states with allocation changed by		
> 20% lower	15	13
10–20% lower	20	16
0–10% lower	22	20
0–10% higher	12	27
10–20% higher	14	8
> 20% higher	16	17

Table 7.4

Correlation of State Characteristics with Substance Abuse Allocations, Changing Population Needs Index Only

Correlation with	Change to Preferred Alternative	
	20% for Prevention	50% for Prevention
State population size	−0.42	−0.45
State percent of population in urban areas	−0.73	−0.83
State percent of population in poverty	0.08	0.13

needs weighting. This is not surprising given the higher prevalence of alcohol dependence predicted in nonmetropolitan states, reflected in our preferred alternative, in contrast to the heavy weighting that the formula currently gives to the urban population. The correlation with urbanicity is even larger for the 50 percent prevention alternative. Figure 7.2 graphs these ratios ordered from low urbanicity states on the left to high urbanicity states at the right. In summary, our preferred needs predictor would move shares away from the larger and more urban states to the smaller and more rural. Explicit incorporation of a prevention component, even when maintaining the current treatment need index, also has the same effect (see Appendix B).

Overall, the difference between the current and the preferred alternative population needs measure is substantially greater for substance abuse than for mental health service allocations.

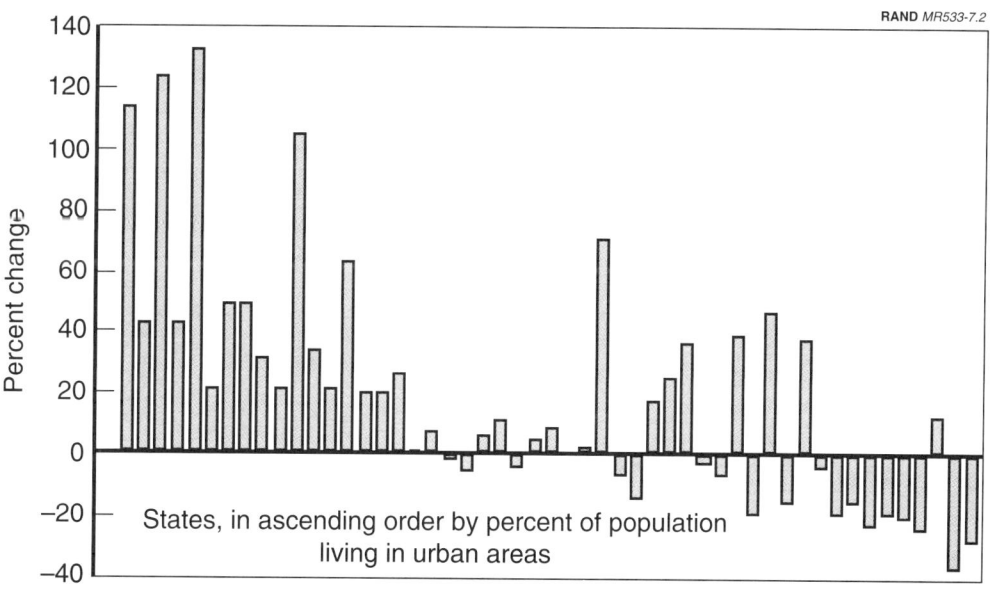

Figure 7.2—Percentage Change in the Substance Abuse Allocation Under the Preferred Alternative Measure of Population Need, by State

COST COMPONENT

Defining a best predictor for the cost component is not as difficult as for the population needs component, in part because the aggregation issue is not present. As Chapter Five explained, we constructed separate cost indexes for substance abuse and mental health services based on cost relationships observed in surveys of SA and MH service providers, but standardized to reflect nationwide average usage of labor and facilities resources; we also developed more relevant wage indexes and updated the rent indexes used in the current COS methodology.

Table 7.5 summarizes how the preferred alternative measure for the cost of mental health services would change state allocation shares relative to the current formula for mental health services. It compares both a constrained and unconstrained version of the preferred measure with the constrained version of the current COSI.[5] When unconstrained, the preferred alternative cost index leads to about a 7 percent shift in state allocations for mental health services, all else being equal. That is, if nothing else changed, about 7 percent of the funds would be added or subtracted from state shares. Further, the shares of 25 percent of the states (13) would change by more than 10 percent. The affected states contain about 28 percent of the U.S. population. Using the preferred alternative cost index with the current system's 0.9 to 1.1 constraints on the index values results in a more moderate 3 percent shift.

Table 7.6 lists the correlations of several state characteristics with the ratio of shares given by the preferred alternative cost index to those given by the current index.

Table 7.5

Effect on Mental Health Allocations of Changing
Cost of Service Index Only

	Preferred Alternative	
	Constrained	Unconstrained
Share of total allocation changed	3	7
Number of states with allocation changed by		
> 20% lower	0	0
10–20% lower	0	7
0–10% lower	14	24
0–10% higher	34	14
10–20% higher	2	6
> 20% higher	1	0
Percent of U.S. population in states with allocation changed by		
> 20% lower	0	0
10–20% lower	0	13
0–10% lower	32	47
0–10% higher	67	26
10–20% higher	1	15
> 20% higher	0	0

---

[5]The constraint on the COSIs refers to the restriction that the range of values taken by the index must lie between 0.9 and 1.1, as currently mandated by the formula.

Table 7.6

Correlation of State Characteristics with Mental Health Allocations, Changing Cost of Service Index Only

Correlation with	Change to Preferred Alternative	
	Constrained	Unconstrained
State population size	−0.26	0.08
State percent of population in urban areas	−0.43	0.11
State percent of population in poverty	0.18	−0.14

Urbanicity and poverty have the strongest relationship, with a higher correlation when the index is constrained than when unconstrained.

Table 7.7 summarizes how state cost-of-service measures for substance abuse services would change under the preferred alternative. Results are very similar for the cost-of-service component evaluation across the mental health and substance abuse formulas. It shows that the preferred alternative leads to about a 7 percent shift in the grants for substance abuse, all else being equal. That is, if nothing else changed, about 7 percent of the funds would be shifted among the states under the preferred alternative. Further, the shares of 27 percent (14/51) of the states would change by more than 10 percent. The affected states include 32 percent of the U.S. population. Using the constraints results in a more moderate 5 percent shift in the total allocation.

Table 7.8 lists the correlations of several characteristics with the substance abuse allocation ratio of the preferred alternative to the current indicator. The largest correlation is with constrained urbanicity. The preferred alternative cost of services index tends to shift substance abuse allocation shares toward less urban states relative to

Table 7.7

Effect on Substance Abuse Allocations of Changing Cost of Service Index Only

	Preferred Alternative	
	Constrained	Unconstrained
Share of total allocation changed	5	7
Number of states with allocation changed by		
> 20% lower	0	0
10–20% lower	2	5
0–10% lower	16	23
0–10% higher	19	11
10–20% higher	10	7
> 20% higher	4	2
Percent of U.S. population in states with allocation changed by		
> 20% lower	1	0
10–20% lower	1	13
0–10% lower	52	53
0–10% higher	38	15
10–20% higher	8	17
> 20% higher	2	2

108 The Substance Abuse and Mental Health Services Block Grant Allotment Formula

Table 7.8

Correlation of State Characteristics with Substance Abuse Allocations,
Changing Cost of Service Index Only

	Change to Preferred Alternative	
Correlation with	Constrained	Unconstrained
State population size	−0.37	−0.18
State percent of population in urban areas	−0.77	−0.42
State percent of population in poverty	0.29	−0.06

the current COSI, when the index is constrained. When unconstrained there is a weaker relationship with any of these three factors.

FISCAL CAPACITY COMPONENT

In Chapter Six, we discussed alternative measures of state fiscal capacity. The current formula uses a three-year average of TTR. The preferred alternative is to use the current year's TTR, not the three-year average. As discussed in Chapter Six, this alternative was not very different for the years where data are available.

In the context of this chapter, the effects of changing from the three-year average TTR to just the most recent year's TTR are negligible. Compared with changing the population need or cost indexes, a change to the preferred fiscal capacity measure has no noticeable effect. For example, only 0.2 percent of the total Block Grant allocation would shift with the change. Because of the small magnitude of the change, we do not produce tables for fiscal capacity as we have for the population needs and COSIs.

INTERACTION OF POPULATION IN NEED AND COST OF SERVICES COMPONENTS: EXPENDITURE NEED

In the previous sections of this chapter, we summarized the relative effects of variations in the three components separately for mental health and substance abuse services. That is, we analyzed each in isolation. Here, we look at interactions between the population need and cost of service components. Since there is no real choice to be made in measuring fiscal capacity, we confine our attention to combining need and cost. Even though we do not analyze fiscal capacity, it should be noted that variations in fiscal capacity can increase or decrease the variability in expenditure needs effects on the allocations across states.

Table 7.9 summarizes how state shares change under the preferred population needs and cost indexes for mental health services compared with shares allocated by the current formula. When population need and costs of services are multiplied, the result is the dollar cost of delivering services to the population in need—termed "expenditure need."

Table 7.9 shows that the preferred alternative expenditure needs measure (when unconstrained) leads to about a 7 percent change in allocations for mental health

Table 7.9

Total Effect on Mental Health Allocations of Changing Population Needs and Cost of Service Indexes

	Preferred Alternative	
	Constrained	Unconstrained
Share of total allocation changed	5	7
Number of states with allocation changed by		
> 20% lower	1	1
10–20% lower	4	7
0–10% lower	18	22
0–10% higher	20	15
10–20% higher	4	3
> 20% higher	4	3
Percent of U.S. population in states with allocation changed by		
> 20% lower	0	0
10–20% lower	6	7
0–10% lower	48	47
0–10% higher	38	30
10–20% higher	4	15
> 20% higher	4	2

services, all else being equal. That is, if nothing else changed, about 7 percent of the funds would be added or subtracted from state shares. Further, the shares of 14 of the states would change by more than 10 percent. These states contain roughly 24 percent of the U.S. population.

Table 7.10 lists the correlations of several state characteristics with the ratio of shares given the preferred to current expenditure needs measure. Poverty has the strongest relationship, with a correlation of 0.68 when the index is constrained and 0.47 when unconstrained. Figure 7.3 graphs these ratios for the unconstrained preferred alternative, with states ordered from low to high poverty levels, showing that allocation shares would be shifted to poorer states.

Next we show the effect of alternative expenditure need measures for substance abuse allocations. Our preferred alternative for expenditure needs is the product of our preferred population need and our preferred cost measures. Table 7.11 summarizes how the preferred alternative measure of expenditure need for substance abuse services would change state allocation shares relative to the current formula for mental health services.

Table 7.10

Correlation of State Characteristics with Mental Health Allocations, Changing Population Needs and Cost of Service Indexes

	Preferred Alternative	
Correlation with	Constrained	Unconstrained
State population size	−0.09	0.09
State percent of population in urban areas	−0.24	0.07
State percent of population in poverty	0.68	0.47

110   The Substance Abuse and Mental Health Services Block Grant Allotment Formula

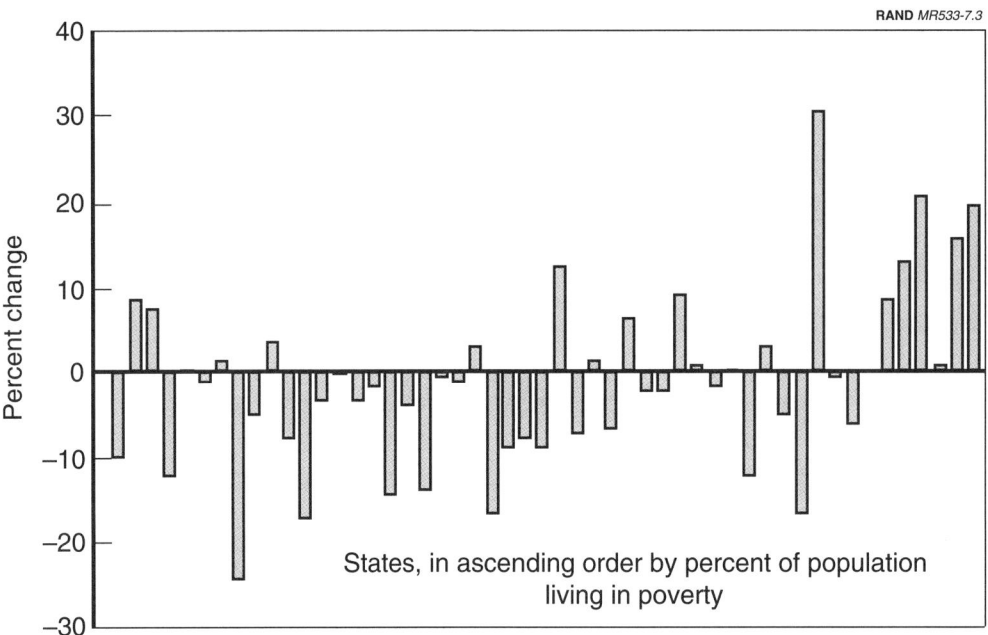

Figure 7.3—Percentage Change in the Mental Health Allocation Under the Preferred
Alternative Measure of Expenditure Need, by State

Table 7.11 shows that the preferred alternative with a 20 percent prevention weight and an unconstrained COSI leads to about a 22 percent change in allocations for substance abuse. That is, if nothing else changed, about 22 percent of the funds would be added or subtracted from state shares. Further, the shares of about three-quarters (38/51) of the states would change by more than 10 percent. These states contain 78 percent of the U.S. population. When using the preferred alternative with a 50 percent prevention weight and a constrained COSI, a smaller percentage of the allocation is shifted (15 percent), and a smaller percentage of the population is in states with shares affected more than 10 percent (58 percent).

Table 7.12 lists the correlations of several characteristics with the ratio of shares from the preferred alternative to those from the current formula. In general, urbanicity has the largest correlation with the change from the current system to one of the alternatives, and state population size is also strongly related. The negative correlations indicate that smaller rural states would in general receive increased shares under the alternatives. Figure 7.4 graphs these ratios ordered from low urbanicity on the left to high urbanicity on the right, using the preferred alternative that weights prevention at 20 percent of total need, and leaves the alternative cost index unconstrained.

Although Figure 7.4 illustrates a very large shift from urban to rural states when the preferred alternative measure of expenditure need is compared to the current formula's allocation, it is important to understand that the current formula tends to favor more urban states. Compared to an allocation that would be based solely on states'

Table 7.11

Total Effect on Substance Abuse Allocations of Changing Population Needs
and Cost of Service Indexes

	Preferred Alternative			
	20% for Prevention		50% for Prevention	
	Constrained	Unconstrained	Constrained	Unconstrained
Share of total allocation changed	19	22	15	17
Number of states with allocation changed by				
> 20% lower	7	7	5	5
10–20% lower	6	7	6	6
0–10% lower	5	9	5	9
0–10% higher	7	4	8	7
10–20% higher	2	2	4	3
> 20% higher	24	22	23	21
Percent of U.S. population in states with allocation changed by				
> 20% lower	2	25	13	15
10–20% lower	25	24	21	24
0–10% lower	11	17	19	20
0–10% higher	14	4	23	12
10–20% higher	12	1	7	14
> 20% higher	18	28	17	15

Table 7.12

Correlation of State Characteristics with Substance Abuse Allocations,
Changing Population Needs and Cost of Service Indexes

	Change to Preferred Alternative			
	20% for Prevention		50% for Prevention	
	Constrained	Unconstrained	Constrained	Unconstrained
State population size	–0.42	–0.38	–0.44	–0.40
State percent of population in urban areas	0.74	–0.66	–0.82	–0.74
State percent of population in poverty	0.12	0.05	0.17	0.10

population size, for example, the current formula tends to distribute larger allocations to urban states and smaller allocations to rural states. This is evident from the strong positive correlation of the difference between population-based allocation shares and allocation shares under the current formula of 0.86. Compared to a purely population-based allocation, the preferred alternative measure of expenditure need tends to distribute larger allocations to rural states and smaller allocations to urban states, but this favoring of rural states is a much smaller effect than the current formula's favoring of urban states. The correlation of the difference between population-based allocation shares and the allocation shares under the preferred alternative expenditure need measure is only 0.32.

Thus, the large shift from urban to more rural states when comparing allocations under the current formula to those using our preferred measure of expenditure need is in part the result of the current formula's heavier weighting of urban population

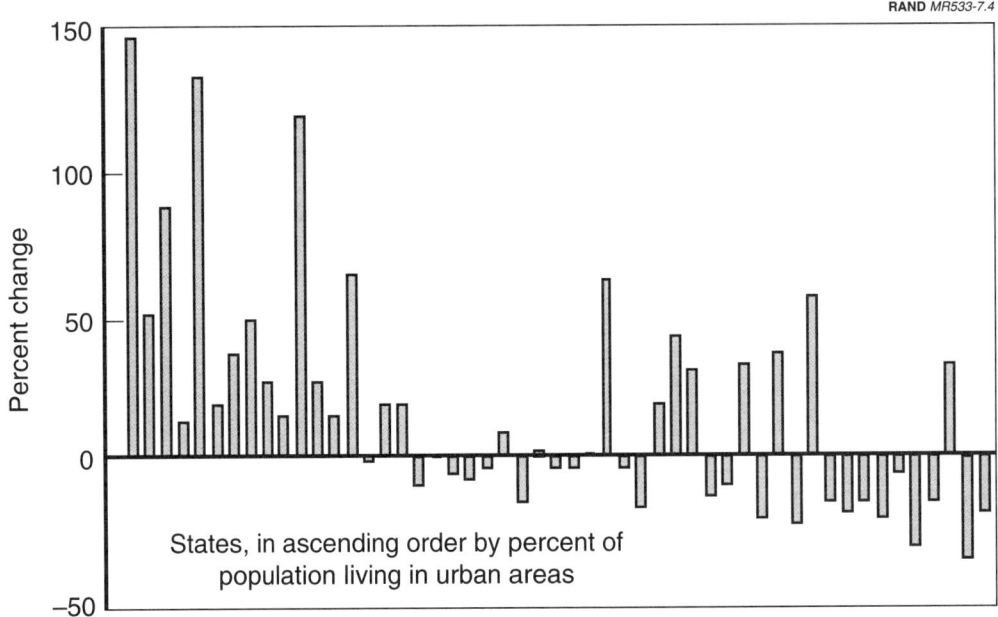

Figure 7.4—Percentage Change in the Substance Abuse Allocation Under the Preferred Alternative Measure of Expenditure Need, by State

needs. This is illustrated in Figure 7.5, which shows the percentage change from a simple population-based allocation for both the current formula and our preferred alternative, with states ordered from low urbanicity on the left to high urbanicity on the right.

POVERTY AND POPULATION NEED FOR SERVICES

The results in this section examine the implications of restricting the definition of the population in need of services to those who are at or below poverty level. Although Congress to date has chosen to view the population in need of services quite broadly, irrespective of poverty level, in practice most of the services funded by the MH and SA Block Grant go to those who are poor and either have no health insurance or have limited insurance benefits that do not cover the MH and SA services they need. In the future, Congress may wish to consider restricting the definition of population need to those who both need services and are unable to privately pay for them. This series of supplementary analyses was conducted to provide preliminary evidence regarding the implications of such a restricted definition of population need. In these analyses, we use the preferred alternative population need and cost of service indicators as above, but additionally define individuals to be in need of services only if they reside in a household that is at or below poverty level.

We first consider the mental health allocation. Table 7.13 shows the effect on the mental health services Block Grant allocation of changing from the current formula to one which uses our preferred measures of mental health population need and cost of services, and in addition, restricts the indicator of population need to those in

Evaluation of the Effects of Alternative Component Definitions in Allotment Formulas 113

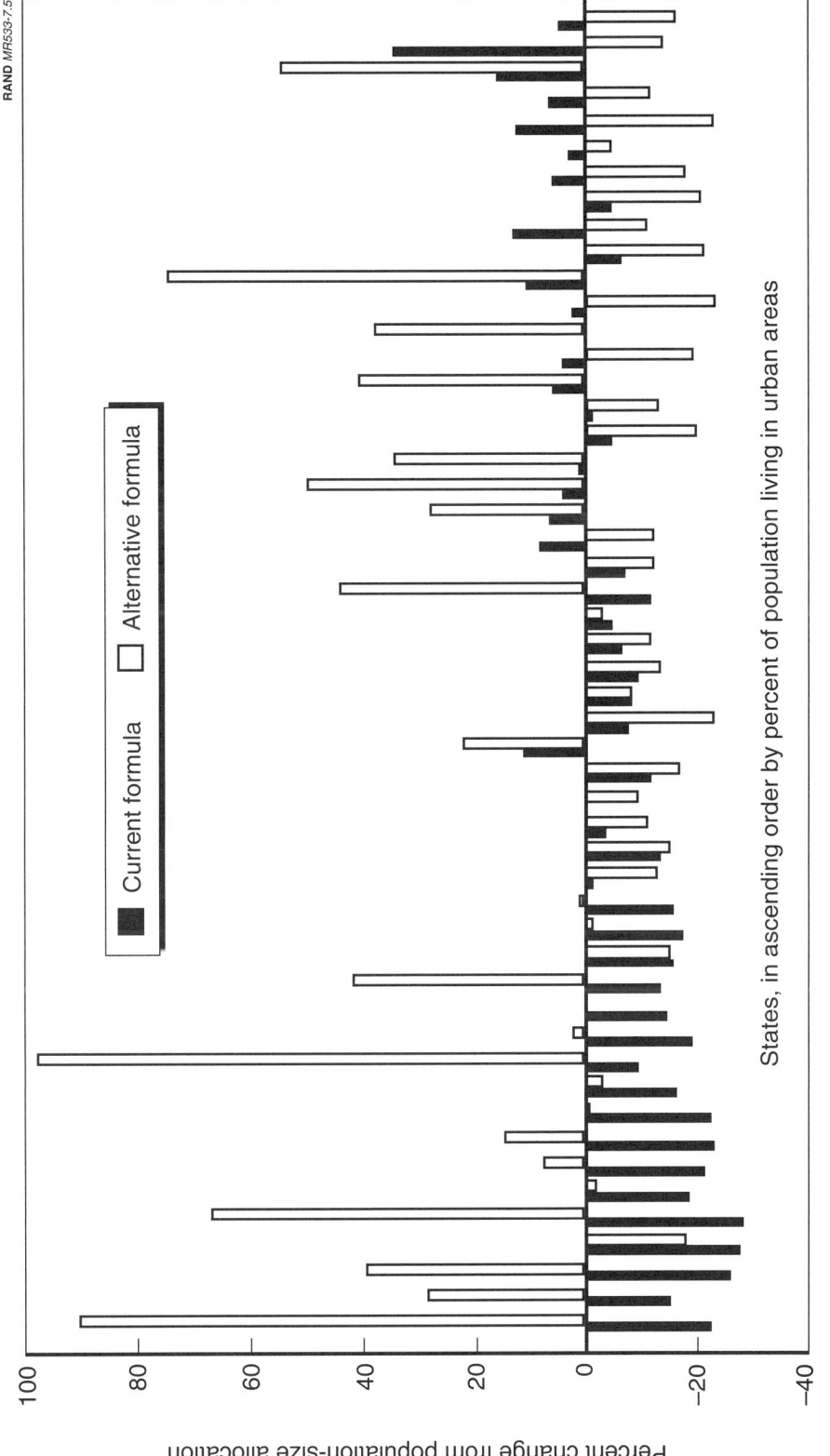

Figure 7.5—Percentage Change in the Substance Abuse Allocation from an Allocation Based Only on Population Size Under the Current Formula and the Preferred Alternative Measure, by State

Table 7.13

Total Effect on Mental Health Allocations of Changing Population
Needs and Cost of Service Indexes and Restricting
Population Need to Poverty Population

	Preferred Alternative	
	Constrained	Unconstrained
Share of total allocation changed	19	16
Number of states with allocation changed by		
> 20% lower	8	10
10–20% lower	8	7
0–10% lower	5	9
0–10% higher	8	8
10–20% higher	6	1
> 20% higher	16	16
Percent of U.S. population in states with allocation changed by		
> 20% lower	20	13
10–20% lower	20	21
0–10% lower	19	27
0–10% higher	10	15
10–20% higher	9	3
> 20% higher	21	21

poverty. The poverty restriction would have a large effect on the mental health allocation, shifting up to 19 percent of the total allocation across states (with the cost of service indicator constrained). The shares of most states (38) would shift by 10 percent or more; with about 70 percent of the population residing in these heavily affected states. The shifts in allocations are highly correlated with state poverty population and urban population. Table 7.14 shows that, relative to the current formula, the alternative that also restricts the population in need to those in poverty would shift the mental health allocation from wealthier to poorer states, and from urban to more rural states. While we would expect shifts in the mental health allotment to be correlated with state poverty level, as we saw previously, this correlation is now particularly high. These results showing major shifts in the mental health allocation contrast with the much smaller shifts that would occur if the population in need were not restricted to those in poverty—as shown above in Table 7.9, only 5 percent of the total mental health allocation would shift in the absence of the poverty population restriction.

Table 7.14

Correlation of State Characteristics with Mental Health Allocations,
Changing Population Needs and Cost of Service Indexes, and
Restricting Population Need to Poverty Population

	Change to Preferred Alternative	
Correlation with	Constrained	Unconstrained
State population size	–0.20	–0.15
State percent of population in urban areas	–0.48	–0.41
State percent of population in poverty	0.90	0.90

Table 7.15 gives parallel results for the substance abuse Block Grant allocations, comparing the allocations using our preferred measures of population need and cost of services, and restricting the population in need to those in poverty-level households. When the preferred indicator of population need is restricted to the poverty population, the substance abuse allocation shifts further from the current formula's distribution. A shift of 29 percent of the allocation would occur across states (with prevention weighted at 20 percent of need and with the cost of service index unconstrained). This compares to a shift of 22 percent of the allocation when the population need index is not restricted to the poverty population (shown in Table 7.11). As expected, the addition of the poverty restriction for the population in need causes the allocation shifts across states to be more strongly correlated with states' percentage of poverty population, as shown in Table 7.16. As before, the substance abuse allocations would be further shifted to smaller and more rural states.

Table 7.15

Total Effect on Substance Abuse Allocations of Changing Population Needs and Cost of Service Indexes, and Restricting Population Need to Poverty Population

	Preferred Alternative			
	20% for Prevention		50% for Prevention	
	Constrained	Unconstrained	Constrained	Unconstrained
Share of total allocation changed	27	29	21	21
Number of states with allocation changed by				
> 20% lower	11	13	8	11
10–20% lower	5	4	5	3
0–10% lower	3	4	4	5
0–10% higher	7	3	8	7
10–20% higher	2	4	4	4
> 20% higher	23	23	22	21
Percent of U.S. population in states with allocation changed by				
> 20% lower	35	40	21	34
10–20% lower	7	6	14	6
0–10% lower	9	8	21	11
0–10% higher	25	11	19	16
10–20% higher	3	4	6	16
> 20% higher	20	31	19	17

Table 7.16

Correlation of State Characteristics with Substance Abuse Allocations, Changing Population Needs and Cost of Service Indexes, and Restricting Population Need to Poverty Population

	Preferred Alternative			
	20% for Prevention		50% for Prevention	
	Constrained	Unconstrained	Constrained	Unconstrained
State population size	−0.37	−0.39	−0.39	−0.42
State percent of population in urban areas	−0.77	−0.80	−0.82	−0.85
State percent of population in poverty	0.55	0.57	0.49	0.53

SUMMARY

We now summarize results to evaluate each of the components of the current formula. Table 7.17 summarizes the percentage of the grant shifted for changes from the current system to the preferred alternative or standard to which it was compared. This is done for need and cost separately as well as together. Changes in the fiscal capacity measure have negligible effect compared with these changes.

As the table shows, a change in the need estimator from the current system to the preferred predictor shifts 5 percent of the total allocation for mental health services and 18 percent for substance abuse services (with prevention need weighted at 20 percent of total need). Changing the cost index from the current method to the preferred predictor alternative (unconstrained) without changing the need estimator would result in a 7 percent shift for mental health and an 8 percent shift for substance abuse services. When both need and cost are changed for mental health services, 7 percent of the total allocation is shifted, not much more than the effect of either the cost index change or the needs change alone.

When both need and cost are changed for substance abuse services, 22 percent of the grant is shifted, more of a shift than either change produces alone. The equal prevention and treatment population needs balance results in an allocation that is similar to the 20 percent prevention needs balance but is somewhat less of a change. This is due to the relatively higher correlation of the prevention population needs index with the current formula's population needs index. When the population need indicator is defined to include need only among the poverty population, and both the need and cost indicators are changed, the mental health and substance abuse service allocations are both shifted even further from the current formula. Restricting the population in need to those in poverty has a much greater effect on the mental health allocation, where the shift across states goes from 7 percent to 19 percent of the allocation, than on the substance abuse allocations, where the shift (when prevention is 20 percent of total need) moves from 22 percent to 29 percent of the allocation.

Alternative population need estimators have a larger effect on the substance abuse services allocations than they have on the mental health services allocations. The cost index has a similar effect in both cases; however, the multiplicative effects of need and cost show that use of both alternative measures has much greater effect on the allocation of funds for substance abuse than mental health services.

Table 7.17

Percentage Shift in Grant Allocations Due to Need and Cost Components

Change	Mental Health	Substance Abuse (20% for Prevention)	Substance Abuse (50% for Prevention)
Need only	5	18	13
Cost only	7	8	8
Need and cost	7	22	17
Poverty need and cost	19	29	21

Chapter Eight
CONCLUSIONS

The goal of this study, as specified in the authorizing legislation, was to evaluate how well the current mental health and substance abuse Block Grant formulas perform in distributing funds equitably across states, and to assess additional factors that might be included in the formulas to improve them. The first consideration in this study, therefore, was to determine more precisely what concept of "equity" Congress intended. A conceptual analysis of the underlying structure of the current Block Grant formulas reveals that they are variants of a taxpayer equity approach to transfer programs in that the design equalizes, across states, the potential tax rates taxpayers would have to pay to support a standard level of service (in this case a standard level of care for individuals with need for mental health or substance abuse services) provided to the population needing services. Although other approaches to equity could be taken, the taxpayer equity approach is reasonable and the basic structure of the formulas appropriately represents this approach. Our study does not question this concept of equity.

However, it is important to realize that the current structure of the formulas considers equity only with respect to the distribution of the Block Grant funds themselves, rather than considering equity across the full range of federal programs that fund mental health and substance abuse services (such as Medicaid and Medicare programs). Because the Block Grant funds are a relatively small share of public expenditures on these services, equalizing taxpayer equity across states in the distribution of Block Grant funds has limited capacity to equalize publicly supported mental health and substance abuse treatment services across states. Indeed, it is entirely possible that the current allocation formula, even with better implementation, exaggerates rather than lessens the differences among states. The authorizing legislation did not give us a mandate for exploring in detail how that problem might be resolved but it would probably involve assessing the distribution of other substance abuse and mental health funds among the states and subtracting those out for each state in calculating what is needed to achieve taxpayer equity.

Another implicit equity decision reflected in the formula is that needs for mental health and substance abuse services are represented as needs for the entire population of the states. Consistent with that assumption is the fact that the mandate for this study referred to population measures of substance abuse and mental illness. Because Block Grant funded mental health and substance abuse services are largely provided to the poor and uninsured, one could reasonably argue that variations across states in need for services should be estimated for this more narrowly defined population. We estimated the consequence of restricting estimates of need to this narrower population and found that indeed it did redistribute substantial additional funds from wealthier to poorer states.

This study's empirical analysis of the appropriateness of the Block Grant formulas accepted as given the underlying structure and implicit equity decisions contained in the current formulas. Such decisions are a matter of policy and not empirical analysis. The study's primary focus, then, was to evaluate how well the key components contained in the current formulas—population needs for services, costs of providing services, and state fiscal capacity—are measured and by implication how these measures (or indexes) might be improved. To carry out this evaluation, we conducted analyses of the best available relevant data to develop a range of alternative measures of each of these components. When the specification of an improved measure depended on policy considerations or intentions of which we were uncertain, we provided alternative measures to examine the sensitivity of our measures to different policy choices. Guided by our best understanding of the intent of the legislation and the results of our analyses, we selected a preferred alternative measure for each key construct, and considered this the "standard" against which to evaluate the adequacy of the measures used in the current formulas. The effects of alternatives different from our preferred ones are contained in the tables and figures of Appendix B.

The heart of our evaluation was a comparison of the Block Grant allocation shares received by the states under the current formulas relative to the distribution of allocation shares received if components of the formulas were indexed using the improved measures developed in this study. Results depended somewhat on specific policy decisions, such as how heavily prevention (as opposed to treatment) was to be weighted when defining population need for substance abuse services, and whether or not constraints should be placed on the range of values taken by the cost of services index. Nonetheless, three general conclusions can be drawn from this study's results irrespective of such policy choices.

1. *Substantial improvements can be made in the measures of both the population needs and cost of services components of the formula.*

The current indicator of population need for substance abuse services overweights urban populations. Our analysis finds that alcohol dependence is more prevalent in rural than metropolitan areas, while drug dependence is no higher in urban areas, once other sociodemographic predictors are taken into account. In addition, the current extra weighting for urban 18 to 24-year-olds is not supported by any evidence that this age group has high demands for treatment services; at the same time, the age group is also too old for primary prevention services. The incorporation of an explicit measure of prevention needs, which have a very different age distribution, also has an effect. When prevention needs are given a high weight the current formula works better, precisely because "use among youth," which drives prevention needs, has less variability among states than abuse/dependence among adults. The current indicator of mental health service needs considers only the population age distribution, which is a poor predictor of state variations in mental health need. The incorporation of other, more powerful sociodemographic predictors, including welfare or disability status, education, and marital status, shows that the current formula tends to overallocate to wealthier states.

The existing cost of services index was developed as a very rough heuristic when few relevant data were available. Newer data allow for a substantially more refined indicator that picks up a great deal more interstate variation, particularly for substance abuse. The true variation in cost of service provision is very great but the current formula, which considers only the cost of inputs (wages and rents) and not economies of scale, inappropriately favors urban areas.

The fiscal capacity component measure, on the other hand, appears to be appropriate and no improvements are indicated.

2. *If improvements in the formula such as those suggested by this study were implemented, the distribution of substance abuse service allocation shares across the states would definitely be heavily affected, and mental health service allocations would be heavily affected depending on how population need is defined.*

For example, if both population needs and cost of service measures were improved, results predict a shift of 17 to 22 percent of the total allocation across states (depending on the emphasis given to prevention versus treatment needs). If only the population needs measure were improved, shifts across states in the substance abuse allotment would still be large (13 to 18 percent of the allocation shares would shift). These shifts would tend to redistribute substance abuse allocation shares from larger urban to smaller and less urbanized states.

If the formula were reconceptualized to take account only of the variation in need across states among persons living in poverty, the redistribution would be even greater. As much as 29 percent of the funds would be redistributed for substance abuse services. Adding the requirement that population need be restricted to those in poverty would lead to a large redistribution of the mental health allocation, 16 percent of the funds, which otherwise would be a relatively small redistribution of 7 percent of the funds.

The decision to constrain cost variation in the formula has nontrivial consequences. Removing the constraints while implementing the more refined cost of service index would reallocate about another 3 percent of total funds as compared to implementing the new index and retaining the constraints; the redistribution would be to more rural states.

3. *Relatively small shifts in allocation shares would result if either or both of the component measures of the mental health formula were improved.*

For example, improvements in both population need and cost of service measures would result in a shift of about 7 percent of the total allocation, generally shifting mental health shares toward poorer states.

While the alternative measures of formula components developed by this study provide a sound basis for making improvements in the Block Grant formulas, the study was not mandated to explicitly generate or recommend new indexes that would be practical to implement. Such recommendations would need to take into account a number of implementation issues, such as whether (a) required data are easily available—for example, the rental cost index used here required, except for census years, complex matching of two datasets with varying definitions of specific metropolitan statistical areas; (b) they are updated frequently enough—for example, the cost of service index developed here depended on the decennial Census; by 1997 this will be substantially dated and some states may well argue that they are being unfairly penalized by use of such aged data; and (c) the time lag between assessment and availability of data is acceptable. These tasks were beyond the scope of the current study.

This study is of course limited by the scope and quality of existing and available data that were relevant to its aims. Three data limitations, in particular, should be noted, all of which concern the measurement of population need for services. First, there are no adequate national data on factors predicting need for mental health services among children, even though children with serious emotional disturbances are a defined target population for services funded by the mental health Block Grants. As a result, our models assume a constant rate of need among children across states (based on the existing but sparse epidemiologic data that are available). Because the proportion of children in the total population varies little across states, however, the incorporation of this nonvariant rate of need into an improved assessment of total mental health population needs had negligible effect. If better epidemiologic data on child mental health needs were available, the incorporation of factors predicting such needs into the formula might have had more effect on our results.

Another limitation of the data is that household surveys fail to include some populations at high risk of heavy drug use, including those who are homeless, transient, and incarcerated. Thus, our estimates of need for substance abuse treatment suffer from inadequate information on these excluded populations who, though small in number relative to the household population, may contain a substantial portion of those in need of treatment.

A third limitation affecting our estimates of state-level population needs for mental health and substance abuse services is that the best available data regarding factors predicting such needs are based on national survey samples. Predictive models based on these samples may not do a good job of estimating need for some states. This would be the case if the state is idiosyncratic (unique factors predict need in this state relative to other states) and not well represented in the national sample. Utah is a prominent example, with its high share of observant Mormons who respect strong strictures against use of any psychoactive substance. Available epidemiologic data relevant to substance abuse population needs contain only broad regional rather than state-level identifiers, thereby limiting investigation of geographic variation that could inform us about such idiosyncrasies. In addition, the samples are designed to allow representation of only broad geographic regions and not individual states; indeed, some sparsely populated states are not even sampled at all. In spite of these limitations, this study provides estimates of population need that fully utilize the most recent and comprehensive data available, and in that respect these estimates provide a reasonable and the best available standard for evaluating the appropriateness of the population needs component of the current formula.

The results of this study regarding the distribution of substance abuse treatment needs across states, where Western and rural states were found to have higher rates of need, raises the issue of whether it is appropriate to give equal weighting to need for treatment across all substances—that is, irrespective of whether the need is for treatment of alcohol, marijuana, cocaine, or heroin dependence. While this study's approach was to weight treatment need equally across substances, based on guidance from SAMHSA and current diagnostic criteria, there is a good rationale for weighting need for alcohol treatment less heavily than need for drug treatment, and perhaps distinguishing among different classes of drugs (for example, marijuana versus harder drugs like heroin). The result of equal weighting of alcohol and drug treatment need is that total estimates of substance abuse treatment need across states are dominated by alcohol dependence, which is approximately three times more prevalent than drug dependence in the household population. Although both alcohol and drug dependence are very costly to society and to the affected individuals, it is likely that the social costs associated with an individual drug abuser are, on average, substantially higher than those associated with an individual case of alcohol abuse. That is because so many of the costs of drug abuse are crime related and are borne by society rather than by the individual.[1]

One could reasonably argue, then, that publicly funded substance abuse services should give higher priority to treating those substance use disorders associated with greater social costs. The substance abuse services Block Grant formula could easily incorporate a measure of population need for treatment that differentially weighted need for alcohol and drug treatment. It would also be possible to implement different weights for treatment of different types of drugs (for example, marijuana versus other drugs). If low-prevalence drugs such as heroin were heavily weighted relative to other substances, however, the household survey data would be inadequate for estimating state variations in treatment need.

If Congress wishes to give further consideration to any of the implicit equity decisions—that is, whether other federal programs funding mental health and substance abuse services should be taken into account in the equity formulation, whether drug treatment need should be given a higher weight than alcohol treatment need, and whether the definition of population needs for services should be restricted to the poor and uninsured population—issues of how to implement the alternative approaches into the current formula would also have to be assessed.

This study should be seen as one more on the path to improving the equity of federal allocations for substance abuse and mental health services by the states. As more data are collected and our understanding of these social problems improve, the formulas will be further refined. However, enough new data and analysis have become

---

[1] On the aggregate and individual costs of alcohol and drug abuse, see Rice (1990).

available since the basics for the formula were developed that it is already possible to significantly improve the allocation of funds by refining the measures used.

Finally, we note that the equity of Block Grant formulas is becoming more salient since Congress passed welfare reform legislation, which turns a number of entitlements, such as AFDC, into state Block Grants. The substance abuse and mental health Block Grant formula is one of the most sophisticated, with its continuing refinement of measures of population in need, and the taxpayer equity structure that takes into account not only population in need, but cost of services and state fiscal capacity. The difficulties experienced over a decade in developing a substance abuse and mental health formula that is both technically sound and can generate political support points to the problems that lie ahead for these much larger Block Grants.

We believe that there are three lessons to be derived from our analysis for the larger issue of developing Block Grant formulas.

First, the substance abuse and mental health allocation formula has been a moving target, driven in large part by increasing sophistication of relevant data and analysis that has exposed the weaknesses of whatever is the current formula. The fact that some state always, and with justification, believes that a revision of the formula to incorporate newer findings would be to its advantage is an important instigating process.

This reflects the fact that there is no "correct" allocation formula. The formula must reflect changing views about equity and knowledge of the beneficiary populations. Our continuing investment in data and research on social problems such as substance abuse and mental health is arguably a major factor in the instability of the formula; that is not an argument against such investments (which are modest enough) but an appreciation of yet another unintended consequence. That is likely to be the case for other Block Grants as well.

Second, we note the tension that comes from bundling of services within a single grant formula. The substance abuse and mental health formula puts drug abuse and alcohol abuse together consistent with the current public health view that legal status is an inappropriate basis for public health responses to substances. Our findings that the current formula gives too heavy a weight to urban states because alcohol abuse and dependence dominate the need measure may lead to a demand for distinguishing the two components of substance abuse treatment need. That may occur with other Block Grant allocation formulas, precisely because they bundle disparate services.

Third, Congress may find itself having to confront revisions in Block Grant formulas on a regular basis. The substance abuse and mental health Block Grants have already been subject to four major revisions since 1981. These revisions involve painful political conflicts, because of the lack of an authoritative and value-free formula. With larger sums and a broader array of services and populations involved, the conflicts may well be even more serious in the future, with an important role to be served by analysis of available data to inform the debate.

Appendix A

CONCEPTUAL ANALYSIS OF THE BLOCK GRANT FORMULA

This appendix examines the conceptual underpinnings of the current SA and MH services Block Grant formula. We show that it is a very minor variation on a generic specification of a formula designed to allocate funds based on what has been called the "taxpayer equity" concept. In the course of the explanation, we also show the equivalence among alternative statements of the taxpayer equity formula; alternative formulations proved convenient in this study to highlight the individual effects of the measures used in the formula.

FORMULAS FOR ALTERNATIVE EQUITY CONCEPTS

For many decades, legislative and judicial bodies at both the state and federal levels have debated concepts of equity for funding a wide variety of programs. The concepts and terminology used in this appendix draw specifically from recent literature concerning federal Block Grant programs similar to the SA and MH services program.

Specifically, a GAO report (1992, pp. 52–59) on Block Grants for maternal and child health describes two alternative standards of equity on which grant allocations may be based. One, labeled "beneficiary equity," would equalize the federally funded share of the cost of providing a standard level of service to all persons in need, regardless of the states in which they reside. The alternative, described as "taxpayer equity," equalizes the potential tax rates taxpayers in all states would have to pay to support that standard level of service.

For both equity standards, a basic concept used in deriving grant formulas is "Expenditure Need," hereafter denoted E. It represents the aggregate expenditure necessary to provide the standard level of service to all persons in need and might be financed by any combination of federal, state, and local funds. For use in grant allocation formulas, E is measured at the state level; the GAO analysis specified it as follows:

$$E_i = P_i * n_i * c_i * \bar{e}, \tag{A.1}$$

where

i = a recipient state or other entity, $i = 1, \ldots, I$[1]

P_i = the total population of state i

n_i = the population in need index for state i

c_i = the cost index for state i (i.e., the ratio of the cost of providing a standard level of service per beneficiary in state i to the national average cost)

$\bar{e}$ = the standard level of service, expressed as a nationwide average expenditure level per capita.

The beneficiary equity criterion is that federal funds should be allocated to support a constant share of E in all states. Alternatively, the taxpayer equity criterion is that federal funding should make up the difference between E and the portion of E that could be funded by state and local governments if they taxed their fiscal capacities at the same (standardized) rate.

A single generic grant formula can represent either concept, as follows:

$$G_i = E_i * [\alpha - \beta * (y_i / (n_i * c_i * \bar{y}))], \quad (A.2)$$

where

α and β = policy parameters

G_i = the grant computed for state i

y_i = the state's per-capita fiscal capacity

$\bar{y}$ = nationwide per capita fiscal capacity.

The choice of an equity concept is implemented by setting a value for β. If β is zero, the grant amount is a constant share of each state's expenditure need and supports the same share of intended services (α) for all beneficiaries; but if β exceeds zero, then the federal share of E varies with each state's fiscal capacity in a way that equalizes potential taxpayer burdens.

Various ways of restating Equation (A.2) provide some insight into how the two equity concepts would affect the distribution of federal funds. First, if we move the $n_i * c_i$ portion of E_i inside the brackets in Equation (A.2), we can rewrite the generic formula as:

$$G_i = \bar{e} P_i [\alpha n_i c_i - \beta f_i], \quad (A.3)$$

---

[1] Hereafter, "state" will be used to refer to any of the fiscal entities represented by i.

where f_i is defined as $(y_i / \bar{y})$ and is readily interpreted as a relative index of state fiscal capacity similar to the indexes of needs and costs. This version of the generic formula emphasizes that the beneficiary and taxpayer equity concepts are variants of a simple per-capita distribution of funds. That is, if per-capita rates of need, cost rates for services, and fiscal capacities were the same for all states, either equity concept would simply allocate funds in proportion to P, total state population. Therefore, we should expect state population size to be a key determinant of funding allocations under either of these concepts, a finding that is confirmed empirically in Chapter Seven.

Alternatively, divide the bracketed term in Equation (A.2) by α to obtain:

$$G_i = (\alpha\bar{e})(P_i n_i c_i)[1 - \rho(y_i / (n_i * c_i * \bar{y})], \qquad (A.4)$$

where ρ is defined as β/α. In this version of the formula, we may interpret $\bar{e}$ as some objectively determined target for the standard level of spending per capita, and α as the portion of $\bar{e}$ policymakers deem appropriate for funding from public (federal plus state and local) sources. Below, we will see that "normalizing" a grant formula to make the sum of the state grants meet a prespecified total federal spending level is equivalent to setting a value for α in Equation (A.4).

Finally, move P_i inside the brackets of Equation A.3 to obtain:

$$G_i = \alpha\bar{e}[n_i c_i P_i - \rho F_i / \bar{y}], \qquad (A.5)$$

where F_i is a state's total fiscal capacity. Now the first term inside the brackets represents a cost-adjusted measure of population in need, and the second term may be interpreted as the number of people the state could afford to serve if it had average costs and taxed itself at an average rate.[2] Since this specification of the fiscal capacity component is independent of the measures of population in need or costs of service, it was used in Chapter Six to evaluate alternative measures of fiscal capacity.

THE CURRENTLY LEGISLATED SA AND MH SERVICES FORMULAS

Public Law 102-321 (July 10, 1992) specifies that the grant award to a state, here denoted B, will be determined as follows:[3]

$$B_i = A(X_i / \sum_i X_i) \qquad (A.6)$$

where A is the total (SA or MH) funding available for distribution according to the formula, and X_i is the product of three terms that represent population in need (here denoted by N_i because we have defined P as total state population), a cost index specified like the one in the generic formulas above (and hence denoted by c_i), and an adjustment for fiscal capacity. In our notation,

---

[2] Notice that F is measured in dollars and $\bar{y}$ is measured in dollars per person. Dollars divided by dollars per person yields a count of people.

[3] The legislation uses U to represent $\sum_i X_i$.

$$X_i = N_i * c_i(1 - .35R\% / N\%), \tag{A.7}$$

where R is a cost-adjusted measure of fiscal capacity, and the "%" notation indicates a ratio of R_i or N_i to the sum of that measure over all states. Below, we will show that Equations (A.6) and (A.7) constitute a variant of the taxpayer equity formula described above.

The current legislation also includes several provisions that are irrelevant to this appendix: Grant awards for substance abuse and mental health services are determined separately, using different values of A and different formulas for calculating N_i. The legislation restricts the values of the cost index and the last term in Equation (A.7)[4] and includes hold-harmless provisions that prevent the formula from reducing grant awards below prior levels. And the legislation requires states to meet various conditions to receive their full grant amounts. In this appendix, however, our interest is in how the legislated formulas compare with the generic formulas for alternative equity concepts, regardless of how the variables in each formula are measured and prior to additional (nonformula) restrictions on the awards.

COMPARISON BETWEEN THE LEGISLATED AND EQUITY FORMULAS

Behavioral Independence

A key feature of a funding formula is whether it is designed to create incentives for recipients by rewarding or penalizing their behavior. For example, matching-grant formulas reward recipient entities for raising their own funds to support a program and hence tend to induce revenue-raising activities. In contrast, the equity concepts outlined above are *not* designed to create incentives for state and local entities. Grant funding is based on a *standardized* level of services (determined by $\bar{e}$) regardless of whether a state provides a higher or lower level of care, on populations *in need* ($n_i P_i$) regardless of whether a state actually serves all of its eligible population, and on the states' fiscal capacities (y_i) regardless of how heavily they tax their residents. The grant awards would vary among states only according to inherent differences in population characteristics, resource costs, and revenue potential.

The SA and MH services grant legislation employs those same provisions. The legislation measures potential population in need based on a state's total population and its age and urbanicity characteristics, uses total taxable resources to measure potential state fiscal capacity rather than actual fiscal effort (see Chapter Six), and mandates the use of a cost-estimation methodology (the HER method described in Chapter Five) that is based on a state's resource prices but not its actual resource utilization. Since a state's actual behavior with regard to SA and MH services delivery or taxation does not enter into the legislated formula, it does not provide incentives for states to modify behavior to influence grant amounts.

---

[4] I.e., it cannot be less than 0.4.

Closed-Ended Funding via Grant "Normalization"

Among the most basic policy decisions about a funding program is whether it will be closed or open-ended. A program is closed if the total funding level is determined in advance and the funding formula allocates that fixed total among recipients. In contrast, a program like Medicare is open-ended because the total funding level is determined by the size of the eligible population and the rules governing levels of support per beneficiary. The SA and MH services legislation clearly provides for a closed-ended funding program, where A is the total funding amount to be expended.

As specified in Equation (A.2), the beneficiary and taxpayer equity concepts appear to be open-ended. That is, if α, β, and $\bar{e}$ were set in advance, the total federal funding for grants would be determined by the sum of the states' grant awards, which in turn are determined by population, cost rates, and (if β is nonzero) fiscal capacity.

However, the beneficiary and taxpayer equity concepts are consistent with a closed-ended program if the parameter α is set so that the funding allocations exactly exhaust the total funding available under the formula, i.e., when

$$\alpha \equiv (A / \sum Z_i) / \bar{e},$$

where

$$Z_i \equiv P_i n_i c_i (1 - \rho y_i / \bar{y}). \tag{A.8}$$

Making this substitution for α in Equation (A.4) yields the following closed-ended generic equity formula:

$$G = (A / \sum Z_i) P_i n_i c_i (1 - \rho y_i / \bar{y}) = A(Z_i / \sum Z_i). \tag{A.9}$$

Notice that Equation (A.9) resembles the legislated SA and MH services formula in Equation (A.6). If the formulas for X_i and Z_i are equivalent, a matter we consider next, then the SA and MH services grant formula matches the equity formula.

Comparing X and Z

Compared with Equation (A.4) for the generic equity formula, the legislated formula replaces $P_i * n_i$ with N_i, and replaces $1 - \rho y_i / (n_i * c_i * \bar{y})$ with $(1 - .35\ R\%/P\%)$. Technically, these replacements distinguish the legislated formula from the generic one. In practice, however, when the fundamental variables (population, persons in need, costs of services, etc.) are measured the same way, these differences in mathematical specification have no observable effect on the actual allocation of a given total funding level, and the legislated formula functions like a closed-end taxpayer equity formula.

128 The Substance Abuse and Mental Health Services Block Grant Allotment Formula

Technically, Z_i in the generic formula differs from X_i in the legislated formula because a count of persons in need is not identical to the product of total population and a needs index. In the generic formula, the need index is defined as:

$$n_i = (N_i / P_i) / \overline{n},$$

where

$$\overline{n} \equiv \sum_i N_i / \sum_i P_i. \tag{A.10}$$

Therefore, $N_i = P_i n_i \overline{n}$ and the legislated formula for X_i implicitly includes the factor $\overline{n}$, which does not appear in the generic formula for Z_i. However, when grants are normalized to match a given funding total, multiplying all state values by a constant such as $\overline{n}$ has no effect on the allocation of funds.[5] Therefore, even when population in need is estimated by an equation that does not make it strictly proportional to state population (as is the case in both the substance abuse and mental health SA and MH services formulas), using that measure in the normalized grant formula does not cause it to differ from the general equity formula.

Similarly, for given measures of fiscal capacity (F) and the cost of service index (c), replacing $1 - \rho y_i / (n_i * c_i * \overline{y})$ with $(1 - .35\, R\%/P\%)$ has no effect on the allocations of grant awards under a normalized formula. In this case, however, the respecification has some effect on our interpretation of the parameter ρ.

Translating the definitions of R% and N% in the SA and MH services legislation into our notation, we have

$$R\% / N\% = [(F_i / c_i) / \sum_i (F_i / c_i)] / [N_i \sum_i N_i] = F_i \sum_i N_i / N_i c_i \sum_i (F_i / c_i), \tag{A.11}$$

whereas rearranging the terms in the generic formula yields:

$$y_i / (n_i * c_i * \overline{y}) = F_i \sum_i N_i / N_i c_i \sum_i F, \tag{A.12}$$

which in turn implies that

$$R\% / N\% = \overline{r} * y_i / (n_i * c_i * \overline{y}), \quad \text{where} \quad \overline{r} = \sum_i F_i / \sum_i (F_i / c_i). \tag{A.13}$$

In any given year, the value of $\overline{r}$ in Equation (A.13) will be constant across all states. Thus, using the legislated formula is equivalent to using the generic formula, where $\rho = 0.35\, \overline{r}$.

---

[5]Mathematically, $P_i n_i / \sum_i P_i n_i = N_i / \sum_i n_i$, which also implies that R%/N% in Equation (A.9) equals R%/P%.

In principle, $\bar{r}$ could vary over time, suggesting that the implied value of ρ would also change if the value 0.35 is held constant under the legislated formula. However, this effect has little operational significance because $\bar{r}$ will rarely (if ever) differ noticeably from 1.0. This conclusion was verified by an analysis of $\bar{r}$ based on actual measures of fiscal capacity and the cost index, including the measures currently being used and the alternatives we considered in this study.

Summary of the Comparison of Formulas

In summary, we have shown that the legislated formula allocates funds independently of state behavior and normalizes the awards to meet a given funding total in a manner that is consistent with a closed-ended form of the generic equity formula. The legislated formula implicitly contains two factors, $\bar{n}$ and $\bar{r}$, that are not found in the generic equity formula. However, under a normalized grant formula, the factor $\bar{n}$ effectively drops out of the formula, and the factor $\bar{r}$ is simply a constant that conceptually modifies the value of the fiscal capacity parameter, ρ, but still renders it (and hence β) nonzero. The conclusion is that the currently legislated formula is a closed-ended application of the taxpayer equity concept.

Appendix B
ALTERNATIVE MEASURES, STATISTICAL ISSUES

In this appendix, we describe the results of alternative models that were not described in Chapters Three, Four, and Seven. In the first section, we consider how definitions of population in need of substance abuse treatment broader than those described in Chapter Four would affect state-level estimates of need. In the second section, we examine how these definitions and the definitions from Chapters Three and Four not treated in Chapter Seven would affect allocations. In the third section, we consider a more complex multipart model of the need for substance abuse services. The last section examines the effects of alternative specifications in the modeling process: weighting, aggregation, and tract-level variables.

HOW DO ALTERNATIVE DEFINITIONS OF POPULATION IN NEED OF SUBSTANCE ABUSE TREATMENT AFFECT STATE-LEVEL ESTIMATES OF NEED?

In Chapter Four, we considered two definitions of population in need of treatment for substance abuse: those who met the DSM-III-R criteria for substance abuse, including either alcohol or drug abuse, and those who met the DSM-III-R criteria for drug abuse only. These are not the only definitions that could be used. A similar dependence measure encompassing both drug and alcohol abuse was developed by researchers in SAMHSA's Office for Applied Studies (OAS). This is summarized as Definition 1 in Table B.1; to differentiate it from our approximation of the DSM-III-R criteria, we call it the OAS dependence criteria and our definition the RAND dependence criteria.

We also considered another definition that broadens the dependence definition by including frequent drug users, and frequent and heavy alcohol users, in addition to persons meeting our "DSM-III-R" dependence criteria (Definition 2 in Table B.1). This definition might be considered the upper bound for any reasonable definition of the population in need of substance abuse treatment. Table B.2 shows the estimated prevalence in the national household population of the percentage of the population aged 12 and older in need of substance abuse treatment, when applying these definitions, as well as showing the RAND dependence definition for comparison.

Table B.1

Operational Definitions of Persons Needing Substance Abuse Treatment Services

Definition 1: Dependence—OAS Definition (DSM-III-R Criteria)
— Experienced 2 or more of the following problems with a specific drug or alcohol in the past year:
  1. Tried to, but unable to cut down use (A-2)
  2. Got less work done at school or on the job (A-5)
  3. Used drug in the past month and had health or psychological problems (i.e., depression, loneliness, nervousness, irritability, or concentration problems) or arguments and fights with family or friends (A-6)
  4. Needed greater quantities to achieve the same effect (A-7)
  5. Withdrawal symptoms (A-8)

Definition 2: Dependence or heavy use
— Dependence defined by the RAND dependence criteria (see Chapter Four)
— *Or* heavy alcohol use (consumed five or more drinks per day on at least five days in the past month)
— *Or* frequent drug use (used a specific type of drug at least once per week in the past year)

Table B.2

Prevalence of Substance Dependence in Household Population

	Percentage with	
Dependence (RAND Definition)	Dependence (OAS Definition)	Dependence or Heavy Use
6.8	5.4	15.7

Table B.3 shows the final reduced regression models for predicting these two alternative measures of need for treatment of substance dependence and substance abuse, as well as that for dependence or heavy use. Across all indicators of need for treatment, five demographic variables were highly predictive: males, white non-Hispanics, those who are separated or unmarried, those aged 18–44, and high school dropouts (followed by high school graduates without a college degree) have higher probability of needing treatment. Regional effects are also important for the two measures of need that focus on the more severe end of the spectrum (the definitions that exclude heavy users per se). Persons living in nonmetropolitan areas are more likely to have substance dependence or abuse than persons living in metropolitan areas. Those living in the Western region of the United States are also more likely to need treatment. For the broader definition that includes heavy substance users with or without problems of dependence, regional variables were not predictive. On the other hand, two additional demographic variables were important predictors of need for treatment: living alone and not attending school full time.

As in Chapter Four, we made simulations to estimate state-level rates of need for substance abuse treatment among adults and prevention needs among adolescents, based on the final predictive models described above. Our indirect estimation method takes the logistic regressions developed above and uses them to estimate the probability of the various substance abuse and prevention need definitions for each person in the 1 percent PUMS. These probabilities are then summed to the state level to get an expected number of persons in need.

Table B.3

Final Models: Factors Predicting Substance Dependence/Substance Abuse

Predictor	Odds Ratios (and 95% Confidence Intervals)					
	Dependence: RAND Definition		Dependence: OAS Definition		Dependence or Heavy Use	
Gender						
Female	1.0		1.0		1.0	
Male	1.8	(1.7–2.0)	1.9	(1.7–2.1)	2.8	(2.7–3.0)
Race						
White, non-Hispanic	1.4	(1.3–1.5)	1.2	(1.1–1.4)	1.4	(1.3–1.5)
Other	1.0		1.0		1.0	
Marital status						
Currently married	1.0		1.0		1.0	
Separated or not married	1.7	(1.6–1.9)	1.7	(1.5–1.9)	1.9	(1.8–2.1)
Age						
12–17 years	1.0		1.0		1.0	
18–34 years	2.2	(1.9–2.5)	1.9	(1.6–2.2)	2.9	(2.5–3.3)
35–44 years			1.5	(1.2–1.9)	2.4	(2.1–2.9)
45–54 years	1.5	(1.2–1.8)				
55–64 years			0.8	(0.6–1.0)	1.1	(0.9–1.3)
65 or older	0.7	(0.5–1.0)				
Education						
0–8 years	1.0		1.0		1.0	
9–11 years	2.5	(2.1–2.9)	2.6	(2.2–3.1)	2.3	(2.0–2.6)
High school graduate	1.9	(1.6–2.2)	2.0	(1.7–2.4)	1.6	(1.4–1.8)
College graduate	1.2	(1.0–1.5)	1.3	(1.0–1.6)	1.0	(0.8–1.1)
Student						
Full-time student					0.6	(0.6–0.7)
Not full-time student					1.0	
Number in household						
Living alone					1.0	
Not living alone					0.9	(0.8–1.0)
Population density						
In MSA	0.7	(0.6–0.8)	0.6	(0.6–0.7)		
Not in MSA	1.0		1.0			
Region						
Northwest			1.0			
North Central	1.0					
South			1.2	(1.1–1.3)		
West	1.6	(1.4–1.7)	1.6	(1.5–1.9)		

Table B.4 presents some descriptive statistics and correlations for the three needs estimators. The various models reflecting different ways of operationalizing need for substance abuse treatment and prevention services give state-level estimates that are not always highly correlated across operational definitions. The two criteria for approximating DSM-III-R dependence (RAND and OAS) contain considerable overlap and provide state-level estimates that correlate very highly. However, estimates based on both of these criteria correlate poorly with estimates that include heavy use as a cause for needing treatment. This is not altogether surprising given that many people satisfied our criteria for heavy use but not for dependence.

Figures B.1, B.2, and B.3 show that including heavy use pushes the Middle West states of Minnesota, Wisconsin, Michigan, Indiana, and Ohio into the top third of

Table B.4
Predicted Prevalence of Substance Dependence/Problems for States: Summary Statistics and Correlation Coefficients

	Treatment Needs Indicators		
	Dependence (RAND Definition)	Dependence (OAS Definition)	Dependence or Heavy Use
Summary statistics			
Mean	7.72	6.72	16.19
Std. dev.	1.70	1.52	0.56
Minimum	5.61	4.57	14.86
Maximum	11.94	10.40	18.08
Correlations			
Treatment needs indicators			
Substance abuse (OAS)	0.9464		
Dependence or heavy use	0.3537	0.2065	

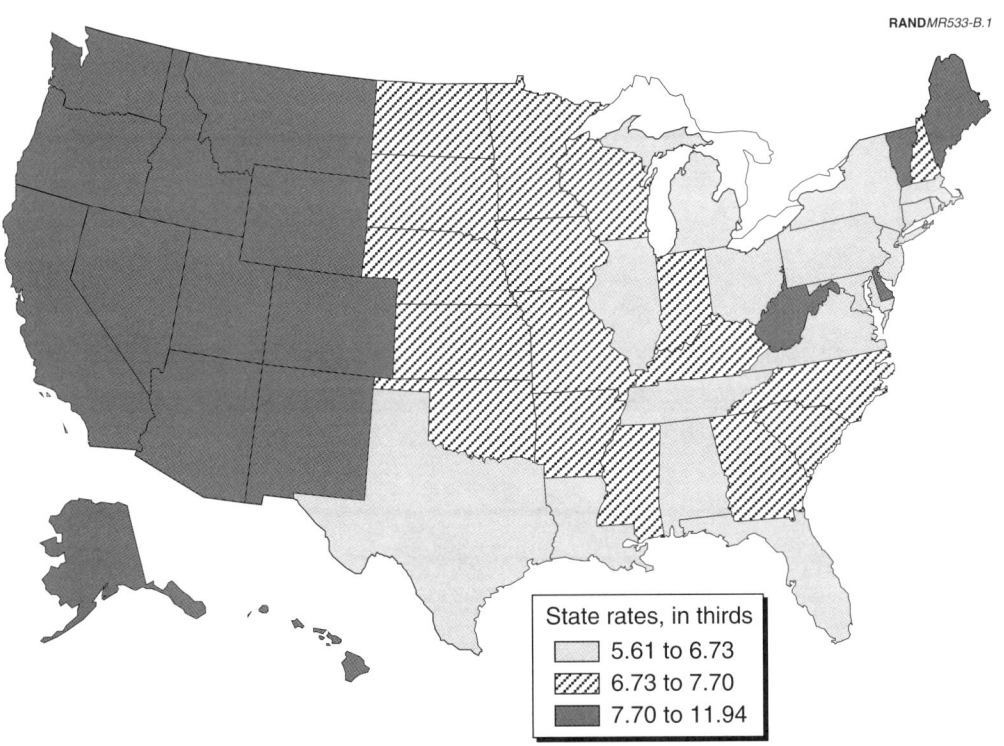

Figure B.1— Percentage of Population Meeting RAND Criteria for Drug or Alcohol Dependence, by State, NHSDA Data

states with the largest rate of need. Also, the new definition moves up Texas, Pennsylvania, Virginia, and Illinois into the middle third. On the other hand, California, Idaho, Montana, and West Virginia move out of the top third. Again, the limitations of this type of modeling are observable in the prediction of a large rate of need for Utah, a state with demographic characteristics not unlike its neighbors (Nevada and Arizona) but with a much lower alcohol consumption rate.

Alternative Measures, Statistical Issues 135

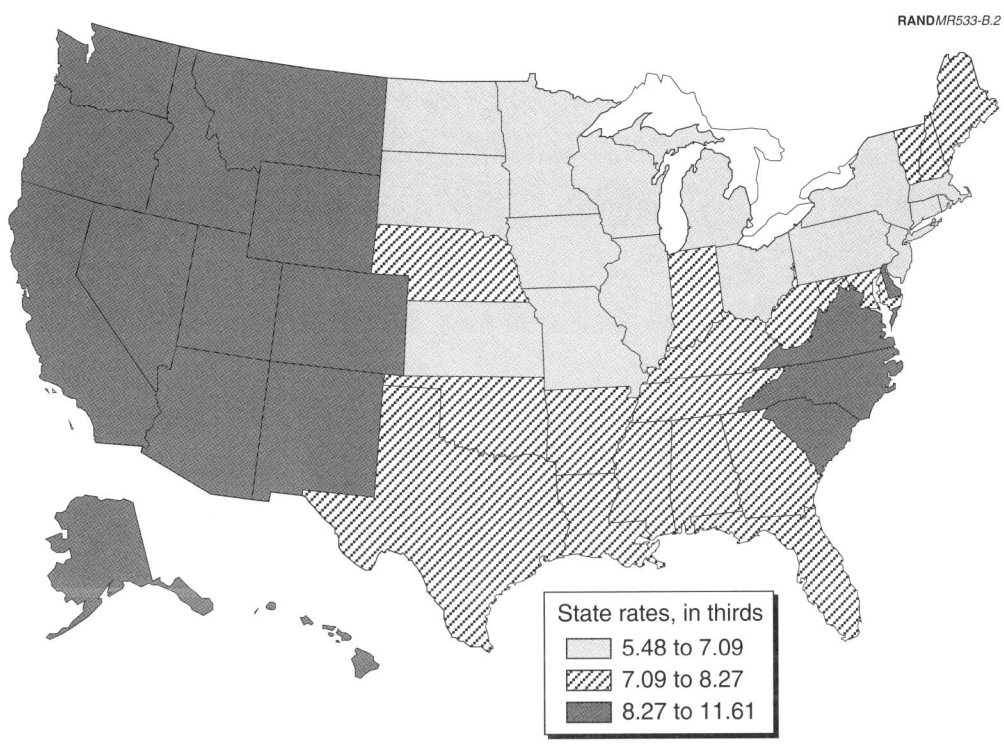

Figure B.2—Percentage of Population Meeting OAS Criteria for Drug or Alcohol Dependence, by State, NHSDA Data

Figures B.4, B.5, and B.6 show the relationship of needs for substance abuse treatment that we estimated for each state, with states ordered by percentage of population in urban areas. These figures illustrate that higher rates of need are predicted for less-urbanized states when definitions of need are based on prevalence of substance dependence. When the definition of need includes heavy use, however, the relationship of need to state urbanicity is reduced.

HOW DO ALTERNATIVE DEFINITIONS OF NEED AFFECT THE ALLOCATIONS?

Chapter Seven examined how the Block Grant allocations would be affected if, instead of the current indicators, our preferred alternative indicators were used. This section shows the effects of the alternatives that were not "preferred," as well as, for comparison, the results of those that were.

Mental Health

In Chapter Three, we described two definitions of serious mental illness: A "broader" definition was based on the DSM-III-R criteria for several mental disorders, a "narrower" definition on these criteria plus additional severity criteria. Severe cognitive impairment was also included in these definitions. These two definitions

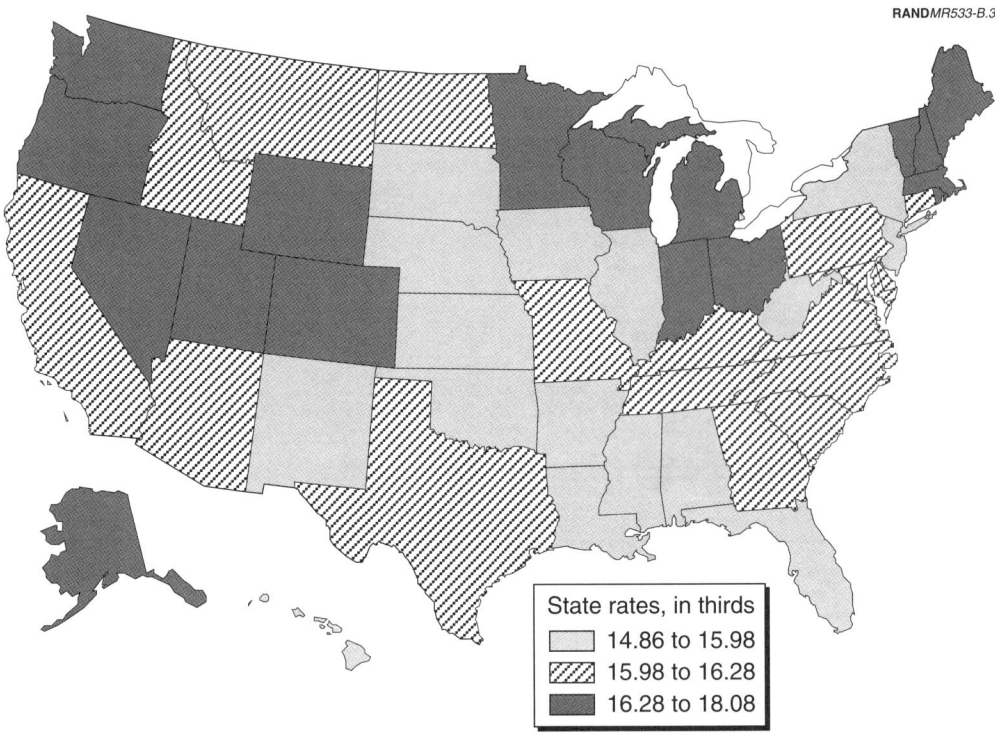

Figure B.3—Percentage of Population Meeting RAND Criteria for Substance Dependence, or Making Heavy Use of a Substance, by State, NHSDA Data

were expanded to four by including a measure of time—mental illness in the last year or in the last month. Each of these four definitions is used in examining data from the ECA and from the NCS.

Population in Need of Mental Health Services. Table B.5 summarizes the shifts in state shares under each of the four definitions of population in need of mental health services using the NCS data and the ECA data. The preferred alternative used in Chapter Seven was the broadly defined 30-day rate from the NCS. The 5 percent of the total shifted by the preferred alternative is in the middle of shifts associated with the eight alternatives. The preferred alternative typically moves states more than the other definitions using the NCS data, but less than the definitions using the ECA data.

Table B.6 presents the correlations between the change in state shares and several state characteristics: population, urbanicity, and poverty. The signs of these correlations are consistent across all eight definitions. All of the changes are negatively associated with urbanicity and positively associated with population and poverty. In seven of the eight cases, the strongest correlation is with state poverty.

Mental Health Expenditure Needs. Table B.7 summarizes the shifts in state shares under the eight definitions of population in need of mental health services combined with the cost of services index currently used and the alternative indicator we

Alternative Measures, Statistical Issues 137

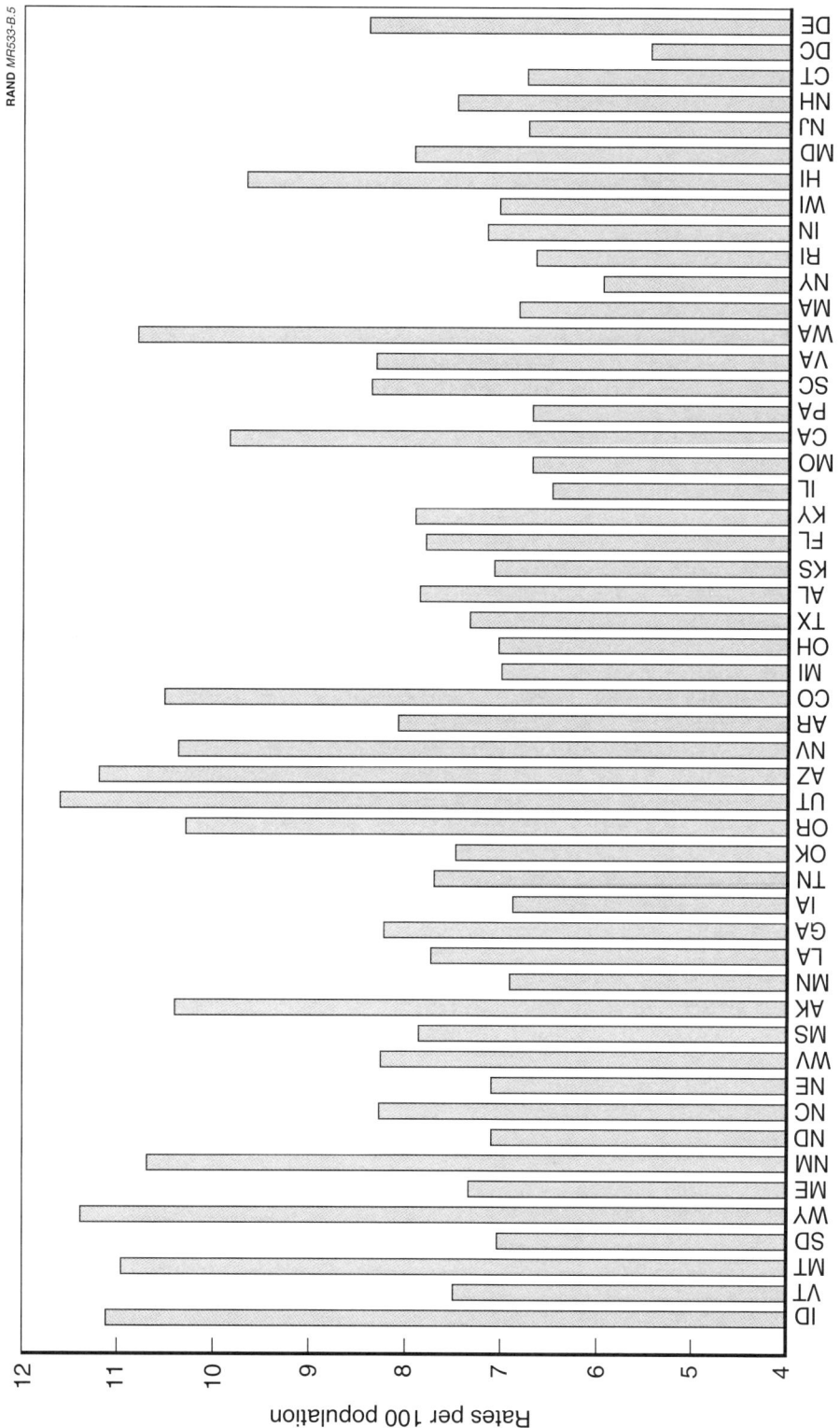

Figure B.4—Percentage of Population Meeting RAND Criteria for Drug or Alcohol Dependence, by State, NHSDA Data

138 The Substance Abuse and Mental Health Services Block Grant Allotment Formula

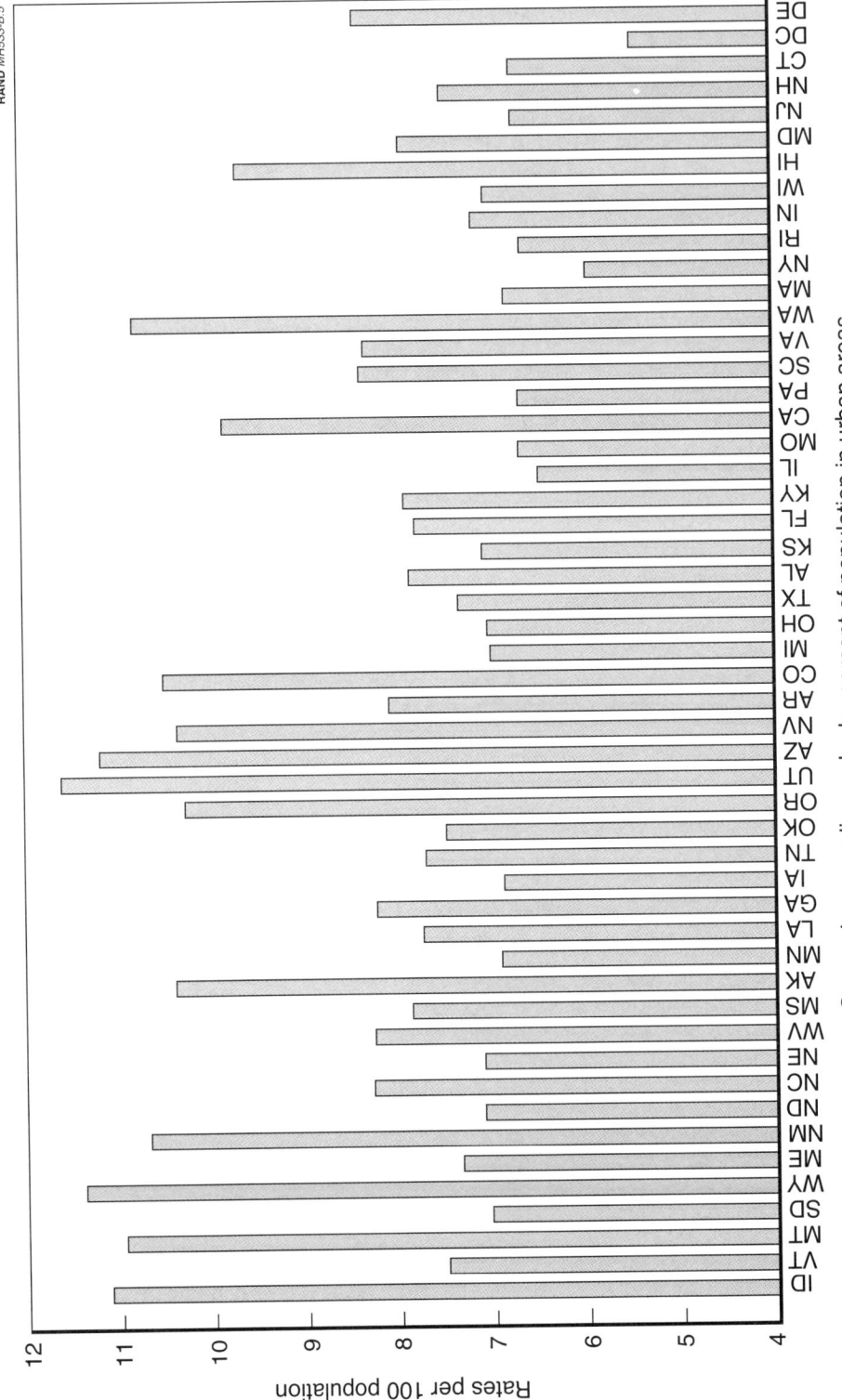

Figure B.5—Percentage of Population Meeting OAS Criteria for Drug and Alcohol Dependence, by State, NHSDA Data

Alternative Measures, Statistical Issues 139

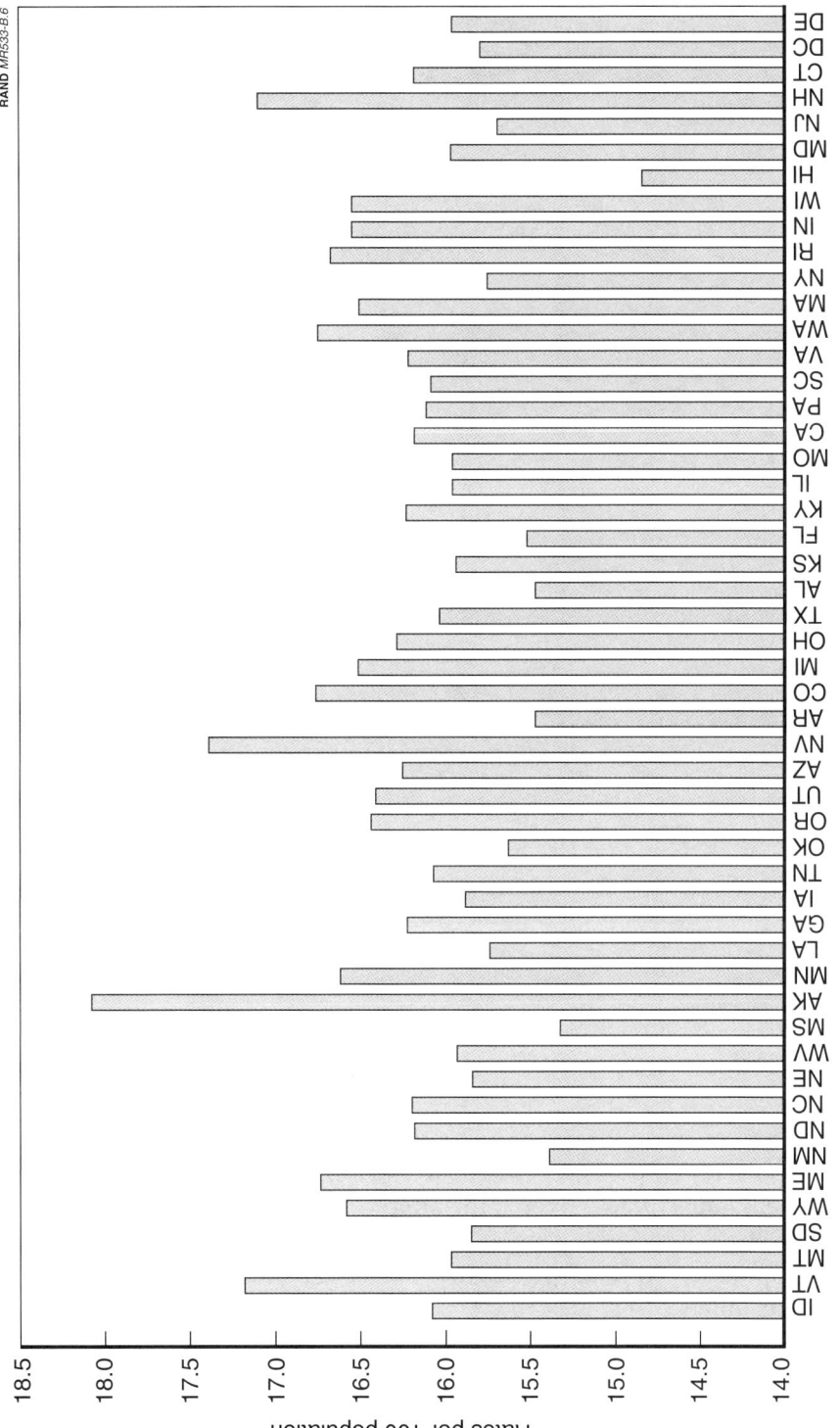

Figure B.6—Percentage of Population Meeting RAND Criteria for Substance Dependence, or Making Heavy Use of a Substance, by State, NHSDA Data

Table B.5

Effect on Mental Health Allocations of Changing Population Needs Index Only

	Current Formula	NCS Data				ECA Data			
		Mental Illness Defined:				Mental Illness Defined:			
		Broadly		Narrowly		Broadly		Narrowly	
		30-Day Rate	12-Month Rate	30-Day Rate	12-Month Rate	30-Day Rate	12-Month Rate	30-Day Rate	12-Month Rate
Share of total allocation changed	0	5	3	4	4	6	4	7	5
Number of states with allocation changed by									
> 20% lower	0	1	0	1	1	1	0	2	2
10–20% lower	0	5	1	3	1	11	4	7	3
0–10% lower	51	20	20	23	24	18	24	20	21
0–10% higher	0	18	30	20	23	14	20	12	18
10–20% higher	0	6	0	3	2	4	3	6	6
> 20% higher	0	1	0	1	0	3	0	4	1
Percent of U.S. population in states with allocation changed by									
> 20% lower	0	0	0	0	0	0	0	1	1
10–20% lower	0	4	0	2	0	10	2	7	4
0–10% lower	1	41	43	46	43	38	33	40	40
0–10% higher	0	47	57	49	55	44	61	39	48
10–20% higher	0	8	0	3	1	5	3	9	7
> 20% higher	0	0	0	0	0	3	0	5	1

Table B.6

Correlation of State Characteristics with Mental Health Allocations, Changing Population Needs Index Only

	NCS Data				ECA Data			
	Mental Illness Defined:				Mental Illness Defined:			
	Broadly		Narrowly		Broadly		Narrowly	
Correlation with	30-Day Rate	12-Month Rate	30-Day Rate	12-Month Rate	30-Day Rate	12-Month Rate	30-Day Rate	12-Month Rate
State population size	0.04	0.00	0.04	0.10	0.09	0.14	0.06	0.07
State percent of population in urban areas	–.03	–.03	.02	.14	.03	–0.09	–.04	–.13
State percent of population in poverty	0.63	0.10	0.60	0.46	0.73	0.83	0.73	0.73

developed in Chapters Five and Seven. These two indicators are shown with and without the 0.9 to 1.1 bounds on the index currently in use (i.e., with or without the indicators being "clipped"). In general, the alternative cost measures increase the shifts for all of the definitions of population in need. None of the alternative measures of population in need produces a set of summary statistics strikingly different from the others.

Table B.8 presents the correlations between the change in state shares and several state characteristics: population, urbanicity, and poverty. There is considerably

Table B.7
Total Effect on Mental Health Allocations of Changing Population Needs and Cost of Service Indexes

	Current Need				Mental Illness Defined Broadly, NCS Data								Mental Illness Defined Narrowly, NCS Data							
					30-Day Rate				12-Month Rate				30-Day Rate				12-Month Rate			
	Current Cost		Alternative Cost		Current Cost		Alternative Cost		Current Cost		Alternative Cost		Current Cost		Alternative Cost		Current Cost		Alternative Cost	
	With Clip	W/O Clip	With Clip	W/O Clip	With Clip	W/O Clip	With Clip	W/O Clip	With Clip	W/O Clip	With Clip	W/O Clip	With Clip	W/O Clip	With Clip	W/O Clip	With Clip	W/O Clip	With Clip	W/O Clip
Share of total allocation changed	0	9	3	7	5	9	5	7	4	10	4	7	4	9	5	7	4	9	4	7
Number of states with allocation changed by																				
> 20% lower	0	1	0	0	1	1	1	1	0	0	0	0	1	1	1	0	1	1	1	0
10–20% lower	0	10	0	7	6	15	4	7	2	14	1	6	4	13	2	8	5	13	2	7
0–10% lower	51	32	14	24	20	21	18	22	23	29	22	22	23	27	24	23	22	29	19	25
0–10% higher	0	2	34	14	18	9	20	15	25	3	24	18	19	5	18	13	21	3	23	11
10–20% higher	0	4	2	6	5	1	4	3	1	0	4	5	3	1	4	6	2	1	5	7
> 20% higher	0	2	1	0	1	4	4	3	0	5	0	0	1	4	2	1	0	4	1	1
Percent of U.S. population in states with allocation changed by																				
> 20% lower	0	0	0	0	0	0	0	0	0	0	0	0	0	0	1	0	0	0	0	0
10–20% lower	0	8	0	13	4	17	6	7	1	19	0	7	3	15	3	7	3	15	3	6
0–10% lower	100	63	32	47	47	43	48	47	52	50	61	46	50	51	58	51	47	53	51	51
0–10% higher	0	2	67	26	43	26	38	30	47	17	37	30	44	19	33	25	48	17	41	22
10–20% higher	0	22	1	15	6	2	4	15	0	0	2	17	3	2	4	17	1	2	5	20
> 20% higher	0	4	0	0	0	12	4	2	0	14	0	0	0	12	1	0	0	12	0	0

Table B.7 (continued)

	Current Need				Mental Illness Defined Broadly, ECA Data								Mental Illness Defined Narrowly, ECA Data							
					30-Day Rate				12-Month Rate				30-Day Rate				12-Month Rate			
	Current Cost		Alternative Cost		Current Cost		Alternative Cost		Current Cost		Alternative Cost		Current Cost		Alternative Cost		Current Cost		Alternative Cost	
	With Clip	W/O Clip	With Clip	W/O Clip	With Clip	W/O Clip	With Clip	W/O Clip	With Clip	W/O Clip	With Clip	W/O Clip	With Clip	W/O Clip	With Clip	W/O Clip	With Clip	W/O Clip	With Clip	W/O Clip
Share of total allocation changed	0	9	3	7	7	10	7	9	4	9	5	8	8	9	8	8	6	8	6	7
Number of states with allocation changed by																				
>20% lower	0	1	0	0	2	7	2	6	0	1	0	0	4	5	2	6	2	3	2	1
10–20% lower	0	10	0	7	9	14	7	9	4	16	4	11	4	14	7	9	3	13	3	10
0–10% lower	51	32	14	24	20	16	20	17	25	24	22	20	22	13	17	16	23	20	20	19
0–10% higher	0	2	34	14	14	7	11	10	21	5	18	13	11	12	13	10	16	11	16	13
10–20% higher	0	4	2	6	3	4	8	6	1	1	5	6	6	3	6	7	6	1	7	6
>20% higher	0	2	1	0	3	3	3	3	0	4	2	1	4	4	6	3	1	3	3	2
Percent of U.S. population in states with allocation changed by																				
>20% lower	0	0	0	0	1	5	2	6	0	0	0	0	2	4	1	6	1	1	1	0
10–20% lower	0	8	0	13	7	14	6	11	2	12	5	16	4	10	8	8	4	12	5	8
0–10% lower	100	63	32	47	47	38	47	41	40	56	39	44	48	35	44	41	49	43	46	42
0–10% higher	0	2	67	26	38	27	32	22	57	7	50	24	32	35	33	35	38	32	38	31
10–20% higher	0	22	1	15	4	6	10	16	1	12	3	16	9	5	9	7	7	7	7	15
>20% higher	0	4	0	0	3	11	3	3	0	12	3	1	5	12	6	3	1	5	3	3

Table B.8

Correlation of State Characteristics with Shifts in Mental Health Allocations, Changing Population Needs and Cost of Service Indexes

	Current Need				Mental Illness Defined Broadly								Mental Illness Defined Narrowly							
					30-Day Rate				12-Month Rate				30-Day Rate				12-Month Rate			
	Current Cost		Alternative Cost		Current Cost		Alternative Cost		Current Cost		Alternative Cost		Current Cost		Alternative Cost		Current Cost		Alternative Cost	
Correlation with	W/O Clip	With Clip	With Clip	W/O Clip	With Clip	W/O Clip	With Clip	W/O Clip	With Clip	W/O Clip	With Clip	W/O Clip	With Clip	W/O Clip	With Clip	W/O Clip	With Clip	W/O Clip	With Clip	W/O Clip
									NCS Data											
State population size	0.35	−0.26	0.08	0.08	0.05	0.26	−0.09	0.09	0.01	0.30	−0.22	0.09	0.05	0.26	−0.12	0.09	0.10	0.29	−0.09	0.14
State percent of population in urban areas	0.57	−0.43	0.11	0.11	−0.02	0.45	−0.24	0.07	−0.01	0.52	−0.37	0.10	0.03	0.50	−0.23	0.12	0.14	0.55	−0.16	0.21
State percent of population in poverty	−0.48	0.18	−0.14	−0.14	0.55	0.09	0.68	0.47	−0.02	−0.37	0.23	−0.08	0.50	0.00	0.64	0.37	0.35	−0.12	0.54	0.23
									ECA Data											
State population size	0.35	−0.26	0.08	0.08	0.10	0.25	−0.02	0.11	0.15	0.38	−0.05	0.16	0.06	0.23	−0.04	0.08	0.08	0.30	−0.06	0.11
State percent of population in urban areas	0.57	−0.43	0.11	0.11	0.03	0.41	−0.12	0.09	−0.08	0.50	−0.32	0.02	−0.03	0.35	−0.18	0.03	−0.12	0.40	−0.31	−0.03
State percent of population in poverty	−0.48	0.18	−0.14	−0.14	0.69	0.28	0.74	0.57	0.75	0.08	0.76	0.46	0.69	0.32	0.74	0.60	0.67	0.19	0.72	0.55

more variability in the correlations from one definition to another than there was in the population needs table. However, the positive correlation with poverty still occurs in most cases.

Substance Abuse

In this section, we show the effect on Block Grant allocations of the alternative definitions of the population in need of substance abuse treatment services described in the first section of this appendix, in combination with the population in need of prevention services described there and in Chapter Four. For comparison, we also include the treatment indicator currently used, the alcohol or drug dependence indicator formulated in Chapter Four, and the drug dependence only indicator from that chapter. Thus, there are five definitions of treatment needs and three definitions of prevention needs. In addition, we again consider the 20 percent and 50 percent weightings of prevention relative to treatment.

Populations in Need of Substance Abuse Treatment or Prevention. Tables B.9 and B.10 summarize the shifts in state shares under each combination of substance abuse treatment needs with prevention needs. Table B.9 shows the 20 percent prevention results and Table B.10 the 50 percent prevention results. The preferred alternative used in Chapter Seven is the dependence/use among youth combination. The 18 percent of the total shifted by the preferred alternative with a 20 percent prevention allocation (Table B.9) is near the upper end of the range of shares moved by the alternatives. The 13 percent of the total shifted by the preferred alternative with a 50 percent allocation (Table B.10) is smaller than that shifted with a 20 percent allocation. Typically, the 50 percent allocation shifts less than the 20 percent allocation.

Tables B.11 and B.12 present the correlations between the change in state shares and three state characteristics: population, urbanicity, and poverty. The signs of these correlations are consistent across all definitions and both treatment/prevention allocations. All of the changes are negatively associated with population and urbanicity and positively associated with poverty. In most cases, the strongest correlation is with state urbanicity. The exception is the drug dependence only definition, which is more highly correlated with state population size than with state urbanicity.

Substance Abuse Expenditure Needs. Tables B.13 and B.14 characterize the shifts in state shares for each combination of the treatment and prevention needs definitions combined with each of the four cost measures. In general, the alternative cost measures increase the shifts for all of the definitions of population in need. The 25 percent shift of our preferred alternative is at the high end of the range of options presented here.

Tables B.15 and B.16 present the correlations between the change in state shares and three state characteristics: population, urbanicity, and poverty. There is considerably more variability in the correlations as we move from one definition to another than there was in the population needs table. However, the negative correlation with urbanicity still appears to be the common theme in most cases.

Table B.9

Effect on Substance Abuse Allocations of Changing Population Needs Index Only (20 Percent Prevention)

	Current Formula Prevention Needs Based on:			Treatment Needs Based on:											
				Drug or Alcohol Dependence (RAND) Prevention Needs Based on:			Drug Dependence Only (RAND) Prevention Needs Based on:			Drug or Alcohol Dependence (OAS) Prevention Needs Based on:			Dependence or Heavy Use (RAND) Prevention Needs Based on:		
	Use Among Youth	Adult Dependence	Number of Youth	Use Among Youth	Adult Dependence	Number of Youth	Use Among Youth	Adult Dependence	Number of Youth	Use Among Youth	Adult Dependence	Number of Youth	Use Among Youth	Adult Dependence	Number of Youth
Share of total allocation changed	3	3	3	18	18	18	24	24	24	19	20	20	9	9	8
Number of states with allocation changed by															
> 20% lower	0	0	0	6	7	7	12	12	12	7	7	7	1	1	1
10–20% lower	1	1	1	5	4	4	2	2	2	4	4	4	3	2	3
0–10% lower	13	15	16	8	7	8	3	5	3	7	7	7	13	13	11
0–10% higher	34	29	31	6	7	6	8	8	10	3	2	3	12	14	15
10–20% higher	3	6	3	4	5	4	9	6	6	8	9	8	10	10	10
> 20% higher	0	0	0	22	21	22	17	18	18	22	22	22	12	11	11
Percent of U.S. population in states with allocation changed by															
> 20% lower	0	0	0	15	17	17	37	37	37	19	19	19	0	0	0
10–20% lower	0	0	0	20	19	19	2	2	2	15	15	15	13	12	13
0–10% lower	42	48	51	22	20	22	11	19	11	23	23	23	37	34	32
0–10% higher	57	49	48	12	14	12	18	11	19	6	4	6	28	35	37
10–20% higher	1	3	1	14	14	14	9	8	8	20	22	20	16	13	13
> 20% higher	0	0	0	16	16	16	23	24	24	17	17	17	6	5	5

146 The Substance Abuse and Mental Health Services Block Grant Allotment Formula

Table B.10

Effect on Substance Abuse Allocations of Changing Population Needs Index Only (50 Percent Prevention)

	Current Formula			Treatment Needs Based on:										
				Drug or Alcohol Dependence (RAND)			Drug Dependence Only (RAND)			Drug or Alcohol Dependence (OAS)			Dependence or Heavy Use (RAND)		
	Prevention Needs Based on:			Prevention Needs Based on:			Prevention Needs Based on:			Prevention Needs Based on:			Prevention Needs Based on:		
	Use Among Youth	Adult Depen-dence	Number of Youth	Use Among Youth	Adult Depen-dence	Number of Youth	Use Among Youth	Adult Depen-dence	Number of Youth	Use Among Youth	Adult Depen-dence	Number of Youth	Use Among Youth	Adult Depen-dence	Number of Youth
Share of total allocation changed	7	9	7	13	15	13	16	17	17	14	15	14	10	11	9
Number of states with allocation changed by															
> 20% lower	1	1	1	4	7	7	4	4	4	6	6	6	2	2	1
10–20% lower	2	6	3	6	3	3	7	6	8	2	4	3	5	7	7
0–10% lower	11	9	13	5	3	5	10	9	8	6	4	6	9	6	7
0–10% higher	17	15	15	9	12	11	5	6	5	9	6	7	11	11	12
10–20% higher	12	12	12	5	3	3	6	8	7	5	12	9	9	10	9
> 20% higher	8	8	7	22	23	22	19	18	19	23	19	20	15	15	15
Percent of U.S. population in states with allocation changed by															
> 20% lower	0	0	0	13	17	17	15	15	15	15	15	15	1	1	0
10–20% lower	4	15	4	16	12	12	19	15	21	7	16	11	24	28	26
0–10% lower	38	33	46	20	12	21	24	20	22	27	17	25	25	14	17
0–10% higher	43	38	36	27	37	30	10	16	8	26	20	25	28	33	36
10–20% higher	11	10	10	8	5	4	18	21	20	7	15	8	13	14	13
> 20% higher	4	4	3	17	17	17	14	13	14	18	16	16	9	9	8

Alternative Measures, Statistical Issues   147

Table B.11

Correlation of State Characteristics with Shifts in Substance Abuse Allocations, Changing Population Needs Index Only (20 Percent Prevention)

	Current Formula Prevention Needs Based on:			Treatment Needs Based on:								
				Drug or Alcohol Dependence (RAND) Prevention Needs Based on:			Drug Dependence Only (RAND) Prevention Needs Based on:			Drug or Alcohol Dependence (OAS) Prevention Needs Based on:			Dependence or Heavy Use (RAND) Prevention Needs Based on:		
	Use Among Youth	Adult Dependence	Number of Youth	Use Among Youth	Adult Dependence	Number of Youth	Use Among Youth	Adult Dependence	Number of Youth	Use Among Youth	Adult Dependence	Number of Youth	Use Among Youth	Adult Dependence	Number of Youth
Correlation with:															
State population size	−0.38	−0.35	−0.35	−0.42	−0.42	−0.41	−0.37	−0.37	−0.37	−0.43	−0.42	−0.42	−0.42	−0.43	−0.42
State percent of population in urban areas	−0.85	−0.83	−0.84	−0.73	−0.72	−0.72	−0.55	−0.56	−0.55	−0.75	−0.74	−0.74	−0.83	−0.83	−0.85
State percent of population in poverty	0.21	0.34	0.35	0.08	0.10	0.10	−0.06	−0.04	−0.04	0.23	0.25	0.24	0.07	0.13	0.13

Table B.12

Correlation of State Characteristics with Shifts in Substance Abuse Allocations, Changing Population Needs Index Only (50 Percent Prevention)

	Current Formula Prevention Needs Based on:			Treatment Needs Based on:								
				Drug or Alcohol Dependence (RAND) Prevention Needs Based on:			Drug Dependence Only (RAND) Prevention Needs Based on:			Drug or Alcohol Dependence (OAS) Prevention Needs Based on:			Dependence or Heavy Use (RAND) Prevention Needs Based on:		
	Use Among Youth	Adult Dependence	Number of Youth	Use Among Youth	Adult Dependence	Number of Youth	Use Among Youth	Adult Dependence	Number of Youth	Use Among Youth	Adult Dependence	Number of Youth	Use Among Youth	Adult Dependence	Number of Youth
Correlation with:															
State population size	−0.41	−0.38	−0.38	−0.45	−0.43	−0.43	−0.43	−0.42	−0.41	−0.46	−0.43	−0.43	−0.43	−0.43	−0.43
State percent of population in urban areas	−0.84	−0.85	−0.84	−0.83	−0.83	−0.82	−0.70	−0.72	−0.70	−0.85	−0.84	−0.83	−0.85	−0.89	−0.89
State percent of population in poverty	0.23	0.37	0.38	0.13	0.19	0.19	0.03	0.1	0.09	0.25	0.30	0.30	0.16	0.27	0.28

Table B.13

Total Effect on Substance Abuse Allocations of Changing Population Needs and Cost of Service Indexes (20 Percent Prevention)

	Prevention Needs Based on:											
	Use Among Youth				Adult Dependence				Number of Youth			
	Cost Needs Based on:				Cost Needs Based on:				Cost Needs Based on:			
	Current Cost		Alternative Cost		Current Cost		Alternative Cost		Current Cost		Alternative Cost	
	With Clip	W/O Clip	With Clip	W/O Clip	With Clip	W/O Clip	With Clip	W/O Clip	With Clip	W/O Clip	With Clip	W/O Clip
Treatment Needs Based on the Current Formula												
Share of total allocation changed	3	7	5	7	3	6	5	8	3	7	5	8
Number of states with allocation changed by												
> 20% lower	0	0	0	0	0	0	0	0	0	0	0	0
10–20% lower	1	5	2	5	1	3	3	6	1	4	3	7
0–10% lower	14	33	16	23	14	35	17	21	15	33	17	20
0–10% higher	32	9	19	11	32	9	16	13	33	10	17	11
10–20% higher	4	1	10	7	4	2	10	7	2	1	11	9
> 20% higher	0	3	4	2	0	2	5	4	0	3	3	4
Percent of U.S. population in states with allocation changed by												
> 20% lower	0	0	1	0	0	0	0	0	0	0	0	0
10–20% lower	0	7	1	13	0	6	5	15	0	7	5	19
0–10% lower	46	63	52	53	40	64	53	42	42	61	51	38
0–10% higher	53	18	38	15	58	19	32	24	57	20	35	23
10–20% higher	1	7	8	17	2	10	8	17	0	7	7	18
> 20% higher	0	5	2	2	0	2	3	2	0	5	1	2
Treatment Needs Based on Drug or Alcohol Dependence (RAND)												
Share of total allocation changed	18	18	19	22	18	18	19	22	18	18	19	22
Number of states with allocation changed by												
> 20% lower	6	5	7	7	9	5	8	8	8	5	8	8
10–20% lower	6	7	6	7	2	7	5	6	3	8	5	8
0–10% lower	7	10	5	9	8	10	4	8	8	9	6	7
0–10% higher	5	9	7	4	5	8	8	4	5	8	6	4
10–20% higher	5	4	2	2	6	5	4	4	6	5	3	3
> 20% higher	22	16	24	22	21	16	22	21	21	16	23	21
Percent of U.S. population in states with allocation changed by												
> 20% lower	22	15	2	25	29	15	21	27	23	15	21	27
10–20% lower	16	24	25	24	7	24	24	19	12	26	24	26
0–10% lower	20	26	11	17	22	27	10	18	22	24	13	13
0–10% higher	10	9	14	4	10	8	15	6	10	9	12	4
10–20% higher	15	3	12	1	16	4	13	1	16	3	13	2
> 20% higher	16	23	18	28	16	23	17	28	16	23	17	27
Treatment Needs Based on Drug Dependence Only (RAND)												
Share of total allocation changed	24	26	26	29	24	26	26	29	24	26	26	29
Number of states with allocation changed by												
> 20% lower	12	12	12	12	12	12	11	12	12	12	11	12
10–20% lower	3	3	2	3	2	3	3	5	2	3	3	4
0–10% lower	3	10	4	9	5	11	4	7	4	11	4	8
0–10% higher	7	7	8	6	8	7	10	6	8	7	9	7
10–20% higher	9	3	6	4	7	2	4	4	8	2	4	3
> 20% higher	17	16	19	17	17	16	19	17	17	16	20	17

Alternative Measures, Statistical Issues 149

Table B.13 (continued)

	Prevention Needs Based on:											
	Use Among Youth				Adult Dependence				Number of Youth			
	Cost Needs Based on:				Cost Needs Based on:				Cost Needs Based on:			
	Current Cost		Alternative Cost		Current Cost		Alternative Cost		Current Cost		Alternative Cost	
	With Clip	W/O Clip	With Clip	W/O Clip	With Clip	W/O Clip	With Clip	W/O Clip	With Clip	W/O Clip	With Clip	W/O Clip
Percent of U.S. population in states with allocation changed by												
> 20% lower	37	38	37	37	37	38	36	37	37	38	36	37
10–20% lower	9	7	2	9	2	7	3	10	2	7	3	9
0–10% lower	10	19	12	17	19	20	12	16	16	20	12	14
0–10% higher	13	6	19	10	11	9	20	9	13	9	20	14
10–20% higher	9	6	5	4	8	3	5	4	9	3	4	3
> 20% higher	24	23	25	24	23	23	25	24	23	23	25	24
Treatment Needs Based on Dependence or Heavy Use (RAND)												
Share of total allocation changed	9	7	9	7	9	7	9	7	8	7	9	7
Number of states with allocation changed by												
> 20% lower	1	1	1	1	2	1	1	1	1	1	1	1
10–20% lower	4	5	3	5	2	4	4	5	3	3	4	5
0–10% lower	14	16	11	13	14	17	12	11	14	18	11	11
0–10% higher	11	15	15	15	11	15	12	15	11	15	13	14
10–20% higher	10	8	8	8	11	8	7	10	11	7	7	11
> 20% higher	11	6	13	9	11	6	15	9	11	6	15	9
Percent of U.S. population in states with allocation changed by												
> 20% lower	0	0	0	0	1	0	0	0	0	0	0	0
10–20% lower	13	10	17	5	13	8	17	10	13	8	17	10
0–10% lower	42	44	36	40	40	45	38	33	39	49	36	33
0–10% higher	23	34	29	42	24	34	26	43	24	32	27	43
10–20% higher	16	10	8	6	17	10	10	8	17	8	10	8
> 20% higher	5	3	9	6	5	3	9	5	5	3	9	5
Treatment Needs Based on Drug or Alcohol Dependence (OAS)												
Share of total allocation changed	19	18	22	24	20	19	22	24	19	19	22	24
Number of states with allocation changed by												
> 20% lower	7	3	9	9	7	4	9	9	7	5	9	9
10–20% lower	5	10	2	4	5	11	3	5	5	9	3	5
0–10% lower	5	7	7	7	5	6	6	6	5	6	6	6
0–10% higher	4	7	1	5	4	6	2	5	4	9	2	5
10–20% higher	8	6	10	5	8	6	10	6	9	4	9	5
> 20% higher	22	18	22	21	22	18	22	20	21	18	22	21
Percent of U.S. population in states with allocation changed by												
> 20% lower	19	5	28	28	19	8	28	28	19	11	28	28
10–20% lower	22	42	6	14	22	43	7	16	22	38	7	16
0–10% lower	14	12	23	16	14	9	21	14	14	10	21	14
0–10% higher	8	10	2	19	7	9	2	8	7	13	2	9
10–20% higher	21	7	25	4	21	7	24	7	22	4	24	4
> 20% higher	17	25	17	28	17	25	17	26	16	25	17	28

Table B.14

Total Effect on Substance Abuse Allocations of Changing Population Needs and Cost of Service Indexes (50 Percent Prevention)

	Prevention Needs Based on:											
	Use Among Youth				Adult Dependence				Number of Youth			
	Cost Needs Based on:				Cost Needs Based on:				Cost Needs Based on:			
	Current Cost		Alternative Cost		Current Cost		Alternative Cost		Current Cost		Alternative Cost	
	With Clip	W/O Clip	With Clip	W/O Clip	With Clip	W/O Clip	With Clip	W/O Clip	With Clip	W/O Clip	With Clip	W/O Clip
Treatment Needs Based on the Current Formula												
Share of total allocation changed	7	5	8	8	8	5	10	10	7	6	8	9
Number of states with allocation changed by												
> 20% lower	1	1	1	1	1	1	2	2	1	0	2	2
10–20% lower	4	4	3	5	6	4	6	6	4	6	2	5
0–10% lower	9	18	13	14	8	15	10	13	10	19	16	15
0–10% higher	17	18	13	15	15	25	11	16	17	19	12	14
10–20% higher	12	7	9	8	13	3	9	5	13	5	5	6
> 20% higher	8	3	12	8	8	3	13	9	6	2	14	9
Percent of U.S. population in states with allocation changed by												
> 20% lower	0	0	1	0	0	0	1	1	0	0	1	1
10–20% lower	9	6	4	12	20	6	19	24	9	7	7	17
0–10% lower	29	43	49	38	24	35	36	26	32	50	51	37
0–10% higher	46	42	30	38	41	55	24	40	45	36	27	23
10–20% higher	11	6	10	7	12	3	11	4	11	6	5	17
> 20% higher	3	2	7	5	4	1	8	6	2	0	9	3
Treatment Needs Based on Drug or Alcohol Dependence (RAND)												
Share of total allocation changed	13	13	15	17	14	13	16	18	13	13	15	18
Number of states with allocation changed by												
> 20% lower	4	2	5	5	8	3	7	6	7	3	6	5
10–20% lower	6	5	6	6	1	6	4	5	2	5	5	7
0–10% lower	5	14	5	9	4	10	2	7	7	13	4	9
0–10% higher	9	8	8	7	12	9	12	8	9	9	10	5
10–20% higher	5	9	4	3	4	11	3	6	4	9	4	5
> 20% higher	22	13	23	21	22	12	23	19	22	12	22	20
Percent of U.S. population in states with allocation changed by												
> 20% lower	13	5	13	15	22	6	17	18	17	6	15	15
10–20% lower	19	16	21	24	2	25	17	16	8	18	19	25
0–10% lower	13	38	19	20	17	26	11	23	27	38	18	22
0–10% higher	31	11	23	12	36	13	32	12	26	11	28	7
10–20% higher	8	21	7	14	6	22	4	17	6	19	4	6
> 20% higher	17	9	17	15	17	7	19	14	17	8	17	24
Treatment Needs Based on Drug Dependence Only (RAND)												
Share of total allocation changed	16	17	17	20	17	17	18	21	17	17	18	21
Number of states with allocation changed by												
> 20% lower	4	4	4	7	4	3	5	7	4	2	5	7
10–20% lower	7	10	7	7	7	12	6	7	7	15	6	9
0–10% lower	9	10	8	11	9	7	8	8	9	6	7	6
0–10% higher	6	6	7	3	5	8	7	8	5	8	8	8
10–20% higher	5	5	5	4	9	5	6	2	7	3	5	3
> 20% higher	20	16	20	19	17	16	19	19	19	17	20	18

Table B.14 (continued)

	Prevention Needs Based on:											
	Use Among Youth				Adult Dependence				Number of Youth			
	Cost Needs Based on:				Cost Needs Based on:				Cost Needs Based on:			
	Current Cost		Alternative Cost		Current Cost		Alternative Cost		Current Cost		Alternative Cost	
	With Clip	W/O Clip	With Clip	W/O Clip	With Clip	W/O Clip	With Clip	W/O Clip	With Clip	W/O Clip	With Clip	W/O Clip
Percent of U.S. population in states with allocation changed by												
> 20% lower	15	7	15	26	15	12	20	26	15	5	20	26
10–20% lower	19	36	19	13	18	32	13	13	19	42	12	18
0–10% lower	26	22	23	27	24	16	18	22	24	16	18	18
0–10% higher	10	6	11	5	9	10	19	11	8	10	20	10
10–20% higher	16	7	17	4	22	7	16	1	20	4	15	3
> 20% higher	16	23	15	26	12	23	15	26	14	24	16	25
Treatment Needs Based on Dependence or Heavy Use (RAND)												
Share of total allocation changed	10	7	11	8	11	6	12	9	9	6	10	8
Number of states with allocation changed by												
> 20% lower	2	2	1	1	2	2	3	3	1	1	2	2
10–20% lower	5	4	7	7	6	4	5	6	6	6	5	4
0–10% lower	10	13	9	11	9	11	7	10	9	13	11	13
0–10% higher	9	16	11	11	8	18	12	10	13	16	10	13
10–20% higher	9	7	6	6	11	9	5	8	7	9	5	6
>20% higher	16	9	17	15	15	7	19	14	15	6	18	13
Percent of U.S. population in states with allocation changed by												
> 20% lower	1	1	0	0	1	1	1	3	0	0	1	1
10–20% lower	24	8	28	18	28	8	29	20	25	9	22	10
0–10% lower	27	40	27	35	23	37	17	30	21	45	31	43
0–10% higher	18	36	25	29	21	42	32	29	34	33	27	33
10–20% higher	19	9	9	8	18	10	8	7	10	10	7	5
> 20% higher	1	5	10	9	9	2	13	10	8	2	12	8
Treatment Needs Based on Drug or Alcohol Dependence (OAS)												
Share of total allocation changed	14	12	16	18	15	14	18	19	14	13	18	19
Number of states with allocation changed by												
> 20% lower	5	2	7	7	6	3	8	8	6	2	8	7
10–20% lower	4	9	3	4	3	7	2	3	3	8	2	5
0–10% lower	5	6	6	7	5	8	5	8	6	7	5	7
0–10% higher	10	12	6	6	5	10	5	4	7	12	7	6
10–20% higher	5	7	6	8	13	9	8	10	10	10	6	8
>20% higher	22	15	23	19	19	14	23	18	19	12	23	18
Percent of U.S. population in states with allocation changed by												
> 20% lower	14	1	19	23	15	3	24	24	15	1	24	23
10–20% lower	12	40	11	13	12	29	6	12	12	32	6	17
0–10% lower	22	14	22	21	22	23	15	22	24	22	15	19
0–10% higher	28	16	21	11	19	16	23	6	25	17	28	9
10–20% higher	6	18	8	19	18	19	12	21	9	20	7	19
> 20% higher	17	11	18	14	15	10	19	15	15	9	19	13

Table B.15

Correlation of State Characteristics with Shifts in Substance Abuse Allocations, Changing Population Needs and Cost of Service Indexes (20 Percent Prevention)

	Use Among Youth				Prevention Needs Based on:				Number of Youth			
					Adult Dependence							
	Cost Needs Based on:				Cost Needs Based on:				Cost Needs Based on:			
	Current Cost		Alternative Cost		Current Cost		Alternative Cost		Current Cost		Alternative Cost	
	With Clip	W/O Clip	With Clip	W/O Clip	With Clip	W/O Clip	With Clip	W/O Clip	With Clip	W/O Clip	With Clip	W/O Clip
Treatment Needs Based on the Current Formula												
Correlation with:												
State population size	−0.35	0.15	−0.37	−0.18	−0.34	0.15	−0.35	−0.17	−0.33	0.18	−0.34	−0.15
State percent of population in urban areas	−0.81	0.09	−0.77	−0.42	−0.83	0.00	−0.75	−0.42	−0.82	0.08	−0.74	−0.39
State percent of population in poverty	0.09	−0.45	0.29	−0.06	0.24	−0.34	0.36	0.13	0.24	−0.36	0.36	0.12
Treatment Needs Based on Drug or Alcohol Dependence (RAND)												
Correlation with:												
State population size	−0.42	−0.34	−0.42	−0.38	−0.42	−0.34	−0.42	−0.37	−0.41	−0.33	−0.42	−0.37
State percent of population in urban areas	−0.76	−0.67	−0.74	−0.66	−0.76	−0.68	−0.74	−0.66	−0.76	−0.67	−0.74	−0.66
State percent of population in poverty	0.06	−0.06	0.12	0.05	0.09	−0.04	0.17	0.07	0.08	−0.04	0.13	0.07
Treatment Needs Based on Drug Dependence Only (RAND)												
Correlation with:												
State population size	−0.37	−0.28	−0.38	−0.31	−0.37	−0.28	−0.38	−0.30	−0.37	−0.27	−0.38	−0.30
State percent of population in urban areas	−0.55	−0.44	−0.57	−0.48	−0.56	−0.45	−0.58	−0.49	−0.55	−0.44	−0.57	−0.48
State percent of population in poverty	−0.08	−0.20	−0.04	−0.10	−0.05	−0.17	−0.01	−0.08	−0.06	−0.18	−0.02	−0.08
Treatment Needs Based on Dependence or Heavy Use (RAND)												
Correlation with:												
State population size	−0.40	−0.20	−0.45	−0.37	−0.41	−0.21	−0.45	−0.37	−0.41	−0.20	−0.45	−0.37
State percent of population in urban areas	−0.78	−0.51	−0.89	−0.75	−0.82	−0.57	−0.90	−0.76	−0.81	−0.54	−0.90	−0.75
State percent of population in poverty	0.03	−0.29	0.17	0.04	0.09	−0.23	0.22	0.09	0.08	−0.25	0.22	0.09
Treatment Needs Based on Drug or Alcohol Dependence (OAS)												
Correlation with:												
State population size	−0.43	−0.36	−0.42	−0.38	−0.42	−0.35	−0.42	−0.38	−0.42	−0.35	−0.42	−0.37
State percent of population in urban areas	−0.78	−0.71	−0.75	−0.68	−0.78	−0.71	−0.75	−0.67	−0.77	−0.71	−0.74	−0.67
State percent of population in poverty	0.21	0.10	0.24	0.18	0.23	0.12	0.26	0.20	0.23	0.12	0.26	0.20

Alternative Measures, Statistical Issues 153

Table B.16

Correlation of State Characteristics with Shifts in Substance Abuse Allocations, Changing Population Needs and Cost of Service Indexes (50 Percent Prevention)

	Use Among Youth				Prevention Needs Based on:				Number of Youth			
					Adult Dependence							
	Cost Needs Based on:				Cost Needs Based on:				Cost Needs Based on:			
	Current Cost		Alternative Cost		Current Cost		Alternative Cost		Current Cost		Alternative Cost	
	With Clip	W/O Clip	With Clip	W/O Clip	With Clip	W/O Clip	With Clip	W/O Clip	With Clip	W/O Clip	With Clip	W/O Clip
Treatment Needs Based on the Current Formula												
Correlation with:												
State population size	−0.40	−0.15	−0.41	−0.32	−0.38	−0.16	−0.38	−0.29	−0.38	−0.11	−0.38	−0.28
State percent of population in urban areas	−0.83	−0.53	−0.85	−0.69	−0.86	−0.61	−0.81	−0.65	−0.86	−0.54	−0.81	−0.63
State percent of population in poverty	0.18	−0.21	0.29	0.15	0.33	0.00	0.38	0.25	0.34	−0.04	0.39	0.25
Treatment Needs Based on Drug or Alcohol Dependence (RAND)												
Correlation with:												
State population size	−0.45	−0.36	−0.44	−0.40	−0.43	−0.35	−0.43	−0.38	−0.43	−0.34	−0.43	−0.38
State percent of population in urban areas	−0.83	−0.75	−0.82	−0.74	−0.84	−0.75	−0.80	−0.72	−0.83	−0.74	−0.80	−0.71
State percent of population in poverty	0.11	−0.04	0.17	0.10	0.18	0.03	0.22	0.15	0.17	0.02	0.22	0.15
Treatment Needs Based on Drug Dependence Only (RAND)												
Correlation with:												
State population size	−0.43	−0.32	−0.44	−0.35	−0.42	−0.32	−0.42	−0.34	−0.42	−0.31	−0.42	−0.33
State percent of population in urban areas	−0.71	−0.58	−0.71	−0.61	−0.72	−0.61	−0.72	−0.62	−0.71	−0.58	−0.07	−0.60
State percent of population in poverty	0.01	−0.16	0.05	−0.03	0.08	−0.07	0.12	0.04	0.07	−0.09	0.11	0.03
Treatment Needs Based on Dependence or Heavy Use (RAND)												
Correlation with:												
State population size	−0.42	−0.28	−0.45	−0.39	−0.42	−0.28	−0.42	−0.37	−0.42	−0.27	−0.43	−0.37
State percent of population in urban areas	−0.84	−0.68	−0.90	−0.80	−0.89	−0.75	−0.88	−0.78	−0.89	−0.73	−0.90	−0.79
State percent of population in poverty	0.12	−0.15	0.23	0.13	0.24	−0.01	0.24	0.22	0.24	−0.04	0.32	0.21
Treatment Needs Based on Drug or Alcohol Dependence (OAS)												
Correlation with:												
State population size	−0.46	−0.38	−0.45	−0.40	−0.44	−0.36	−0.43	−0.38	−0.44	−0.36	−0.43	−0.38
State percent of population in urban areas	−0.86	−0.79	−0.83	−0.75	−0.85	−0.78	−0.80	−0.72	−0.84	−0.77	−0.80	−0.72
State percent of population in poverty	0.23	0.09	0.27	0.20	0.28	0.15	0.31	0.24	0.28	0.15	0.31	0.24

AN ALTERNATIVE MULTIPART MODEL FOR NEED FOR SUBSTANCE ABUSE TREATMENT

A key assumption behind our indirect estimation procedure is that of exchangeability. Exchangeability implies that we can exchange NHSDA respondents with other members of the U.S. population who have similar characteristics, e.g., a young white male high school drop-out from the NHSDA sample can be exchanged for all other young white male high school drop-outs in the United States. There are reasons to doubt the validity of this assumption. For example, it is well known that people living in metropolitan areas have different drug use patterns than people with similar characteristics living in other areas. One example of this is that adolescents growing up in small metropolitan areas (fewer than one million residents) are more likely to use marijuana than their counterparts living in other areas (Johnson, O'Malley and Bachman, 1996).

Because the basic exchangeability assumption is an open question, we fit an alternative model for predicting drug or alcohol dependence that relaxed this assumption. This section describes that model and the results of using such a model to estimate the population in need of drug treatment for each state. The state estimates are then used to generate alternative definitions of need for treatment and prevention services.

A Multipart Model of Drug or Alcohol Dependence

Our alternative model is a multipart model. A separate model was fit for people from large metropolitan areas (over one million residents), other metropolitan areas, and non-metropolitan areas. This model assumes that exchangeability is limited to people from regions of equal metropolitan status. Thus, an NHSDA respondent who is a young white male high school dropout residing in a large metropolitan area is exchangeable only for other young white male high school dropouts living in large metropolitan areas. In this section we give justifications for such a model.

As discussed in Chapter Four, previous research has found that metropolitan size is correlated with the probability of both drug and alcohol use. Thus, exchangeability across regions of differing metropolitan status is a dubious a priori assumption and any model should account for metropolitan status. Inclusion of metropolitan status dummy variables in our previous regression models was one approach to accounting for this predictor. However, such an approach assumes that the influence of metropolitan status is roughly linear. Our alternative approach allows for alternative functional forms.

On the other hand, in 1991, the NHSDA oversampled the population of many large MSAs. This was the result of designed oversampling of six specific MSAs and oversampling of Hispanics. Thus, fitting the multipart model corresponds to adjusting for oversampling in the NHSDA sample. Fitting the model with sampling weights is an alternative approach to making such an adjustment. However, estimates from the multipart model may be more precise and if metropolitan status has nonlinear effects, weighting cannot produce the correct model.

Exchangeability may be most justifiable at the smallest level of aggregation available in the sample. Thus, we could model the probability of dependence at the household or segment (the second-stage sampling unit level). Given small segment samples, this is not really feasible. However, we did fit separate models for each primary sampling unit (PSU), the next smallest unit. These PSU fits showed considerable variation in the parameter estimates. Thus, hierarchical modeling that fits models for each PSU and then models the PSU-level fits, might be justifiable. Our only available PSU-level identifiers are metropolitan status and region. Thus, our multipart model can be considered an approximation to such hierarchical modeling.

Analysis Methods and Results

The multipart model involved three separate analyses. The sample was split into three subsamples: large metropolitan, other metropolitan, and nonmetropolitan. Parallel analyses were then conducted on all three subsamples. For each subsample, predictors were found using the algorithm outlined in Chapter Four. A large main-effects model including all predictors in Table 4.4 was fit to each subsample of data. The models were then reduced using backward selection, and the AIC criteria and interaction among remaining effects were explored.

The resulting models are given in Table B.17. Although the models for the three strata are similar, there are some differences. In all three strata, people who were under 45 years old, those who were not married, and those who were male and had limited educational attainment were the most likely to need treatment. Adolescents attending school had lower odds of needing treatment. Although whites had greater odds of needing treatment in all metropolitan areas, it was Hispanics who were at increased risk for needing treatment in the nonmetropolitan areas.

Other factors were less consistent across the three strata. For example, full-time employment reduced the odds of needing treatment only for residents of nonmetropolitan areas. Likewise, people with higher incomes or more children in the household were less likely to need treatment in large metropolitan areas but not elsewhere. Similarly, welfare recipients were more likely to need treatment only in large metropolitan areas. Overall, males had a greater chance of needing treatment; however, in nonmetropolitan areas the marginal effect of being male was small and increased risk was mostly for Hispanic males and males with low educational attainment. Similarly, low educational attainment increased a person's odds of drug or alcohol dependence, but in small metropolitan areas the effects were present only for males. Regional differences also varied across the strata. Metropolitan respondents from the Middle and South Atlantic and East Central states had lower odds of needing treatment. On the other hand, nonmetropolitan residents in the Mid-Atlantic states and the West South Central regions had relatively greater odds of needing treatment.

Table B.17

Final Model: Factors Predicting Drug or Alcohol Dependence (RAND)

Predictors	Odds Ratios (and 95% Confidence Intervals)		
	Large Metropolitan	Other Metropolitan	Non-Metropolitan
Gender			
Female	1.0	1.0	1.0
Male	2.0 (1.5–2.6)	1.4 (0.9–2.2)	0.5 (0.3–0.9)
Race			
White, non-Hispanic	1.7 (1.5–1.9)	1.9 (1.4–2.6)	
Hispanic			2.1 (1.4–3.1)
Other		1.0	1.0
Marital status			
Currently married	1.0	1.0	1.0
Separated or not married	2.0 (1.6–2.4)	2.3 (1.9–3.0)	2.2 (1.7–2.9)
Age			
12–44	1.6 (1.4–1.9)	2.5 (1.7–3.8)	4.3 (2.7–6.9)
45 or older	1.0	1.0	1.0
Education			
0–8 years and a student	0.3 (0.2–0.4)	0.3 (0.2–0.4)	0.2 (0.1–0.4)
Dropped out before high school			1.2 (0.7–2.0)
High school dropout		0.9 (0.7–1.4)	
High school graduate and not a student	1.3 (1.1–1.6)		1.0 (0.7–1.4)
Completed some college and not a student		0.5 (0.4–0.7)	
Other		1.0	
Work status			
Working full-time			0.7 (0.5–0.8)
Other			1.0
Welfare status			
Welfare recipient	1.4 (1.2–1.7)		1.8 (1.4–2.3)
Not welfare recipient	1.0		1.0
Geographic region			
Mid-Atlantic[a]			1.9 (1.1–3.3)
East Central[b]	0.6 (0.5–0.6)	0.4 (0.3–0.6)	
South Atlantic[c]			
West South Central[d]			1.9 (1.5–2.5)
Other	1.0	1.0	1.0
Gender by marital status			
Male and not married	0.7 (0.5–0.8)		
Other	1.0		
Gender by race			
Male and Hispanic			1.9 (1.1–3.3)
Male and white		0.6 (0.4–0.9)	1.0
Other		1.0	
Gender by education			
Male 0–8 years and a student	0.5 (0.3–0.9)		
Male and dropped out before high school	1.4 (1.1–1.8)		6.0 (3.0–12.3)
Male and high school dropout		2.3 (1.5–3.5)	
Male, high school graduate, not a student			3.4 (1.9–5.9)
Male and some college and not a student			
Other		1.0	
Gender by region			
Male and Mid-Atlantic			
Male and East North Central		1.8 (1.1–2.8)	
Male and East South Central			
Other		1.0	
Age by race interactions			
12–44 years and white			2.8 (1.2–6.6)
Other			1.0
Log income	1.0 (0.9–1.0)		
Number of children in household	0.9 (0.8–1.0)		0.7 (0.7–0.8)

[a]NY, PA, and NJ.
[b]OH, MI, IN, IL, WI, KY, TN, AL, and MS.
[c]MD, DE, WV, VA, NC, SC, GA, and FL.
[d]TX, AR, and LA.

State-Level Estimates of Need for Substance Abuse Treatment

This section presents the results of using the multipart model given in Table B.17 to estimate treatment needs at the state level using the indirect estimation techniques described in Chapter Four. The results of this simulation are then combined with the state-level prevalence estimates to create alternative indexes of need for treatment and prevention services. These indexes are subsequently compared with the current Block Grant formula.

Table B.18 presents descriptive statistics for the resulting state-level estimates of need for treatment. The multipart model was used to estimate need as defined by our DSM-III-R dependence measure given in Chapter Four and Table B.18 compares the multipart model results to those from Chapter Four. The two models produce different state-level estimates of need. Using the multipart model, we estimate that on average roughly 7 percent of a state's population needs treatment. The corresponding estimate from Chapter Four was 8 percent. The correlation coefficient between the two sets of estimates of rate of need is only 0.09. This is very small, indicating not only that the two models produce different estimates for each state but that the rank orderings of the states is also quite different.

Figure B.7 shows a map of the multipart model estimates of the rate of need for treatment. Although the map differs from those given in Chapter Four, there are some similarities. The Pacific Coast states and the southwest have a relatively high prevalence of need for treatment regardless of the model. On the other hand, the multipart model also estimates high prevalence for Texas and Louisiana, whereas in Chapter Four, these states' estimates were among the lowest third.

Figure B.8 shows the multipart model estimates of rate of need for treatment for each state with states ordered by percentage of urban population. There appears to be a weak positive relationship between the size of a state's urban population and the rate of need for treatment.

Table B.18

Predicted Prevalence of Substance Dependence for States:
Summary Statistics and Correlation Coefficient Between
Alternative Models of Need for Treatment Defined
as Drug or Alcohol Dependence

	Drug or Alcohol Dependence (RAND)	
	Original Model (Chapter Four)	Alternative Model
Mean	7.72	6.98
Standard deviation	1.70	1.52
Minimum	5.61	4.80
Maximum	11.94	10.59
Correlation	.0906	

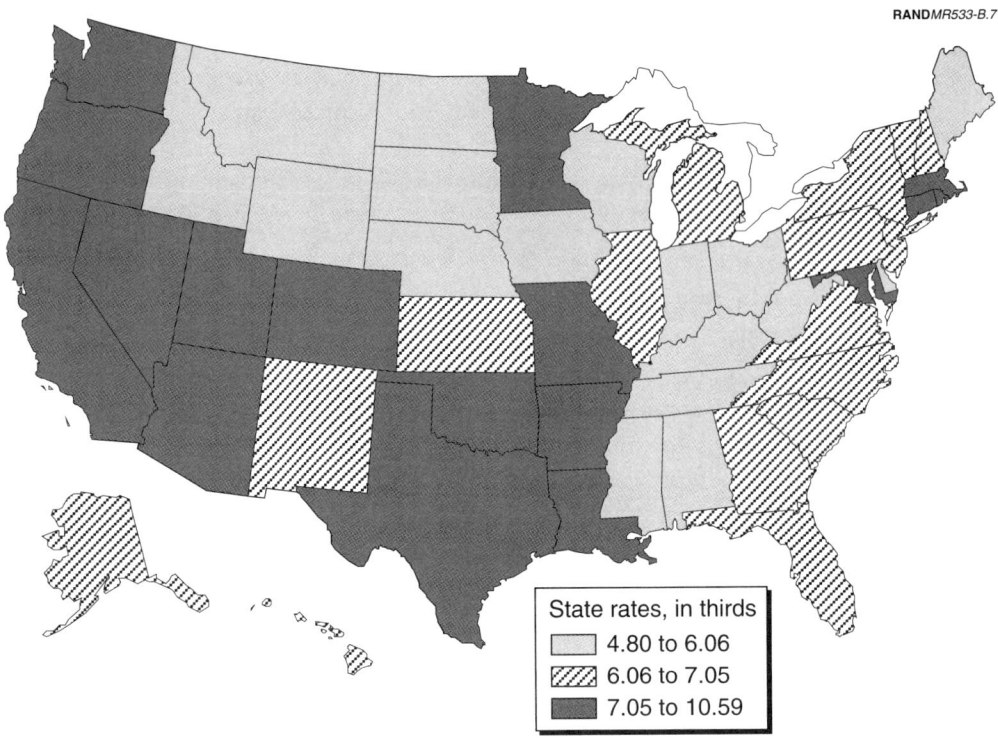

Figure B.7—Alternative Model of the Percentage of Population Meeting RAND Criteria for Dependence

HOW WOULD ALTERNATIVE APPROACHES TO THE POPULATION NEEDS MODELING AFFECT OUR RESULTS?

In Chapters Three and Four and in the previous sections of this appendix, we considered how alternative needs measures and alternative choices for their correlates would have affected our conclusions. In this section, we consider three other issues and how they would affect our conclusions. First, we take up the issue of whether to use sample weights in the fitting of the logistic regression models. Second, we examine the effect of using aggregate, rather than individual-level, correlates for the state-level estimation. Third, we explore, insofar as is possible, the effects of not having used tract-level community variables for our indirect estimation.

Weighted Versus Unweighted Analysis

The literature on weighting for regression is sparse and embodies no definitive conclusion. For simple summaries like crosstabs, sample weights are clearly the correct weights to use. The question is whether sample weights should be used in multivariate analyses or whether other weighting needs (e.g., variance weights) take precedence in the modeling setting. Our view is that sample weights should not be

Alternative Measures, Statistical Issues 159

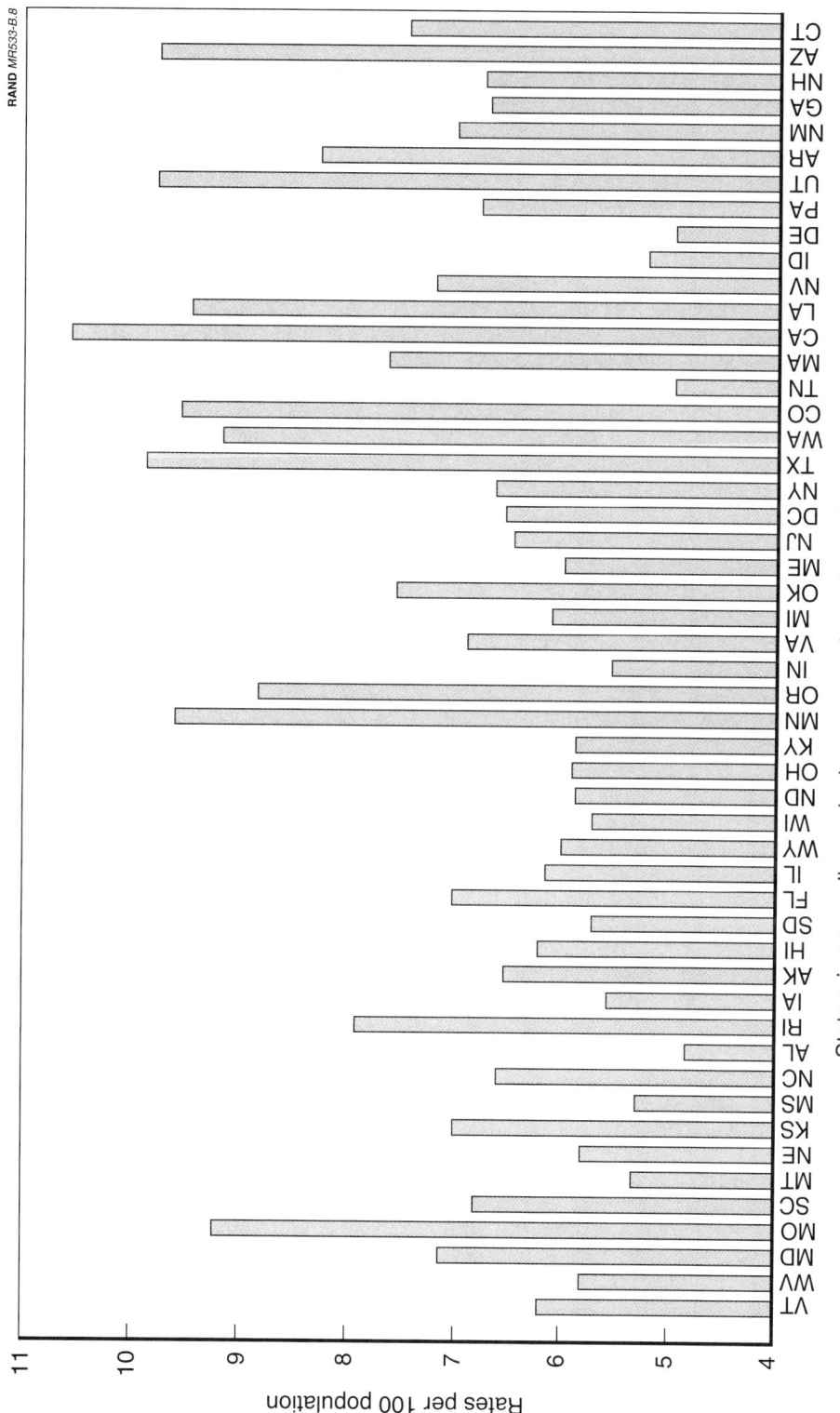

Figure B.8—Alternative Model of the Percentage of Population Meeting RAND Criteria for Dependence, by State

160 The Substance Abuse and Mental Health Services Block Grant Allotment Formula

used in regression. We do examine, however, how modeling with sampling weights would have affected our conclusions.

Table B.19 presents summaries that compare the indirect estimates from weighted and unweighted models for both mental health and substance abuse. Although there are significant differences in the means, standard deviations, and ranges, the correlations between the weighted and unweighted state estimates are quite large. These correlations (0.99 and 0.94) are the relevant comparison for the index construction used in the formulas. We conclude that the decision to use or not to use sample weights does not have a meaningful effect on study results.

Table B.19

Predicted Prevalence of Mental Illness and Substance Dependence for States:
Summary Statistics and Correlation Coefficients Between Weighted and
Unweighted Models of Preferred Definitions of Need for Treatment

	SMI, Past Month (NCS Data)		Drug or Alcohol Dependence (RAND)	
	Original Model (Chapter Four)	Weighted Model	Original Model (Chapter Four)	Weighted Model
Mean	10.95	9.36	7.72	7.11
Standard deviation	0.63	.54	1.70	1.36
Minimum	9.55	8.28	5.61	5.89
Maximum	12.99	11.16	11.94	10.41
Correlation	0.9908		0.9363	

State-Level Aggregate Data

Recall from Chapters Three and Four that our indirect estimation method takes the logistic regressions and uses them to estimate the probability of mental illness or substance abuse for each person in the PUMS. These probabilities are then summed to the state level to get an expected number of persons at need.

$$\text{PIN} = \sum p_i \quad \text{where} \quad p_i = \frac{1}{1 + e^{-x\beta}},$$

PIN is the estimated population in need, β is from the logistic regressions, and x is an individual in the PUMS data.

This process requires a large amount of computation because the calculations are performed for a large sample of individuals. An obvious alternative is to put state-level averages into the regression equations and do a single calculation for each state. This would produce the same answer if the indirect estimates were from ordinary regressions instead of logistic regressions. The nonlinearity of logistic regressions calls into question the applicability of this approach.

We explored this issue by recalculating state-level estimates from state averages. Table B.20 presents summaries for both mental health and substance abuse comparing results from Chapters Three and Four with estimates from the aggregate method.

Table B.20

Predicted Prevalence of Mental Illness and Substance Dependence for States:
Summary Statistics and Correlation Coefficients Between Individual and
Aggregate-Level Estimates

	SMI, Past Month (NCS Data)		Drug or Alcohol Dependence (RAND)	
	Original Model (Chapter Four)	Aggregate Calculation	Original Model (Chapter Four)	Aggregate Calculation
Mean	10.95	9.59	7.72	5.63
Standard deviation	0.63	0.47	1.70	1.26
Minimum	9.55	8.74	5.61	4.11
Maximum	12.99	11.54	11.94	8.76
Correlation	0.9784		0.9979	

Although some of the summaries differ, the correlations between the individual level and aggregate estimates are quite high (0.978 and 0.998). It is the correlations that are relevant for the indexes in the formula.

These results are encouraging. They suggest that not much would be lost by implementing the much simpler aggregate method, a quite feasible approach for actual formula implementation.

Using Neighborhood Characteristics in Our Epidemiological Models

The epidemiological models considered in Chapters Three and Four used only individual-level characteristics to predict an individual's probability of needing either mental health or substance abuse treatment. There is, however, a general belief that environmental variables, such as neighborhood characteristics, are also associated with increased risk of need for treatment. In this section we discuss models for predicting need that included Census-tract-level variables to serve as a proxy for environment characteristics. We include alternative models for both the preferred definition of substance dependence (backwards selection for our mental health preferred alternative model resulted in no included Census-tract-level variables). We use the relative R^2 to compare these alternative models to the models given in Chapter Four. Because the PUMS data do not include tract-level variables, the new models could not be used to generate state-level synthetic estimates. In this section we will only discuss the preferred substance abuse alternative.

Alternative Models for Drug or Alcohol Dependence. The alternative model for drug or alcohol dependence was found by augmenting our model from Chapter Four with Census-tract-level variables and using backwards deletion to select the best fitting model. Interactions between individual and tract-level variables were also explored. In this section, we describe the Census tract variables that we explored and the final model we selected. We then compare this model with the model for the preferred definition given Chapter Four.

We considered environmental variables that described the socioeconomic status of the neighborhood from which the survey respondents lived. Our best estimate of neighborhood characteristics were characteristics of the respondents Census tract from the 1990 Census. The tract-level variables measured the percentage of the tract's population or housing units with a given socioeconomic characteristic. For example, we measure the percentage of people aged 16 to 64 with disabilities and the percentage of housing units which are rented. Table B.21 lists the tract-level variables we considered.

Table B.22 gives the odds ratios for our model for predicting drug or alcohol dependence using both individual and tract-level variables. For comparison, the table also contains the odds ratios for the original model given in Table 4.5 of Chapter Four. Eight tract-level variables (or interactions including tract-level variables) remain in the final model. Given a person's individual characteristics, residing in a neighborhood (Census tract) with a large percentage of single-person households, a large percentage of the families living below the poverty line, or a high median value for

Table B.21

Census-Tract Variables Examined as Predictors of Need for Drug or Alcohol Abuse Treatment

Gender by marital status	Percent of females currently married
	Percent of females separated, divorced, or widowed
	Percent of females never married
	Percent of males currently married
	Percent of males separated, divorced, or widowed
	Percent of males never married
Age	Percent under 18 years
	Percent 19 to 24 years
	Percent 25 to 34 years
	Percent 35 to 44 years
	Percent 45 to 54 years
	Percent 55 to 64 years
	Percent 65 years or older
Household composition	Percent living alone
	Percent female-headed household with no spouse and children under 18
Education (persons over 18)	Percent 0 to 8 years of school
	Percent 9 to 12 years of school
	Percent high school graduates
	Percent attended college, no degree
	Percent associates degree
	Percent bachelor's, graduate, or professional degree
Work status	Percent females 16 years or older in labor force
	Percent males 16 years or older in labor force
Race	Percent Hispanic origin
	Percent white (non-Hispanic)
	Percent black (non-Hispanic)
	Percent other race (non-Hispanic)
Poverty	Percent of families below poverty line
Public assistance	Percent households with public assistance income
Disabilities	Percent persons 16 to 64 with a work disability
Housing	Percent housing units owner-occupied
	Percent housing units rented
	Median value owner-occupied housing units
	Median rent for rental units

Table B.22

Final Model: Factors Predicting Drug or Alcohol Dependence
Using Census-Tract Variables

	Odds Ratios (and 95% Confidence Intervals)	
Predictors	Original Model (from Chapter Four)	Alternative Model
Gender		
Female	1.0	1.0
Male	1.8 (1.7–2.0)	2.2 (1.7–2.7)
Race		
White, non-Hispanic	1.4 (1.3–1.5)	1.3 (1.2–1.5)
Other	1.0	1.0
Marital status		
Currently married	1.0	1.0
Separated or not married	1.7 (1.6–1.9)	1.7 (1.6–1.9)
Age		
12–17	1.0	1.0
18–44	2.2 (1.9–2.5)	2.3 (2.1–2.7)
45–64	1.5 (1.2–1.8)	1.6 (1.4–1.9)
65 or older	0.7 (0.5–1.0)	1.0
Education		
0–8 years	1.0	1.0
9–11 years	2.5 (2.1–2.9)	2.4 (2.1–2.7)
High school graduate	1.9 (1.6–2.2)	1.6 (1.4–1.9)
College graduate	1.2 (1.0–1.5)	1.0
Population density		
In MSA	0.7 (0.6–0.8)	1.4 (1.0–1.7)
Not in MSA	1.0	1.0
Geographic region		
West[a]	1.6 (1.4–1.7)	1.5 (1.4–1.7)
Other	1.0	1.0
Tract-level variables[b]		
Percent 1 person households		2.0 (1.6–2.5)
Percent of housing units rented		2.9 (1.4–6.1)
Percent of families living below poverty level		2.0 (1.4–2.9)
Percent of households with public assistance income		0.5 (0.4–0.7)
Median value of owner-occupied housing units		1.3 (1.1–1.5)
Male by percent of 1-person households		0.6 (0.5–0.8)
Male percent of families living below poverty level		1.4 (1.1–1.9)
MSA by percent of housing units rented		0.2 (0.1–0.4)

[a]Includes: AK, AZ, CA, CO, HI, ID, MT, NM, NV, OR, UT, WA, and WY.

[b]All tract-level variables are continuous. Odds ratios are for 5th and 95th percentiles.

owner-occupied housing units increases the likelihood of drug or alcohol dependence. Residing in a tract with a large proportion of families receiving public assistance decreases the likelihood of drug or alcohol dependence. Also, the effects of percentage of single-person households are much smaller for males than for females and the effects of living in a neighborhood with a large percentage of families living below the poverty line is somewhat greater for males than for females. For people living in metropolitan areas, the likelihood of needing substance abuse treatment decreases as the percentage of rented housing units increases. For people outside of MSAs, the likelihood of need for treatment increases as the proportion of renters increase.

Adding tract-level variables to the model has little effect on the estimated odds ratios for variables included in the original model given in Chapter Four. The only predictor with any appreciable change in estimated odds ratio is the MSA indicator variable. In the original model, living in an MSA decreased the odds of drug or alcohol dependence. The alternative model shows that effects of living in an MSA are dependent on the proportion of rented housing units in the neighborhood where a person resides. Living in an MSA increases the odds of being drug or alcohol dependent for people in neighborhoods with less then 18 percent of all housing units rented, but it decreases the odds of dependency for people from neighborhoods with a greater proportion of rented units.

Overall, adding tract-level variables does little to improve the predictive accuracy of our model. The relative R^2 for comparing the original model from Chapter Four to our expanded model is 0.90. Thus, our original model is 90 percent as accurate as the expanded model. Also, as noted above, including tract-level variables in the model does not change the qualitative interpretation of the person-level predictors included in the original model.

Appendix C
COST OF SERVICE REGRESSION ANALYSIS

This appendix presents the regression analysis we conducted to obtain the "alternative" cost of service indexes described in Chapter Five. The analyses were conducted using data from the 1991 NDATUS and the 1992 NRPMHS. We begin by outlining the cost model underlying the regression specification, then describe the data sources and variables, and conclude with the regression results. As in Chapter Five, this appendix uses "state" to mean each of the 50 states and the District of Columbia.

THE REGRESSION MODEL

The total cost of providing services to all beneficiaries (i.e., clients) in a state is simply the sum of expenditures for labor, capital (e.g., facilities), and miscellaneous resources. Using the subscript T to indicate totals over all beneficiaries in a state, the cost equation is:

$$C_T = WL_T + RK_T + MX_T, \tag{C.1}$$

where W is the wage of labor (L), R is the rental rate for capital (K), and M is the price of miscellaneous resources (X). Equation (C.1) lays the foundation for specifying a regression equation to be estimated using SA and MH services survey data. To derive the regression specification, we introduce several additional considerations.

First, we note that Equation (C.1) is an identity (i.e., the total cost exactly equals the sum of expenditures on resources). However, we do not directly estimate that equation. Instead, we estimate the relationship between funding and resource costs. (This is a practical necessity for analyzing substance abuse costs because NDATUS survey data report funding, not expenditures.) Funding can differ from actual expenditures for several reasons, including differences in timing between funding receipts and outlays for resources. Letting ε_T represent the "error" or discrepancy between funding and costs, the equation for funding, F_T, is:

$$F_T = C_T + \varepsilon_T. \tag{C.2}$$

Because Equation (C.2) includes a stochastic variable, it can serve as the basis for regression analysis.

If we attempted to estimate Equation (C.2) directly, we would expect to observe heteroskedasticity in the errors. That is, we would expect the discrepancy between funding and expenditures to vary with the overall level of funding. To avoid that undesirable property, we restate the equation in terms of funding and costs per beneficiary served:

$$F = C + \varepsilon$$
$$= WL + RK + MK + \varepsilon, \qquad (C.3)$$

where

$$\begin{aligned}
F &= F_T / B_T, \\
C &= C_T / B_T, \\
L &= L_T / B_T, \\
K &= K_T / B_T, \\
X &= X_T / B_T, \\
\varepsilon &= \varepsilon_T / B_T,
\end{aligned}$$

and B_T is the total number of beneficiaries served. An advantage of this specification is that it does not require complete data on all delivery organizations within a state; a sample of organizations can be used if they provide representative estimates of the per-client variables used in the regression.

If we estimated Equation (C.3) using resource expenditures per client (WL, RK, and MX) as explanatory variables, we would expect the coefficients of all those variables to equal 1.0. However, we do not observe WL, RK, or MX. Instead, using the data described below, we observe labor utilization per client (L), an indicator of space utilization per client (S, a proxy for K), and indexes for the variation in wages and rents; we do not observe either M or X.

Accordingly, our analysis is based on assuming that:

- The wage index, w_i, and the rent index, r_i, properly measure proportional variation around the interstate means of wages and rents, $\overline{w}$ and $\overline{r}$, respectively. That is, we assume that $W = \overline{w} * w_i$ and $R = \overline{r} * r_i$.

- As in Pope (1990), the prices of resources other than labor and rents are constant, so that an index for them would equal 1 for all states. That is, $M = \overline{m}$, where $\overline{m}$ denotes the interstate mean of prices for miscellaneous resources.

- At least for a given type of beneficiary, the quantity of miscellaneous resources used per beneficiary is constant across states. That is, $X = \overline{X}$.

Based on the foregoing assumptions, the basic form of the equation to be estimated is:

$$F = \alpha(w_i L) + \beta(r_i S) + \gamma + \varepsilon, \qquad (C.4)$$

where α, β, and γ are parameters to be estimated. According to this model, the estimates of α and β should correspond to $\overline{w}$ and $\overline{r}$. The estimate of γ should be a cost that is constant per beneficiary, corresponding to $\overline{m}\,\overline{X}$.

Equation (C.4) would be a satisfactory specification if we assume that all beneficiaries are homogeneous, but we are particularly interested in the hypothesis that there are systematic differences in the costs of delivering care to urban and rural beneficiaries. To see how this affects the specification, let us initially consider just the labor input.

Suppose that each state's total clients include some numbers of rural and urban beneficiaries, so that $B_T = B_R + B_U$. Suppose further that there is a systematic difference between the labor input per beneficiary. Then we may write:

$$L_T = L_0 B_T + (L_U - L_0) B_U$$

or

$$L = L_0 + (L_U - L_0) B_U / B_T, \quad (C.5)$$

where L_0 is statewide average amount of labor per beneficiary (including labor used for both urban and nonurban beneficiaries) and L_U is the amount of labor used specifically to serve urban beneficiaries. Now, if there is a systematic difference between the amounts of labor used by rural and urban beneficiaries, the term in parentheses in Equation (C.5) might exhibit two patterns: The difference might be a constant across states, or it might be proportional to the statewide average use of labor, L_0. If the difference is simply a constant, then the "constant" cost per beneficiary in Equation (C.4) would appear to be linearly related to the urban share of a state's beneficiaries; otherwise, the effect would appear as a nonzero parameter for a term reflecting an interaction between $w_i L$ and the urban share of beneficiaries.

Generalizing from this, we considered regression specifications in which funding per beneficiary varies with the urbanicity of a state's clients, with interactions between the labor variable and urbanicity, and with interactions between the space variable and urbanicity. However, perhaps because of the high correlations between the urbanicity variable and the urbanicity interaction terms, using the interaction terms did not significantly improve the fit of either the substance abuse or mental health regressions. Thus, the general specification reported below for both types of services was:

$$F = \alpha'(w_i L_0) + \beta'(r_i S) + \gamma' B_U / B_T + \varepsilon'. \quad (C.6)$$

THE DATA

We used the same interstate wage and rent indexes for both the substance abuse and mental health service analyses. The 5 percent household sample from the 1990 Census provided mean wages for workers in SA and MH services-related occupations and industries (see Chapter Five); the wage index is the ratio of the mean wage in each state to the population-weighted average of the state-level means. As described in Chapter Five, we used the Pope (1990) methodology to develop the rent index, but updated the values using the 1990 Census and the 1990 Fair Market Rents published by the Department of Housing and Urban Development; again, the index was formed by taking ratios of each state's rent value to the population-weighted mean of those values across all 51 states. Both the rent and wage indexes were rescaled to yield a mean of 1.0 over all 51 state observations. The values of the wage and rent indexes appear in Table C.1.

Other variables for the substance abuse analysis were obtained from the NDATUS. This is an annual survey that requests information on funding (by source), clients served, the shares of clients who are "urban," "suburban," or "rural," and the numbers of staff (by category) from all organizations that provide substance abuse services in the United States.[1] We obtained a copy of the data file generated from the 1991 survey for this study. It contained records for nearly 11,300 responding organizations in the 50 states and Washington, D.C.

Because many NDATUS respondents provide incomplete or inaccurate information, aggregations of NDATUS responses generally do not agree with other sources of information. (In particular, the NDATUS is known to underreport aggregate funding by state.) For our purposes, however, it was not necessary for the NDATUS to provide complete data on the entire population of substance abuse service providers. Instead, we needed state-level estimates of funding per client, staffing per client, clients per provider, and urbanicity—estimates that could be obtained from a *sample* of providers in each state. Therefore, we dropped records that contained incomplete data on the variables of interest.

We dropped a total of 3,834 records due to incomplete data—1,531 records that omitted funding, 36 records that omitted total clients, 2,266 records that lacked both funding and client counts, and one additional record that lacked staffing information. Records dropped solely due to missing client counts appeared to have lower funding than the records we kept, but were so few in number that omitting them should not affect the representativeness of the sample. The records dropped solely due to lack of funding data appeared to have relatively small client loads, but the difference was not statistically significant.

More importantly, the share of clients reported as "urban" or "suburban" was the same for the records that were dropped for lack of funding as for the sample we used in our analysis. We cannot say much about the 20 percent of the NDATUS observations that lacked both client and funding data, except that they were not concentrated in just a few states; our sample of records with complete data accounted for half or more of the providers in each state.[2]

---

[1]Both NDATUS and NRPMHS also cover providers in U.S. territories and possessions, but we omitted those providers in this analysis.

[2]With two slight exceptions: We dropped 34 of Washington, D.C.'s, 65 respondents (52 percent), and 111 of Indiana's 218 respondents (51 percent).

Table C.1

1990 Wage and Rent Indexes

State	SA and MH Services-Related Wage Index	1990 Rent Index
Alabama	0.909	0.726
Alaska	1.107	1.182
Arizona	1.018	1.085
Arkansas	0.915	0.748
California	1.240	1.447
Colorado	1.046	0.948
Connecticut	1.212	1.229
District of Columbia	1.140	1.414
Delaware	1.026	1.234
Florida	1.084	1.004
Georgia	1.017	0.912
Hawaii	1.163	1.370
Idaho	1.001	0.927
Illinois	1.045	1.136
Indiana	0.968	0.975
Iowa	0.888	0.862
Kansas	0.971	0.832
Kentucky	0.905	0.800
Louisiana	1.002	0.841
Maine	0.853	1.007
Maryland	1.195	1.244
Massachusetts	1.088	1.409
Michigan	1.070	0.955
Minnesota	0.963	0.979
Mississippi	0.908	0.753
Missouri	0.924	0.832
Montana	0.774	0.891
Nebraska	0.841	0.805
Nevada	1.179	1.289
New Hampshire	0.955	1.418
New Jersey	1.205	1.262
New Mexico	0.936	0.935
New York	1.143	1.192
North Carolina	0.881	0.790
North Dakota	0.894	0.806
Ohio	0.963	0.852
Oklahoma	0.909	0.779
Oregon	0.999	1.009
Pennsylvania	1.001	1.017
Rhode Island	1.033	1.128
South Carolina	0.934	0.769
South Dakota	0.786	0.751
Tennessee	0.954	0.797
Texas	1.017	0.872
Utah	1.182	0.823
Vermont	0.941	1.081
Virginia	1.014	1.095
Washington	1.043	1.041
West Virginia	0.918	0.812
Wisconsin	0.953	1.025
Wyoming	0.887	0.907

NDATUS respondents report numbers of personnel by occupation (e.g., psychiatrists, social workers, administrators) and status (paid versus volunteer). NDATUS also provides a standard formula for converting numbers of personnel to full-time-equivalent staff. For each provider in our final sample, we applied the NDATUS formula to the counts of paid personnel, summing over all occupations (including administrative staff).

To calculate the state-level variables used in our regressions, we summed over all records in each state to get funding, staffing, and client totals and then computed the per-client funding and staffing rates; in effect, this generates a client-weighted statewide average over all sampled providers.

To measure client urbanicity, we multiplied each provider's client total by the sum of the shares described as "urban" and "suburban,"[3] then summed the results over all the sampled providers in each state, and finally divided by the statewide count of total clients. About 10 percent of the records in our sample did not report urban and suburban shares; in those cases, we substituted the 1990-Census-based measure of percentage of statewide population residing in MSAs.

Because NDATUS does not report information on facilities or office space, we used the units per client as a proxy. For each state, we computed the ratio of the total number of reporting units to the statewide total number of clients.

Table C.2 reports basic statistics for the NDATUS data used in our analysis—the dependent variable (F), the explanatory variables used in the regression, and the underlying variables from which the explanatory variables were computed. The table shows statistics for the 50 observations (49 states and the District of Columbia) actually used in the final COS regression analysis; North Dakota was dropped because its value for funding per client was well outside the range for other states and appeared to distort the regression results. This explains why the means shown for the rent and wage indexes do not equal 1.0.

Table C.2

Descriptive Statistics for Substance Abuse Analysis Variables

Variable	Minimum	Maximum	Standard Deviation	Median	Mean
Funding per client (F)	$2,138.9	$27,507.5	$4,335.4	$6,235.1	$7,297.4
Rent index (r_i)	0.733	1.462	0.202	0.962	1.004
Wage index (w_i)	0.774	1.240	0.112	1.000	1.002
Labor per client (L_0)	0.055	0.489	0.085	0.166	0.185
Units per client (S)	0.004	0.045	0.009	0.012	0.014
Client urbanicity (B_U / B_T)	0.193	0.993	0.168	0.715	0.693
$w_i L_0$	0.056	0.471	0.080	0.161	0.183
$r_i S$	0.003	0.052	0.010	0.011	0.015

NOTE: Values are based on 50 observations—the District of Columbia and all states except North Dakota. The means shown here are the simple, unweighted averages.

---

[3] A few respondents estimated urban-suburban-rural shares that did not sum to 100 percent; we rescaled these estimates to yield the proper sum.

The analysis of mental health services used the same wage and rent indexes described above, but measures of labor and space resources were taken from the NRPMHS. It surveys mental health service providers nationwide, asking questions about funding, staffing, and client loads similar to those asked by NDATUS. Unlike the NDATUS, however, the NRPMHS asks about the type of services provided (e.g., inpatient versus outpatient) instead of client urbanicity, includes questions about expenditures as well as funding, and does not distinguish between paid and unpaid (volunteer) staffing. Furthermore, the 1992 NRPMHS data file we received had been cleaned and edited before its release; we found all but 51 of the 5,335 records sufficiently complete to be used in our analysis.

We computed state-level mental health funding and staffing per client using the same procedures as for NDATUS. As a proxy for client urbanicity, we used the share of each state's population residing in MSAs from the 1990 Census. We also computed expenditures per client to compare it with funding, and found that the two measures were very similar in value. And we computed inpatients as a share of total clients,[4] included that as an explanatory variable in some regressions, but found that it did not improve the fit of the equation; this was not surprising because the simple correlation between inpatient share and the wage-weighted wage measure is very high (0.71).

Table C.3 presents descriptive statistics for the variables used in the mental health analyses. Here, the table covers 48 observations because three—in this case, the District of Columbia and Maryland as well as North Dakota—were outliers eliminated from the final regression equation.[5] For general information only, the table includes statistics for expenditures per client and inpatients per client.

THE REGRESSION RESULTS

Tables C.4 through C.6 present the results of applying ordinary least squares regression to Equation C.6 using the substance abuse data described above.

The first pair of tables indicate that the regression equation is an effective predictor of substance abuse spending, explaining better than 70 percent of the interstate variation in funding. We would expect labor and space inputs to be excellent predictors of costs, especially when the resource quantities are adjusted for wage and rent variation.

---

[4]We also tried a measure of residential patients, including residential care as well as hospital inpatients, with similar results.

[5]When the District of Columbia and Maryland are included in the regression, the coefficient on the rent-weighted space variable is larger and highly significant statistically, while the coefficient on wage-weighted labor is smaller. Overall, the effects on the final COSI are virtually indistinguishable from the results based on the regression reported in the text.

Table C.3

Descriptive Statistics for Mental Health Services Analysis Variables

Variable	Minimum	Maximum	Standard Deviation	Median	Mean
Funding per client (F)	$4,050.4	$11,771.5	$1,969.1	$7,387.3	$7,309.4
Expenditure per client	$4,130.2	$12,152.0	$1,996.1	$7,379.2	$7,120.3
Rent index (r_i)	0.726	1.447	0.198	0.952	0.990
Wage index (w_i)	0.774	1.240	0.109	0.985	0.995
Labor per client (L_0)	0.079	0.212	0.034	0.140	0.141
Units per client (S)	0.001	0.003	0.001	0.002	0.002
Population urbanicity (U)	0.204	1.000	0.217	0.674	0.635
$w_i L_0$	0.078	0.242	0.040	0.141	0.141
$r_i S$	0.001	0.003	0.001	0.002	0.002
Inpatients per client	0.013	0.077	0.016	0.043	0.046

NOTE: Values are based on 48 states, excluding North Dakota, the District of Columbia, and Maryland. The means shown here are the simple, unweighted averages.

Table C.4

Substance Abuse Regression Statistics

Multiple R	0.8697462
R square	0.75645846
Adjusted R square	0.72481839
Standard error	2184.5481
Observations	50

Table C.5

Substance Abuse Regression: Analysis of Variance

	Degrees of Freedom	Sum of Squares	Mean Square	F Statistic	Significance F
Regression	3	696679630	232226543	48.6618522	2.5816E-14
Residual	47	224295768	4772250.39		
Total	50	920975399			

Table C.6

Substance Abuse Regression: Coefficient Estimates

Variable	Coefficient	Standard Error	t Statistic
Intercept	Suppressed	N/A	N/A
Client urbanicity	−1877.72	970.66	−1.9344
$w_i L$	43433.89	5095.95	8.5232
$r_i S$	43243.28	43369.36	0.9971

On the other hand, the dependent variable in the regression represents funding levels rather than actual expenditures, the available measures of resources and rents are less than ideal, and the regression aggregates observations to the statewide level. Considering those limitations, the high explanatory power of the regression appears to justify our speculation that SA and MH services survey data can be used effectively to relate costs to state and client characteristics.

Table C.6 shows the final substance abuse regression coefficients and their t statistics. As indicated, we suppressed the constant term ("intercept") because the urbanicity measure captures costs that are fixed per client (but that differ depending on whether clients are from an urban setting); preliminary results showed that an intercept would not be statistically significant. The wage-weighted labor differs from zero at better than 95 percent confidence and the client urbanicity coefficient nearly achieves that standard. Although the t statistic on the coefficient for rent-weighted space is not high, we retained the variable to avoid biasing the urbanicity coefficient.[6]

Similarly, Tables C.7 through C.9 report the regression statistics and coefficients for mental health services.

A review of the residual plots from each regression showed no pivotal outliers or other properties that would raise concerns about the use of ordinary least squares regression. On the whole, the regression results support the view that the methodology and specification we used are appropriate for the purposes of projecting interstate cost-of-service variations for substance abuse and mental health services.

Table C.7

Mental Health Regression Statistics

Multiple R	0.90867
R square	0.82567
Adjusted R square	0.7957
Standard error	840.204
Observations	48

Table C.8

Mental Health Regression: Analysis of Variance

	Degrees of Freedom	Sum of Squares	Mean Square	F Statistic	Significance F
Regression	3	150460871.7	50153623.91	71.04480405	6.67692E-17
Residual	45	31767461.48	705943.594		
Total	48	182228333.2			

Table C.9

Mental Health Regression: Coefficient Estimates

Variable	Coefficient	Standard Error	t Statistic
Intercept	Suppressed	N/A	N/A
U	–1152.4	672.58	–1.7134
$w_i L_0$	47044.8	3561.90	13.2078
$r_i S$	807097	169803.32	4.7532

---

[6]Also, as we noted above, preliminary analyses showed that changing the regression sample sometimes caused the coefficient on rS to become significant without substantially affecting the resulting COSI estimates.

THE COST OF SERVICE INDEXES

Chapter Five described how we used the foregoing regression results to construct standardized COSIs for SA and MH services. One step in that procedure entailed substituting the interstate average values for the labor and space variables in the regression equations. Those values were not the simple means over the regression samples as shown in Tables C.2 and C.3 but were the population-weighted means. In the SA COSI, the weighted means were 0.1341 and 0.0103 for labor and space, respectively; in the MH COSI, the corresponding values were 0.1500 and 0.0015.[7]

To enable the COSI to reflect interstate variation in urbanicity, we needed a measure of urbanicity that varies among states but is also independent of actual state decisions about making services accessible to urban versus rural clients. In the mental health index, the standardized measure of client urbanicity is each state's overall population urbanicity from Census data. For the substance abuse equation, however, we estimated a predicted value of client urbanicity derived from a regression of the urbanicity reported by NDATUS on the state Census measure. The results of this regression appear in Tables C.10 through C.12.[8] The results indicate that, in general, the clientele of substance abuse programs is slightly more likely to be urban or suburban than the overall state population. For example, Census data indicate that the average (unweighted) MSA share of statewide population is about 65 percent whereas NDATUS suggests the average urbanicity of statewide substance abuse clienteles is 69 percent.

Table C.10

Substance Abuse Urbanicity Regression Statistics

Multiple R	0.84479
R square	0.71367
Adjusted R square	0.70783
Standard error	0.09007
Observations	51

Table C.11

Substance Abuse Urbanicity Regression: Analysis of Variance

	Degrees of Freedom	Sum of Squares	Mean Square	F Statistic	Significance F
Regression	1	0.99078	0.99078	122.131	6.6E-15
Residual	49	0.39751	0.00811		
Total	50	1.38829			

---

[7] The text reports rounded values. The values actually used in the computation were not rounded.

[8] We considered regression specifications in which client urbanicity might simply be proportional to Census urbanicity (i.e., the intercept would be suppressed) as well as nonlinear relationships. However, for the range of Census urbanicity observed in the 51 states, a piecewise linear specification appeared to do very well in explaining the client urbanicity variation.

Table C.12

Substance Abuse Regression: Coefficient Estimates

Variable	Coefficient	Standard Error	t Statistic
Intercept	0.28212	0.03914	7.20775
Census urbanicity	0.63219	0.05721	11.0513

Finally, Table C.13 reports the COSI we derived for substance abuse and mental health services as well as a normalized version of the index reported in the original HER study (described and cited in Chapter Five).[9] The HER index differs from ours because wages and rents have changed since 1980 as well as because our indexes use weights derived from regression analyses. The relative importance of these differences is discussed in Chapter Five.

---

[9]The average of the original HER index values was 0.972. Normalizing (i.e., dividing all values by the mean so their average becomes 1.0) increases the index values across the board, rendering them more comparable to the normalized COSI developed in this study.

Table C.13

Normalized Cost of Service Indexes

State	Normalized HER Index	Substance Abuse Index	Mental Health Index
Alabama	0.898	0.863	0.867
Alaska	1.566	1.198	1.166
Arizona	1.031	0.995	1.009
Arkansas	0.838	0.937	0.917
California	1.181	1.247	1.250
Colorado	1.048	1.010	1.009
Connecticut	1.104	1.203	1.193
District of Columbia	1.075	1.118	1.145
Delaware	1.225	1.048	1.060
Florida	0.946	1.037	1.039
Georgia	0.930	1.012	1.002
Hawaii	1.103	1.199	1.196
Idaho	0.947	1.100	1.057
Illinois	1.127	1.022	1.036
Indiana	0.940	0.951	0.960
Iowa	0.901	0.906	0.904
Kansas	0.877	0.978	0.963
Kentucky	0.905	0.915	0.907
Louisiana	0.992	0.977	0.969
Maine	0.874	0.898	0.908
Maryland	1.051	1.184	1.180
Massachusetts	1.105	1.078	1.109
Michigan	1.068	1.041	1.035
Minnesota	0.997	0.948	0.958
Mississippi	0.837	0.952	0.927
Missouri	0.967	0.893	0.900
Montana	0.959	0.823	0.833
Nebraska	0.894	0.835	0.845
Nevada	1.125	1.193	1.187
New Hampshire	0.952	1.006	1.039
New Jersey	1.166	1.180	1.181
New Mexico	0.972	0.958	0.955
New York	1.156	1.122	1.125
North Carolina	0.875	0.861	0.866
North Dakota	0.894	0.917	0.907
Ohio	0.986	0.910	0.920
Oklahoma	0.933	0.886	0.887
Oregon	1.058	0.990	0.994
Pennsylvania	1.022	0.955	0.973
Rhode Island	1.004	0.985	1.010
South Carolina	0.866	0.912	0.907
South Dakota	0.788	0.811	0.813
Tennessee	0.903	0.921	0.919
Texas	0.966	0.968	0.969
Utah	1.023	1.167	1.123
Vermont	0.869	1.037	1.021
Virginia	0.920	1.006	1.016
Washington	1.108	1.014	1.021
West Virginia	0.994	0.955	0.936
Wisconsin	0.946	0.940	0.956
Wyoming	1.089	0.944	0.933

BIBLIOGRAPHY

Achenbach, T. M., and C. S. Edelbrock, *Manual for the Child Behavior Checklist and Revised Child Behavior Profile*, Burlington, Vermont: University of Vermont, Department of Psychiatry, 1983.

Achenbach, T. M., and C. S. Edelbrock, *Manual for the Teacher's Report Form and Teacher Version of the Child Behavior Profile*, Burlington, Vermont: University of Vermont, Department of Psychiatry, 1986.

Advisory Commission on Intergovernmental Relations, *RTS 1991: State Revenue Capacity and Effort*, Report number M-187, Washington, D.C., 1993.

Advisory Commission on Intergovernmental Relations, *State Fiscal Capacity and Effort, 1988*, Report number M-170, Washington, D.C., 1990.

Advisory Commission on Intergovernmental Relations, *Tax Capacity of the Fifty States: Methodology and Estimates*, Report number M-134, Washington, D.C., 1982.

Akaike, H., "Information Theory and an Extension of the Maximum Likelihood Principle," in B. N. Petrov and F. Csaki (eds.), *Second International Symposium on Information Theory*, Budapest: Akademia Kiado, pp. 267–281, 1973.

American Medical Association Center for Health Policy Research, *Physician Marketplace Statistics, Fall 1990*, Chicago, Illinois, 1990.

American Psychiatric Association, *Diagnostic and Statistical Manual of Mental Disorders* (3rd ed., DSM-III), Washington, D.C.: American Psychiatric Association, 1980.

American Psychiatric Association, *Diagnostic and Statistical Manual of Mental Disorders* (3rd ed. revised, DSM-III-R), Washington, D.C.: American Psychiatric Association, 1987.

Anthony, J. C., and J. E. Helzer, "Syndromes of Drug Abuse and Dependence," in L. N. Robins and D. A. Regier (eds.), *Psychiatric Disorders in America: The Epidemiologic Catchment Area*, New York: Free Press, pp. 116–154, 1991.

Arnao, G., "Some Questions About the U.S. 1990 National Household Survey on Drug Abuse," *Journal of Drug Issues*, Vol. 21, pp. 879–881, 1991.

Aronson, J. R., and J. L. Hilley, *Financing State and Local Governments*. Washington, D.C.: The Brookings Institution, 1986.

Barro, S. M., "State Fiscal Capacity Measures: A Theoretical Critique," in H. C. Reeves (ed.), *Measuring Fiscal Capacity*, Boston, Massachusetts: Oelgeschlager, Gunn, and Hain, 1984.

Bird, H. R., G. Canino, M. Rubio-Stipec, M. S. Gould, J. Ribera, M. Sesman, M. Woodbury, S. Huertas-Goldman, A. Pagan, A. Sanchez-Lacay, and M. Moscoso, "Estimates of the Prevalence of Childhood Maladjustment in a Community Survey in Puerto Rico," *Archives of General Psychiatry*, Vol. 45, pp. 1120–1126, 1988.

Blazer, D., et al., "Alcohol Abuse and Dependence in the Rural South," *Archives of General Psychiatry*, Vol. 44, pp. 736–740, 1987.

Breiman, L., J. H. Frieman, R. A. Olshen, and C. J. Stone, *Classification and Regression Trees*, Belmont, California: Wadsworth International Group, 1984.

Burnam, M. A., et al., "Six-Month Prevalence of Specific Psychiatric Disorders Among Mexican Americans and Non-Hispanic Whites in Los Angeles," *Archives of General Psychiatry*, Vol. 44, pp. 687–694, 1987.

Caetano, R., "Acculturation and Drinking Patterns Among U.S. Hispanics," *British Journal of Addiction*, Vol. 82, 1987, pp. 789–799.

Caetano, R., and M. M. Mora, "Acculturation and Drinking Among People of Mexican Descent in Mexico and the United States," *Journal of Studies on Alcohol*, Vol. 49, No. 5, pp. 462–471, 1988.

Cahalan, D., "Problem Drinking Among American Men Aged 21–59," *American Journal of Public Health*, Vol. 62, pp. 1473–1482, 1972.

Carnevale, J., and J. Fastrup, "The Alcohol, Drug Abuse and Mental Health Services Block Grant Formula," unpublished manuscript, 1991.

Chambers, W. J., J. Puig-Antich, M. Hirsch, et al., "The Assessment of Affective Disorders in Children and Adolescents by Semistructured Interview: Test-Retest Reliability of the Schedule for Affective Disorders and Schizophrenia for School-Age Children, Present Episode Version," *Archives of General Psychiatry*, Vol. 42, pp. 696–702, 1985.

Cohen, P., N. Velez, M. Kohn, M. Schwab-Stone, and J. Johnson, "Child Psychiatric Diagnosis by Computer Algorithm: Theoretical Issues and Empirical Tests," *Journal of the American Academy of Child and Adolescent Psychiatry*, Vol. 26, pp. 631–638, 1987.

Costello, A., C. Edelbrock, R. Kalas, M. Kessler, and S. Klaric, *NIMH Diagnostic Interview Schedule for Children (DISC)*, Rockville, Maryland: National Institute of Mental Health, 1984.

Eaton, W. W., A. Dryman, and M. M. Weissman, "Panic and Phobia," in L. N. Robins and D. A. Regier (eds.), *Psychiatric Disorders in America: The Epidemiologic Catchment Area Study*, New York: Free Press, pp. 155–179, 1991.

Fastrup, J. C., "Analysis of Grant Targeting Under the Alcohol, Drug Abuse, and Mental Health Services Block Grant Formula," unpublished manuscript, 1991.

Federal Committee on Statistical Methodology, *Indirect Estimators in Federal Programs*, Statistical Policy Working Paper 21, Washington, D.C.: Office of Management and Budget, Statistical Policy Office, 1993.

Federal Register (Friday, July 17, 1992), Vol. 57, No. 138, Proposed Rules (p. 31682).

Folstein, M., J. C. Anthony, I. Pahrad, B. Duffy, and E. M. Gruenberg, "The Meaning of Cognitive Impairment in the Elderly," *Journal of the American Geriatrics Society*, Vol. 33, pp. 228–235, 1985.

Folstein, M. F., S. E. Folstein, and P. R. McHugh, "Mini-Mental State: A Practical Method for Grading the Cognitive Status of Patients for the Clinician," *Journal of Psychiatric Research*, Vol. 12, pp. 189–198, 1975.

Garrison C. Z., C. L. Addy, K. L. Jackson, R. E. McKeown, and J. L. Waller, "Major Depressive Disorder and Dysthymia in Young Adolescents," *American Journal of Epidemiology*, Vol. 135, pp. 792–802, 1992.

George, L. K., R. Landerman, D. G. Blazer, and J. C. Anthony, "Cognitive Impairment," in L. N. Robins, and D. A. Regier (eds.), *Psychiatric Disorders in America: The Epidemiologic Catchment Area Study*, New York: Free Press, pp. 291–327, 1991.

Gill, A. M., and R. J. Michaels, "The Determinants of Illegal Drug Use," *Contemporary Policy Issues*, Vol. 9, pp. 93–105, 1991.

Grant, B. F., "Prevalence of the Proposed DSM-IV Alcohol Use Disorders: U.S., 1988," *British Journal of Addiction*, Vol. 87, pp. 309–316, 1992.

Grant, B. F., et al., "DSM-III-R and the Proposed DSM-IV Alcohol Use Disorders, U.S. 1988: A Nosological Comparison," *Alcoholism: Clinical and Experimental Research*, Vol. 16, No. 2, pp. 215–221, 1992.

Harford, T. C., et al., "Alcohol Use and Dependence Among Employed Men and Women in the U.S. in 1988," *Alcoholism: Clinical and Experimental Research*, Vol. 16, No. 2, pp. 146–148, 1992.

Helzer, J. E., "Epidemiology of Alcoholism," *Journal of Consulting and Clinical Psychology*, Vol. 55, No. 3, pp. 284–292, 1987.

Helzer, J. E., "Psychiatric Diagnoses and Substance Abuse in the General Population: The ECA Data," in *Problems of Drug Dependence*, NIDA Research Monograph DHHS Publication No. (ADM)88-1564, pp. 405–415.

Helzer, J. E., A. Burnam, and L. T. McEvoy, "Alcohol Abuse and Dependence," in L.N. Robins and D. A. Regier (eds.), *Psychiatric Disorders in America: The Epidemiologic Catchment Area*, New York: Free Press, pp. 81–115, 1991.

Helzer, J. E., et al., "Alcoholism: A Cross-National Comparison of Population Surveys with the Diagnostic Interview Schedule," in R. M. Rose and J. Barrett (eds.), *Alcoholism: Origins and Outcome*, New York: Raven Press, pp. 31–47, 1988.

Herd, D., "Drinking by Black and White Women: Results from a National Survey," *Social Problems*, Vol. 35, No. 5, pp. 493–505, 1988.

Herd, D., "Subgroup Differences in Drinking Patterns Among Black and White Men: Results from a National Survey," *Journal of Studies on Alcohol*, Vol. 51, No. 3, pp. 221–232, 1990.

Herjanic, B., and W. Reich, "Development of a Structured Psychiatric Interview for Children: Agreement Between Child and Parent on Individual Symptoms," *Journal of Abnormal Child Psychology*, Vol. 10, pp. 307–324, 1982.

Hilton, M. E., "Drinking Patterns and Drinking Problems in 1984: Results from a General Population Survey," *Alcoholism: Clinical and Experimental Research*, Vol. 11, No. 2, pp. 167–175, 1987.

Hilton, M. E., "Trends in U.S. Drinking Patterns: Further Evidence from the Past 20 Years," *British Journal of Addiction*, Vol. 83, pp. 269–273, 1988.

Horwath, E., J. Johnson, and C. D. Hornig, "Epidemiology of Panic Disorder in African-Americans," *American Journal of Psychiatry*, Vol. 150, pp. 465–469, 1993.

Hosmer, D., and S. Lemeshow, *Applied Logistic Regression*, New York: J. Wiley & Sons, 1989.

Hughes, A. L., "The Prevalence of Illicit Drug Use in Six Metropolitan Areas in the U.S.: Results from the 1991 National Household Survey on Drug Abuse," *British Journal of Addiction*, Vol. 87, pp. 1481–1485, 1992.

Institute for Health and Aging, *Review and Evaluation of Alcohol, Drug Abuse and Mental Health Services Block Grant Allotment Formulas*, San Francisco, California, 1986.

Johnston, L. D., P. M. O'Malley, and J. G. Bachman, *National Survey Results on Drug Use from the Monitoring the Future Study, 1975–1995. Volume I: Secondary School Students*, Rockville, Maryland: National Institute on Drug Abuse, 1996.

Kandel, D. B., "The Social Demography of Drug Use," *The Milbank Quarterly*, Vol. 69, No. 3, pp. 365–414, 1991.

Kashani, J. H., N. C. Beck, E. W. Hoeper, C. Fallahi, C. M. Corcoran, J. A. McAllister, T. K. Rosenberg, and J. C. Reid, "Psychiatric Disorders in a Community Sample of Adolescents," *American Journal of Psychiatry*, Vol. 144, pp. 584–589, 1987.

Keith, S. J., D. A. Regier, and D. S. Rae, "Schizophrenic Disorders," in L. N. Robins and D. A. Regier (eds.), *Psychiatric Disorders in America: The Epidemiologic Catchment Area Study*, New York: Free Press, pp. 33–52, 1991.

Kessler, R. C., K. A. McGonagle, S. Zhao, C. Nelson, M. Hughes, S. Eshleman, H-U Wittchen, and K. S. Kendler, "Lifetime and 12-Month Prevalence of DSM-III-R Psychiatric Disorders in the United States," *Archives of General Psychiatry*, Vol. 51, pp. 8–19, 1994.

Kincaid, J., "Fiscal Capacity and Tax Effort of the American States: Trends and Issues," in *Public Budgeting and Finance*, Autumn 1989.

Kopstein, A. and J. Gfroerer, *Drug Use Patterns and Demographics of Employed Drug Users: Data from the 1988 National Household Survey on Drug Abuse*, National Institute on Drug Abuse Research Monograph, Vol. 100, pp. 11–24, 1990.

Manderscheid, R., et al., "The National Reporting System for Mental Health Statistics: History and Findings," in *Public Health Reports*, Vol. 101, No. 5, pp. 532–539, September-October 1986.

Nam, C. B., and M. G. Powers, "Variations in Socioeconomic Structure by Race, Residence, and the Life Cycle," *American Sociological Review*, Vol. 30, pp. 97–103, 1965.

National Advisory Mental Health Council, "Health Care Reform for Americans with Severe Mental Illnesses: Report of the National Advisory Mental Health Council," *American Journal of Psychiatry*, Vol. 150, pp. 1447–1465, 1993.

Norton, R., and J. Colliver, "Prevalence and Patterns of Combined Alcohol and Marijuana Use," *Journal of Studies on Alcohol*, Vol. 49, No. 4, pp. 378–380, 1988.

Pope, G. C., *Adjusting the Alcohol, Drug Abuse, and Mental Health Services Block Grant Allocations for Poverty Population and Cost-of-Service*, Needham, Massachusetts: Health Economics Research, March 30, 1990.

Regier, D. A., et al., "Comorbidity of Mental Disorders with Alcohol and Other Drug Abuse: Results from the Epidmiologic Catchment Area (ECA) Study," *Journal of the American Medical Association*, Vol. 264, No. 19, pp. 2511–2518, 1990.

Regier, D. A., W. E. Narrow, and D. S. Rae, "The Epidemiology of Anxiety Disorders: The Epidemiologic Catchment Area (ECA) Experience," *Journal of Psychiatric Research*, Vol. 24, pp. 3–14, 1990.

Regier, D. A., W. E. Narrow, D. S. Rae, R. W. Manderscheied, B. Z. Locke, and F. K. Goodwin, "The de facto US Mental and Addictive Disorders Service System: Epidemiologic Catchment Area Prospective 1-year Prevalence Rates of Disorders and Services," *Archives of General Psychiatry*, Vol. 50, pp. 85–94, 1993.

Rice, D. P., *The Economic Costs of Alcohol, Drug Abuse and Mental Illness: 1985*, Washington, D.C.: Department of Health and Human Services, 1990.

Roberts, R. E., and E. S. Lee, "Occupation and the Prevalence of Major Depression, Alcohol, and Drug Abuse in the United States," *Environmental Research*, Vol. 61, pp. 266–278, 1993.

Robins, L. N., J. E. Helzer, J. Croughan, and K. Ratcliff, "The National Institute of Mental Health Diagnostic Interview Schedule," *Archives of General Psychiatry*, Vol. 38, pp. 381–389, 1981.

Robins, L. N., J. Wing, H-U Wittchen, and J. E. Helzer, "The Composite International Diagnostic Interview: An Epidemiologic Instrument Suitable for Use in Conjunction with Different Diagnostic Systems and in Different Cultures," *Archives of General Psychiatry*, Vol. 45, pp. 1069–1077, 1988.

Sheehan, M. F., "Dual Diagnosis," *Psychiatric Quarterly*, Vol. 64, No. 2, pp. 107–134, 1993.

Sidney, S., "Evidence of Discrepant Data Regarding Trends in Marijuana Use and Supply, 1985–1988," *Journal of Psychoactive Drugs*, Vol. 22, No. 3, pp. 319–324, 1990.

Treno, A., R. N. Parker, and H. D. Holder, "Understanding U.S. Alcohol Consumption with Social and Economic Factors: A Multivariate Time Series Analysis, 1950–1986," *Journal of Studies on Alcohol*, Vol. 54, pp. 146–156, 1993.

U.S. Department of Labor, Bureau of Labor Statistics, *Employment Cost Indexes and Levels, 1975–90*, Bulletin 2372, Washington, D.C., 1990.

U.S. Department of Health and Human Services, *Report to Congress on the Study of Equitable Formulas for the Allocation of Block Grant Funds*, Washington, D.C.: U.S. Government Printing Office, 1982.

U.S. Department of Health and Human Services, Public Health Service, Alcohol, Drug Abuse, and Mental Health Administration, *National Drug and Alcoholism Treatment Unit Survey (NDATUS): 1989 Main Findings Report*, Washington, D.C., 1990.

U.S. Department of the Treasury, Office of State and Local Finance, *Federal-State-Local Fiscal Relations: Report to the President and the Congress*, Washington, D.C.: U.S. Government Printing Office, 1985.

U.S. General Accounting Office, *Improvements in the Alcohol, Drug Abuse, and Mental Health Block Grant Distribution Formula Can Be Made Both Now and in the Future*, Washington, D.C.: U.S. Government Printing Office, 1984.

U.S. General Accounting Office, *Drug Treatment: Targeting Aid to States Using Urban Population as Indicator of Drug Use*, Washington, D.C.: U.S. Government Printing Office, 1990.

U.S. General Accounting Office, *Mental Health Grants: Funding Not Distributed in Accordance with State Needs*, Testimony before the Subcommittee on Health and *the Environment, Committee on Energy and Commerce, U.S. House of Representatives*, Washington, D.C.: U.S. Government Printing Office, 1991.

U.S. General Accounting Office, *Maternal and Child Health: Block Grants Should Be Distributed More Equitably*, Washington, D.C., 1992.

U.S. House of Representatives, *House Conference Report No. 97-208, Legislative History, P.L. 97-35*, Washington, D.C.: U.S. Government Printing Office, 1981.

U.S. Public Law 97-35, *Omnibus Budget Reconciliation Act of 1981*, Washington, D.C.: U.S. Government Printing Office, 1981.

U.S. Public Law 98-509, *Alcohol Abuse, Drug Abuse, and Mental Health Amendments of 1984*, Washington, D.C.: U.S. Government Printing Office, 1984.

U.S. Public Law 100-690, *Anti-Drug Abuse Act of 1988*, Washington, D.C.: U.S. Government Printing Office, 1988.

U.S. Public Law 102-321, *ADAMHA Reorganization Act*, Washington, D.C.: U.S. Government Printing Office, 1992.

U.S. Senate, Committee on Labor and Human Resources, *Senate Report No. 97-158, Legislative History, Omnibus Budget Reconciliation Act of 1981, P.L. 97-35*, Washington, D.C.: U.S. Government Printing Office, 1981.

U.S. Senate, Committee on Labor and Human Resources, *Senate Report No. 98-381, Legislative History, Alcohol Abuse, Drug Abuse, and Mental Health Amendments of 1984, P.L. 98-509*, Washington, D.C.: U.S. Government Printing Office, 1984.

U.S. Senate, Committee on Labor and Human Resources, *Senate Report No. 102-131, Legislative History, ADAMHA Reorganization Act, P.L. 102-321*, Washington, D.C.: U.S. Government Printing Office, 1992.

Weissman, M. M., M. L. Bruce, P. J. Leaf, L. P. Florio and C. Holzer, "Affective Disorders," in L. N. Robins and D. A. Regier (eds.), *Psychiatric Disorders in America: The Epidemiologic Catchment Area Study*, New York: Free Press, pp. 53–80, 1991.

Weissman, M. M., and J. K. Myer, "Affective Disorders in a United States Community: The Use of Research Diagnostic Criteria in an Epidemiological Survey," *Archives of General Psychiatry*, Vol. 35, pp. 1304–1311, 1978.

World Health Organization, *Composite International Diagnostic Interview (CIDI), Version 1.0*, Geneva, Switzerland, 1990.